The Wall Street Jungle

The Wall Street Jungle

by Richard Ney

Grove Press, Inc., New York

To the students of America
Whose values are the cement of our society.

Preface

Most of us enter the investment business for the same sanity-destroying reasons a woman becomes a prostitute: it avoids the menace of hard work, is a group activity that requires little in the way of intellect, and is a practical means of making money for those with no special talent for anything else.

With money one achieves status and power of a kind no other means can reach—which in itself would not be unworthy if the methods used to obtain it merited our respect. They don't. It should not surprise us, therefore, that these methods are less than explicit; or that the interests of the Stock Exchanges are solely in their billion-dollar speculations, without regard to their social obligations or the needs of a legitimate auction market.

There is a difference between what is legal and what is legitimate. Once understood, this distinction illuminates an environment in which larceny hides its nakedness in the toggery of law and order, custom and routine. We find it in the no man's land of rules and regulations that sanction Stock Exchange members' manhandling of credit and of stock prices on behalf of their own speculations. Short selling, big block fees, special brokerage incentives, and the specialists' investment and trading accounts, are only a few of the methods used to keep the members of the financial establishment established, at the expense of the individual investor.

Much that is painful in our society is due to the public's belief in the cant of the Exchange's chief organs of opinion. Indeed, hidden behind a façade of pompous jargon and noble affectations, there is more sheer larceny per square foot on the floor of the New York Stock Exchange than any place else in the world. It is the legacy of a communal effort that has become a property right, handed down from father to son to grandson. It is sustained by the exclusive allegiance of its high priests to a tradition that wars against reason and that has become so powerful that anyone setting himself against it on behalf of a higher loyalty soon finds he has set himself against a power that is identical to that of government itself.

Clearly, the lunatic economics of this larceny appeal to the criminal. The story is told that after he had been deported to Italy, Lucky Luciano granted an interview in which he described a visit to the floor of the New York Stock Exchange. When the operations of floor specialists had been explained to him, he said, "A terrible thing happened. I realized I'd joined the wrong mob."

Acknowledgments

Success in life is due less to our talents than to the fact that others have behaved decently toward us. In this sense, my debts are enormous. I owe much to my teachers who, more than a quarter century ago, struggled to educate me to a more dramatic understanding of the laws of mind and nature. I owe a great deal to Joseph Wood Krutch, Lionel Trilling, and many others at Columbia University. They made each of their students believe they were born to a role as large as their country's destiny. Their unfailing wisdom sustained me in my search for leadership. They made it possible to recognize the cramping bias of a generation that had become enfeebled by success. My deepest intellectual debt is to Lucky Roberts. His great understanding of literature provided the gateway out of one world and into another. It was his knowledge of publishers that directed me to Grove Press, which treated me with the utmost generosity, encouragement, and forbearance. Nor can I fail to direct the reader's attention to two dear friends, Mia Miyashiro and Joan Gluck, my untiring secretaries. They offered me loyalty and trust. They transcribed my scrawled notes and countless drafts with great skill and affection. To all these and to many others who helped either by accident or design—to Charles Champlin and Marshall Berges—to Teresa Calabrese, Chuck Stone, Robin White, and John Peck—to Everett Noonan and Bernard Goldman—to Paul, Kip, Archie, Bill, and Pauline—each of you left your imprint on my mind, my character, and my work.

Contents

The Wall Street Jungle

1

The Specialist
or
The Legend of Big Brother

**A stock is only worth what
its specialist is willing to pay for it.**

Some people claim that "investment adviser"—which is what I am—is just a high-class name for a croupier. I agree. I deal in a big floating crap game, one that is played every weekday in the richest and most exclusive casino in the world: the New York Stock Exchange.

Who are this casino's pit bosses, the men who decide how the game will be played and, frequently, who will win? Who, for example, on the morning of August 8, 1967, opened Chicago and Northwestern Railroad down 39 points? Who, on October 21, 1968, opened one of the preferred stocks of TRW, Inc., 28 points lower than its closing price on the previous day it traded, on a transaction of only 100 shares? And who, on February 4, 1970, opened Memorex 29½ points lower than its previous closing price? [1]

Who are the people in this favored spot who decide that one investor shall receive $2,800 less for his TRW

—an electronics company—and another $3,900 less for his 100 shares of Chicago and Northwestern Railroad? When the huge Lockheed C5A cargo plane and Boeing SST contracts were announced, who were the men who made use of public demand for these stocks to subsequently send them *down?* Who sets limits to the market's vital disorders? Who are the men who move at the center of its convulsions and officiate at its requiems? The New York Stock Exchange and the American Stock Exchange call them "specialists."

Specialists are brokers who work at the market's center and who act as its leaders. The rise of the specialist as a permanent fixture of the market was almost unnoticed. For a long time, the community in which he functioned was virtually unaware of his existence. But it is he who, to a great extent, controls the market's rises and falls. In this book I will attempt to show that the statement "The stock market, by bringing together buyers and sellers from all over the world, reflects their composite judgment of the present and future value of the stock" [2] is false. I will try to show that a significant cause of the market's day-to-day fluctuations is, in fact, the manipulations of the specialist. I propose to illuminate the shadows in which the specialist hides, demonstrate his effect on stock values and prices, and distinguish between the facts and the sophisticated fictions promulgated about him by the Securities and Exchange Commission and the Stock Exchanges.

Who is the specialist?

A specialist is the "broker's broker"; the specialist or a member of his team is always on the Stock Exchange floor near the signboard of the stocks in which he specializes. Orders for buying or selling his specialty stocks on the New York Stock Exchange go through him. Regular brokers bring him their customers' orders to buy or sell shares in his stocks. Often the order is to sell at a price that is not current: when the stock of XYZ Company is selling at $50 a share, a customer might give his broker an order to sell 100 shares at $51. Instead of waiting at the XYZ specialist's post until the price matches his customer's sell order, the broker generally gives the order to the specialist and goes about his business. The specialist's job is then to sell that customer's 100 shares when the price reaches $51, if it does. For this service he takes a small fraction of the broker's commission.

The specialist is the man who, according to Stock Exchange theory, is supposed to determine the price of his specialty stock within the perimeters of existing supply and demand. If there are orders to buy it at $50 and orders to sell it at $51, he is supposed to set the "market price" somewhere in between.

The New York Stock Exchange says of the specialist's function, that he:

> . . . must maintain fair and orderly markets in the stocks which he handles, insofar as it is reasonably practicable for him to do so. He does this by buying or selling for his own account when there is a temporary disparity between supply and demand and when he has no competing public order. In this way he contributes to price continuity and to the liquidity of the market and enables investors' orders to be executed at more favorable prices.[3]

A report on the American Stock Exchange states that the specialist "exercises a significant influence on the public appraisal of a security, since he is the one who quotes the market."[4] A team of Securities and Exchange Commission investigators[5] saw him as the individual who exercises decisive "control over the market." These investigators, writing in the Special Study Report of the SEC, concluded that the specialist system "in broad terms, appears to be serving its purposes satisfactorily" [6]; even so, they provide a warning. They say that the

> New York Stock Exchange has pioneered in the development of surveillance techniques regarding specialists' performances and has devoted considerable energy to this area. Nevertheless, its present techniques are not sufficiently refined to deal adequately with certain important aspects of the specialists' role and obligations . . .[7]

At present, there are about 360 New York Stock Exchange members registered as specialists. They are organized into 110 specialist units of between one and nine specialists each. Specialist units may operate as individuals, partnerships, corporations, so-called joint accounts, or "combined books." Partnerships are the favored method of operation. Those units that choose the corporate method do so partly because, in a corporate structure, the specialist's short-term gains are subject to corporate rather than individual income taxes. In highly volatile stocks, this kind of tax treatment provides numerous advantages when specialists trade for their own accounts. In general, the internal composition of a specialist unit is determined by the specific tax, trading, or credit advantages to be gained by the specialists involved.

The New York Stock Exchange, as one might expect, vehemently defends the specialist system. The NYSE is the Big Board and as such always stands ready to provide a catalogue of virtues describing the public-spirited impulses of its members and how well self-regulation succeeds. It fails to mention that the conflicts of interest operating in the Exchanges have proven incapable of resolution under existing codes and practices. In theory, the Exchanges are governed by a highly moral code of financial conduct; in fact, they pit the specialist's financial interests against those of his customers.

The New York Stock Exchange and the regulatory

bodies of the federal government have failed to face the basic fault in the specialist's *modus operandi*—namely, that there is a conflict of interest built into his function. He is meant to be the representative—in the key position on the Stock Exchange—of the public, but at the same time he gains his income by trading against the public. Theoretically, then, he must adhere to a golden mean. But it is one thing to preach the golden mean and quite another to achieve it. In fact, the weight, scope, and power of the Exchanges' public relations programs have caused investors to remain in complete ignorance of how specialists operate and how their operations affect the investor.

It is necessary to show that both the New York Stock Exchange and the SEC have failed to create the kind of approach that would contribute to the development of a sane and safe auction market. In the course of this book we will acquire a new perspective on the meanings of such words as "stabilization" and "liquidity," and we will see that, far from stabilizing the market, the specialist system is so constructed that a specialist may exploit an emergency situation—or any announcement, be it good or bad—to enrich his own account.

As for the much-vaunted "liquidity" his efforts are said to foster, we will show that when the investor's ability to buy or sell stock at a moment's notice requires the specialist's services, the cost of those services runs high. In such a market, investors compete not with each other but with specialists; specialists competing with investors determine the prices at which investors will buy and sell stock.

All of us who have invested in the market have, at one time or another, followed this pied piper. Too many of us forget that the piper demands not only that we follow whatever tune he plays—but that somewhere along the way we pay him.

The New York Stock Exchange tries to present itself as having a highly moral code. From my vantage point it would seem that the Exchange's rituals have more to do with providing a casino-like facility for gambling than anything else—and the tables are rigged.

One of the rigging devices is called the "specialist's book." In it the specialist lists the public's buy and sell orders that are above or below a stock's then-existing price. This list can be used to by-pass the functions of supply and demand. A close study of the specialists' use of short selling to acquire stock for their own investment accounts shows clearly that the game is weighted heavily in the specialists' favor.

Then there are those transactions between specialists and member firms which, contrary to what the public generally believes, never appear on the tape. Such transactions are routine on the Exchange in big-block sales and accumulations.

The Exchange maintains that it has, largely through experience, evolved a complex system of rules for self-control. We will see how effective self-regulation is when we examine the events following the assassination of President Kennedy, when specialists made substantial profits and the money came out of the pockets of individual investors.

The rules of the New York Stock Exchange and the SEC grant specialists vast authority to impose an arbitrary structure upon the prices of stocks. In the following dialogue between a specialist and an SEC investigator, the specialist tells how he uses this authority:

Q: You supplied 600 [shares] at 43?

A: That is right.

Q: If you hadn't done that——

A: It could have sold at any price. I mean, had I wanted to, I could have sold 100 at 43, 100 at 43¼,

100 at 43½, 100 at 43¾, 100 at 43⅞, and so on;
and just done anything I wanted to. I just didn't. I
figured 43 was a very equitable price for the buyer.[8]

He is talking here about the specialists' usual game—
chipping away at eighths or quarters of a point. Investors
in a stock stand to lose—or occasionally to gain—$12.50
with every chip, on each 100 shares, and specialists often
deal in hundreds of thousands of shares per day. Specialists can also use an ax with great effect. Where an
ax is used, the investors' money drops like autumn leaves.
There's quite a contrast between the way the market
actually operates and the New York Stock Exchange's
typical statements about it:

Stock prices change because of the law of supply and
demand . . .
  If more people want to buy than sell, the price of a
stock goes up . . .
  In the long run, the price of a stock tends to reflect
the value of a company . . .[9]

Sometimes specialists transgress even the very flexible
regulations imposed on them by the Exchange and the
SEC and resort to practices even more questionable than
those already described. Even when this happens, they
are seldom severely punished. For example, one of the
most powerful units on the floor is Bill Meehan's at Post
Twelve.[10] In 1968, for instance, he handled such heavy-
weights as Amsted Industries, Bell Intercontinental, Commercial Solvents, Deere, Ford, Fairchild Camera, Georgia Pacific, Ideal Cement, Glen Alden, Jim Walter,
National Cash Register, Oklahoma Gas and Electric,
Oklahoma Natural Gas, Radio Corporation of America,
Southwestern Public Service, and Texas Eastern Trans-
mission. The titular head, founding father, and guiding
genius of this firm, Michael J. Meehan, was a specialist
who revealed himself as a master of price control.

After an investigation into the shifting subtleties of Michael Meehan's activities in July, 1937, the SEC alleged that his activities were in violation of the law. The SEC stated its decision regarding Meehan in these words: "The gravity of his conduct leads us to conclude that the penalty should be expulsion from all the national securities exchanges of which he is a member. An order to this effect will accordingly issue." [11]

It is worth noting that the SEC used the words "gravity of his conduct" instead of a harsher, perhaps more accurate phrase. It is also worth noting that Meehan was allowed to resign, instead of being expelled, and that his firm remained intact and kept its place on the floor.

In his brilliant and wide-ranging book, *The Rich and the Super-Rich,* Ferdinand Lundberg goes to the core of the problem of crime among the privileged rich. He draws on the work of a noted criminologist, Professor Edwin Sutherland, to help us understand why the punishment doesn't fit the crime when the criminal is a member of the establishment:

Most offenses open to members of the upper socio-economic class other than those traditionally proscribed, as he [Sutherland] found, were dealt with by special administrative tribunals. The offenses were mostly variants of fraud or conspiracy. Where they were committed against the broad public they called for relatively light penalties, seldom prison terms . . .

Even when a member of the upper socio-economic class was found guilty of a stigmatic crime [one involving violence or *direct* theft] and was about to be sentenced, there was a marked difference in language of the judge . . . The judge (as quoted by Sutherland) typically said: "You are men of affairs, of experience, of refinement and culture, of excellent reputation and standing in the business and social world." They were in fact, as the judicial process had just disclosed, *criminals* . . .

When Sutherland inquired closely he found, contrary to the established supposition, that many members of the upper classes did commit offenses for which the government held them accountable. But, in most cases special arrangements had been made to handle them with kid gloves and in many cases to administer by way of punishment a slap on the wrist.

Nor was the reason for differential formulation and application of the law hard to find. The class whose members were being proceeded against was the class that had the dominant influence in the government and supported the political parties at the top. It was, indeed, their government and their political parties engaged in running their very own plantation.[12]

There is little question that specialists' income puts them among society's elite. Figures provided by the Special Study Report of the SEC (Part 2, p. 68) purport to show the gross income in 1959 and 1960 of all New York Stock Exchange specialist units:

1959	AMOUNT	PERCENTAGE OF TOTAL
Commissions	$19,590,000	48
Trading Profits	21,237,000	52
Total	$40,827,000	100
1960		
Commissions	$18,919,000	55
Trading Profits	15,769,000	45
Total	$34,688,000	100

If these figures seem surprisingly modest, it is because the SEC did not go far enough. Specialists do indeed trade for the benefit of their trading accounts, the figures for which are shown above. But they also trade on behalf of their own investment accounts and the accounts they maintain in partnership with other specialists, brokers, and their own financing firms.[13] They also market stocks for big-block institutional clients, thus further augmenting their incomes. It becomes apparent that the SEC figures barely scratch the surface.

The latest figures available are ten years old. More recent income figures would doubtless reflect the enormous increase in the volume of specialist trading since 1959 and 1960.

Many specialists have sufficiently large incomes to buy jet airplanes as a way to reduce their taxes. Along with other individuals with high incomes, specialists form partnerships to buy diesels or jets and then lease them to railroads or airlines for the 7 per cent tax credit on capital goods purchases to reduce personal income taxes.

Heads of corporations must report to the SEC their profits and losses as they trade in the stock of their companies. Yet specialists are not required to report their profits in trading their specialty stock either in their segregated tax accounts or in their other investment accounts, as co-stockholders in their financing firm, as owners of a specialist financing firm, or from countless other areas of taxable and nontaxable income.[14]

Since the SEC insists that the specialist operate in the public interest, why isn't his income public knowledge? If the SEC were to make public the income figures for specialists, we might gain some insight into their "affirmative contributions to the market." According to the Special Study Report (Part 2, p. 121):

Some specialists testified that under certain circumstances a specialist has a broad right to liquidate his position, although such transactions might not represent an affirmative contribution to the market and may even serve to destabilize the market and depress prices. The reason advanced was that if a specialist faces financial difficulties he has the right to sell his inventory as a

> matter of business survival. A prominent specialist and former chairman of the board of governors [of the NYSE] apparently believes that specialists are permitted an almost unlimited right of liquidation: "After all, you could ruin a man if he couldn't get out." Whether such a "right of liquidation" is sanctioned by . . . Exchange rules is, however, not entirely clear.

It doesn't really matter, though, whether it's clear, for Exchange rules are, on the whole, not very strict.

In 1964, subsequent to the publication of the Special Study Report, there were disquieting rumors that major reforms of the specialist system were about to take place. The Exchange's top negotiating team of specialists met with Commissioner Ralph Saul and other members of the SEC in Washington and on Wall Street. Their stated purpose was to consider the Special Study Report's recommendations concerning the specialist system. The meetings were ordered to be held *behind closed doors*. Then, on September 24, 1964, the New York Stock Exchange issued a memorandum to its members:

> The interchange of ideas [between the Exchange and the SEC] . . . provided the basis for modifying or substantially changing a number of the recommendations originally made by the SEC Special Study Group. However, where a Special Study recommendation appeared to offer the prospect of improving the specialist system, the Board has not hesitated to endorse it and take appropriate steps towards implementing it.

Where the SEC investigating team's recommendations threatened the specialist system with reform they were "modified." Where they strengthened the system they were "endorsed."

In Washington and Wall Street, today's government-business love affairs are pregnant with tomorrow's economic arrangements; hence it is not surprising that former Commissioner Ralph Saul—who had conducted the SEC's 1962–1963 investigation of the securities market and the specialist system—was installed as President of the American Stock Exchange in 1966.

Public scandals occur more frequently on the American Stock Exchange than on the New York Stock Exchange. The difference in power and separation of activities between the two Exchanges has never been adequately explored. Basically, because of the regulations governing the listing of companies on each Exchange, each Exchange can be said to be much like an individual with a distinct personality. The companies on the NYSE, which are mature and seasoned, enjoy the security of a well-financed middle age, while the newer companies on the Amex, which have less capital and less experience, suffer from each little crisis of adolescence. The NYSE consists of highly individuated and consistent personalities, the Amex of men and companies that are one way today and another tomorrow. It is understandable therefore that big money, in the form of mutual funds, pension funds, foundations, and other institutional accounts, tends to restrict most of its trading to the more predictable potentials of the NYSE. The range of the NYSE's financial power and the degree of its political control and dominion over the economic resources of the United States are related to its access to this institutional business.

Yet the motives, functions, and activities of the specialists on both Exchanges have much in common. Both groups seem more concerned with the narrow questions of how they can increase their profits, power, privilege, and status, than with the larger issues of public service. The devices and skills that are employed by the Amex specialist to exploit his public customers are also employed by the NYSE specialist. Both groups are sustained by the same web of myths, and both groups observe the most famous of Machiavelli's precepts: If one is to lead other men, one must be willing to throw overboard accepted codes of morality whenever necessary, while at the same time making a show of observing these codes.

More fundamental than these considerations is the fact that the political power and financial status of the NYSE tend to reinforce each other. The rule of the dollar is more absolute in New York than anywhere else in the world; thus, it has been a simple matter for the NYSE to establish a situation in which it is able to assert increasing influence over governmental agencies that are meant to regulate it. Thus we find that members of the NYSE retain as their legal representatives the law offices of New York Senators and Congressmen. It has also been revealed that members of the NYSE contributed to the income of a Supreme Court justice by making donations toward paying his lecture fees.[15] Because of its influence in high places the Exchange can grossly exploit the basic and universal interests of investors. The world of the NYSE is a closed world of almost absolute power.

The American Stock Exchange is, by comparison, less powerful. The powers external to the Amex allow it only a limited authority. If, after a major decline in the market, the public clamors for blood, it will most likely be a member of the Amex who is offered to them as a scapegoat. It will be claimed that because the regulations governing the listing of companies on the Amex are less stringent, the dealings of the specialists on this Exchange are more open to question, and that they are more likely to be derelict in fulfilling their obligations. When in the course of a dinner party I discussed with Keith Funston, then the President of the NYSE, the manipulations that had been going on in a highly active stock, his response was, "Oh, but *that* was on the *American* Stock Exchange." Let there be no mistake about it, however: the manner in which each of these Exchanges is regulated has its locus in the dollar.

If one hears of more scandals on the American Exchange than on the NYSE, it is probably because the names of some persons involved in scandals on the New York Exchange are discreetly hushed up. For example, the stock in Douglas Aircraft recently went down more than $300 million in value. There were insiders who got the bad news in advance of the public and the other stockholders and were able to get out at a high price—all this without so much as one member of the NYSE being cited.[16] Indeed, one brokerage firm that was cited by the SEC was allowed to settle the charges against it in order to avoid hearings by "consenting to the order without admitting the allegations." This kind of protection, commonly offered to specialists on the NYSE and not to those on the Amex, is the basic difference between the two Exchanges.

Financier Louis Wolfson, as he was preparing to serve a one-year sentence for violation of the securities laws, had this to say (as quoted in the *Wall Street Journal,* April 22, 1969):

> You've got more crooks in Wall Street than in any other industry I've ever seen.

NOTES, chapter 1

1 During the afternoon of February 5, an official of Memorex stated he knew of no corporate development to account for the stock's opening 29½ points lower. At one point during the day Memorex was down 38¼ points. Two days earlier the company had reported sharply higher earnings ($1.87 for 1969 *vs.* $1.35 for 1968). On February 4, true to form, the *Wall Street Journal* reported ". . . several analysts were disturbed that . . . fourth period net was up only four cents . . ."

[2] Merrill Lynch, Pierce, Fenner & Smith, *How to Read a Financial Report,* rev. January, 1961, p. 28.

[3] New York Stock Exchange, *The Specialist on the New York Stock Exchange, An Explanation Primarily for Corporate Officials,* undated, p. 3.

[4] *Staff Report on the Organization, Management, and Regulation of Conduct of Members of the American Stock Exchange,* January, 1962, p. 23.

[5] This team, the Special Study group, was formed when Congress, in September, 1961, directed the SEC to make a study and investigation of the adequacy with which the rules of national Securities Exchanges and associations protect the interests of investors and to submit a report on or before January 3, 1963.

[6] Part 2, p. 167.

[7] SEC, *Report of the Special Study of Securities Markets,* Part 2, pp. 170–171, July 17, 1963. This document will hereafter be referred to as the Special Study Report or SSR.

In the January, 1962, SEC *Staff Report on the Organization, Management, and Regulation of Conduct of Members of the American Stock Exchange* the specialist's crucial position was also described as follows (p. 23): "In his unique capacity the specialist stands at the heart of the Exchange market mechanism. He has intimate knowledge of the past market action of the stocks in which he specializes. He also has sole access to the specialist book showing outstanding orders both below and above the market which affords him a great competitive advantage over the public."

Page 19 of this report states: "Specialists have been shown to be the dominant group in the government of the Exchange." This, of course, is even more true of the NYSE.

[8] Emphasis added. Special Study Report, Part 2, p. 136.

[9] These particular statements are quoted in John G. Fuller, *The Money Changers* (New York: Dial Press, 1961), p. 137.

[10] Typically, a specialist unit controls 6 to 15 stocks; two of the most powerful units handle between 36 and 40 stocks each.

[11] SEC File No. 4–232, July 31, 1937, *In the Matter of Michael J. Meehan.*

[12] New York: Bantam Books, 1969, pp. 125–126. Lundberg's magnum opus bears heavily on the workings of the financial establishment and its control over both houses of Congress.

[13] Specialists' trading accounts, investment accounts, and "joint" accounts are defined and explained in Chapter 4.

[14] They report profit and loss in their *trading* accounts to the NYSE, which holds the reports.

Specialists' various "segregated accounts" are described in Chapter 4.

[15] *Wall Street Journal*, September 18, 1968.

[16] Merrill Lynch, as a firm, was later cited, but none of its officers who are members of the NYSE was named—only the smaller fish.

2

The Specialist's Book

**Using his book, the specialist
chops off more heads than Alice's Red Queen.**

One of the specialist's greatest advantages over the average investor is that the specialist is in the right place at the right time. An investor who wants to buy or sell has a choice between giving his broker a *market order* (an order to buy or sell at the best price available when the order reaches the trading floor), a *stop order* (an order to buy or sell that becomes a market order as soon as the price of the stock reaches the price specified by the buyer or seller), a *limit order* (an order to buy or sell at a specific price or better), or a *stop limit order* (an order to buy or sell that becomes a limit order as soon as the stock reaches the price specified by the buyer or seller).[1]

These orders are all entered in what is called the "specialist's book"—a source of incomparable privilege. It is a loose-leaf binder approximately 4 inches by 11 inches. The book is used to record customers' orders (placed with the specialist by brokers) ⅛ of a point apart—that is, from, say, 35, 35⅛, 35¼ . . . to 35⅞. Orders to buy or sell stock are entered by the specialist in the sequence in which they are received, at the appropriate price, with a notation of the number of shares.

The specialist's book gives him yet another crucial advantage over investors. He *knows* (investors can only guess) when it will be safe to play. For instance, if there are stop limit orders on his book to buy 700 shares at 60¼, which might be the "break-out" point of the trading range that had existed between 50 and 60, he's safe in buying 700 shares at the "current market price" of 58.

The speculator is easily persuaded by his broker to enter a stop order to "protect" himself from loss. "You bought the stock at 49—it's now 53, enter a stop at 52 and you'll have covered all commission costs and still be ahead." The broker, of course, takes a commission on this deal, and brokers make their living from commissions.

On the subject of the prediction value of the book, the Special Study Report is again worth examining:

> The specialist's book has an importance beyond that of a mere repository of unexecuted agency orders. It serves as an indicator of public interest in a particular security. For example, a book containing many orders reasonably close to the market indicates that, at the time, the stock is an active one of wide interest. On the other hand, a light book may indicate that a stock is less active, or that if active, it may be volatile in character.
>
> A much-argued point has been whether the number of buy-and-sell orders contained on the book is an indicator of immediately forthcoming market trends. At the time of the Pecora hearings some specialists argued that the book was almost valueless from this point of view. The same argument was made in 1935, when the Commission had under consideration a rule which would have required complete disclosure of the book, and the same point was reiterated during the Segregation Study. In fact, it was argued that the contents of the book are apt to be misleading since many orders are not in the book—some are held by floor brokers and others are in brokerage offices and not yet transmitted to the floor.

Nevertheless, it seems clear that in certain instances the book is an important indicator. A book that has a great many sell-stop orders suggests that the stock will suffer a quick decline when these orders are reached. In addition, a large number of limit orders immediately below or above the market may indicate that, in the very short run, there is a floor or ceiling to the stock's price.

Some specialists testified that the trend of the market is indicated by the orders on the book—that a book which contains many sell orders is characteristic of a stock which will increase in price, while a book containing many buy orders indicates that the price will decline. One specialist stated that this theory has greater validity when limit orders to sell are filling in after a stock has reached a low or limit orders to buy are entered when a stock has just gone through a sharp rally.[2]

The specialist who stated "a book containing many buy orders indicates that the price will decline" was pointing out—albeit obliquely—the most important of all the auction market's paradoxes: that demand, as stated earlier, may tend to send the price of a stock not up but down.

How much time and attention a specialist gives to each order and whether he will use the book to benefit the customer or himself often depends on the name of the firm forwarding the order. The name of the ordering firm is jotted down at the same time as the number of shares and the price ordered. Knowing the name of the firm tells him, for example, whether the order originated with his own or an allied company. Not to put too fine a point on it, knowing the order's origin makes it possible for the specialist to decide whether he will give it his best or worst effort.

One of the Exchange's rules is that no order given to a specialist in his specialty stock shall indicate the account for which it is entered. The rule was made to ensure equal treatment for all buyers; the following discussion from the Special Study Report suggests the difference between the way a specialist handles just any broker's order and the way he approaches one from a mutual fund, from officials of the companies whose stocks he specializes in, or from an "intimate friend."

It is necessary to distinguish between several different kinds of situations. Some specialists are partners in member firms which regularly do business with the public, maintaining board rooms and providing all the services usually associated with a public commission business. Other specialists introduce accounts to their clearing agent and obtain a split of commissions. At least two specialists have arrangements with mutual funds whereby all the fund's orders are transmitted through the specialist, who then channels the orders to the member firms which are to receive reciprocal business. Finally, many specialists have a public business restricted to friends and business acquaintances, occasionally officials of the companies in whose stock the specialists are registered. This last may be illustrated from the testimony of one specialist:

Q: Can anyone call up and give your firm an order?

A: Not without checking with us on the floor. That is why we have the phone. The order would not be accepted if we don't know the person.

Q: You have to know the person personally or one of your partners?

A: Right.

Q: Will you accept orders from any acquaintance of yours?

A: No.

Q: What is the classification of persons?

A: Intimate friends. We are not in the commission business. This is just an accommodation.[3]

In this same section, on pages 154–155, the SSR stated:

> No matter what method was used to transmit the order to the floor, most specialists stated that they were aware when orders arriving at their posts originated through their own firm, either because the order slip would bear their firm's name or because *there would be some special notation on the form.*[4]

The NYSE rules now prohibit a specialist from taking orders for sale or purchase of shares of his specialty stock directly from officers of the company. There seems to be no check, however, on whether he takes such orders indirectly, and there are several easy methods for doing so. The Special Study Report, taking off into the friendly dark, says,

> the specialist is in the same position as others who might seek to use knowledge of the contents of the book for their own profit, except insofar as his activities are circumscribed by rules.
>
> Thus, in executing his brokerage functions, the specialist has a powerful tool, available to him only, giving him insight into the possible course of the market. The justification for the special treatment can lie only in the need for such information for the most effective conduct of his dealer activities, which, as has been indicated, provide the basis for the fulfillment of his responsibilities to maintain a fair and orderly market.[5]

Existing rules notwithstanding, specialists have been known to discuss the prices and amounts at which stop and limit orders have been entered in their books with other members. Members then learn the prices at which blocks of stock can be purchased or sold by them.

Anyone who has stumbled through the investment world long enough will recognize the absurdity of rules that trust to the value judgments of human nature. Obviously, instinct and impulse and consciousness, as well as unconsciousness, will be operating as the specialist employs his book for the benefit of friends, family, and big-block customers. Indeed, it would be pointless for a big-block customer to have placed an order with a specialist for 200,000 shares of his stock unless consultation with the specialist showed that the book could be counted on to supply the bulk of such an order.

Attorney General Robert Kennedy's 1960–1961 investigation into the activities of Alexander Guterma, who at the time had already been convicted of stock fraud, raised critical questions concerning the manner in which specialists manipulated their stocks. The immediately desirable aspects of their operations seemed suddenly not quite so desirable, and the undesirable aspects had become even more undesirable.

Because of Kennedy's revelation by way of Guterma, the SEC was obliged to launch an investigation of the Amex. Pursuant to an order of the SEC, the investigation was held behind closed doors. It produced the *Staff Report on the Organization, Management, and Regulation of Conduct of Members of the American Stock Exchange* in January, 1962; and it revealed that, on either the American or New York Stock Exchange, when there was to be a secondary distribution, it was routine practice for brokers to ask the specialists, prior to the date of the offering, what the aggregate bids on the book were between the market price and the estimated offering price.[6] Commenting on this, the Staff Report stated emphatically:

> the possibility of abuse in connection with the disclosure of non-public information on the specialist book in secondary offerings as revealed by the instant investigation is substantial. For example, the underwriter, issuer, or selling stockholder may adjust the offering price or the time of offering because of the receipt of such non-public information in order to benefit themselves.[7]

When the SEC asked what specialists thought of the idea of disclosing to nonmembers the orders that might be on their books, one anonymous specialist said: "If the public became aware of unusually large orders, the tendency very likely would be for the public to want to be on the same side of the block. The execution of the block would be more difficult therefore and the fluctuations accentuated." [8] Yet the specialist is in the same position as the nonmember who would use knowledge of the book, if he had it, for his own profit. What the specialist is saying here, in fact, is that his monopoly of information provides him with an unusual trading advantage. It's obvious, but it's seldom stated so openly.

When it is worth his while, a specialist can hang ten thousand traders from the branch of one rumor. When he has enough orders on his book—say, from a price of 60 down to 50—the specialist can build up activity in his stock, then spread another rumor counteracting the rumor used to advance the stock. Once that rumor has been sent through brokers' boardrooms across the country (via the Dow Jones News Service, called "the broad tape"), enough sell orders can be counted on to enable him to have it announced over the ticker tape that "Due to an excess of sell orders trading was halted." He can then re-open the stock 10, 20, 30, or more points lower at the market's close. The following morning the specialist can open this same stock 10 or more points higher. Meanwhile it will have been possible for him to have sold out his inventory at the top and then established a short position for himself. By halting trading and re-opening his stock lower at the close, he is able to cover his short sales [9] and add to his long position. Occasionally he may even allow favored customers to do the same thing. Such an operation is totally against the law. But where are the checks that would discover and prevent it? Laws that are not enforced are meaningless.

Further, investors—even official investigators—do not have access to any but the most indirect, unspecific information. Anyone who wants to know what happened or is happening in the Exchange is obliged to burrow underground.

Burrowing once again, we see how specialists can use the information in their books, in the following example. The specialist in Fairchild Camera is Bill Meehan (he is also the specialist in RCA and many other stocks). On January 10, 1967, it appeared, from the price change and the number of shares, that his specialist unit had sold Fairchild short at 124¾. From that price it dropped to 120⅝, where it closed.

Few specialists fire a salvo to announce the end of a bull market in their stocks. Certainly Meehan doesn't. Many investors, who had seen Fairchild move down from its high at the 135 level, had probably entered stop orders with their brokers to sell it if it sold under 120.[10] On the following morning, Fairchild opened not at 120, not at 119, but at 116⅝. It is impossible to know, of course, what Meehan was doing that day, but this opening made it seem likely that Meehan's unit had indeed sold short the previous day. The opening of the stock at 116⅝ suggested that he now had not only covered any short sales but had also added stock to his trading account in preparation for a sharp rise in the price of Fairchild.[11]

Investors who had had their orders to sell executed at the 116⅝ opening now saw Fairchild move back up to 125⅜, where Meehan closed it.

Meehan's book provides specific knowledge about the number of shares available to him and at what prices. It would be useful, no doubt, to know what you can acquire under 120. His book also told him the price Fairchild Camera would have to drop to if the sell orders were to be executed in one transaction.

There is very little—far from enough—public information on short selling by specialists. We cannot be certain of what Meehan was doing, yet anyone who invests needs to try to predict; the investor must, therefore, put together such evidence as he can get, to form a working theory. An SEC bulletin shows the total of each day's short sales by all specialists together; the bulletin comes out, however, about two months after the fact. The pattern of movement in Fairchild that day coincided with what I have found to be, usually, short selling by a specialist.

For a striking example, see (on pp. 28–29) the DJIA and short sales by specialists for October 22, 1969. On that date the market, and many stocks, approximated their 1969 highs; to the accompaniment of a big increase in public buying, specialist short sales jumped from 746,840 shares to 1,016,950 shares. Note too the increase on that day in member short sales on and off the floor. Public demand for particular stocks not only made it possible for specialists and other members to sell out their holdings in these stocks (from their trading and segregated accounts) but to then sell these stocks short into the bargain.

The specialist's book makes it possible for him to sell at the top, and buy big blocks for himself and his big-block customers at the bottom.[12] For example, there was a rumor that a merger of Chicago and Northwestern Railroad with Essex Wire was imminent, and on Friday, August 4, 1967, the stock of Northwestern rose from 165½ to 171. At that price level, big blocks, representing informed money, began to move across the tape. When big blocks move after the kind of percentage gain in price that had occurred in Chicago and Northwestern in the previous week, it is an indication that the specialist unit has begun to unload its stock and the stock of its big-block customers.

On Monday, August 7, the Henderson specialist unit opened Chicago and Northwestern Railroad at 170. This

ROUND-LOT STOCK TRANSACTIONS ON THE NEW YORK STOCK EXCHANGE
(SHARES)

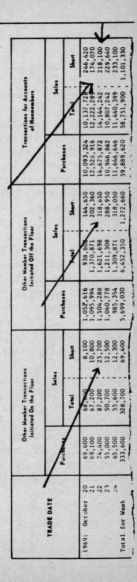

TRADE DATE	ALL ROUND-LOT SALES		Transactions of Specialists (except for Odd-lot Accounts) in Stocks in Which They are Registered			Round-lot Transactions for Odd-lot Accounts of Odd-lot Dealers and Specialists		
	Total	Sales Short	Purchases	Sales Total	Sales Short	Purchases	Sales Total	Sales Short
1969: October 20	13,544,510	1,039,530	2,177,030	2,110,160	640,360	148,940	231,020	0
21	16,406,090	1,134,070	2,553,810	2,560,100	746,840	220,270	245,570	0
22	19,331,120	1,579,400	2,882,910	3,177,090	1,016,950	193,650	300,890	0
23	14,786,070	1,230,140	2,558,690	2,452,710	699,050	164,740	264,110	0
24	15,434,140	1,241,130	2,572,700	2,373,180	677,680	163,940	255,090	0
Total for Week	79,558,930	6,224,270	12,745,140	12,729,300	3,780,880	891,540	1,296,680	0

TRADE DATE	Other Member Transactions Initiated On the Floor			Other Member Transactions Initiated Off the Floor			Transactions for Accounts of Nonmembers		
	Purchases	Sales Total	Sales Short	Purchases	Sales Total	Sales Short	Purchases	Sales Total	Sales Short
1969: October 20	69,600	68,900	8,100	1,052,616	938,605	144,650	10,093,324	10,137,728	246,420
21	69,100	67,200	10,800	1,095,994	1,370,871	202,360	12,525,916	12,222,289	174,070
22	74,400	87,200	25,700	1,504,288	1,621,698	318,650	14,675,872	14,144,242	218,100
23	55,000	50,700	12,500	1,060,778	1,211,308	288,950	10,946,862	10,807,242	229,640
24	65,500	55,600	12,300	985,354	1,309,871	318,050	11,646,646	11,440,399	233,100
Total for Week	333,600	328,700	69,400	5,699,030	6,452,350	1,272,660	59,889,620	58,751,900	1,101,330

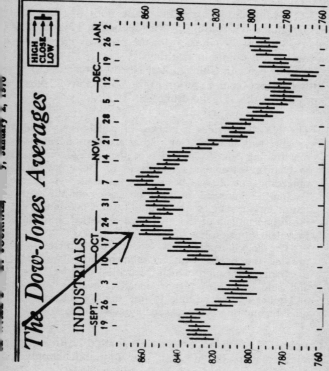

The Dow-Jones Averages

was down a full point from the Friday close—on only
300 shares. Henderson closed it that afternoon at 159,
down 11 points from the opening. After the close it was
announced that the merger with Essex had been called
off. Tuesday the stock didn't trade until just before the
end of that day's trading. It was opened at 120 on 45,000
shares—*down 39 points from the previous day's close*—
a total of 50 points in two days.[18]

The investor in Chicago and Northwestern could draw
little comfort from a section in the SSR (Part 2, page 78)
aptly titled the "Dealer Function":

The NYSE provides a market in which every traded
security can be bought or sold at any time during normal trading hours. The price of the transaction ought
to bear a reasonable relationship to the immediately
preceding one. It has been the consistent view of the
Exchange, expressed on many occasions and under different circumstances, that liquidity and continuity are
the prime indicia of the quality of a market. Exchange
President Funston has stated:

"The sole purpose of a modern marketplace is to
provide the public with an efficient and dependable
mechanism through which securities can be bought
and sold . . . This means, ideally, that every buyer
and seller should be able to find his opposite number
quickly, and at a price reasonably close to the last sale."

On page 79 of this report the SSR quoted Keith Funston:
"[If] specialists did not fill gaps in public supply and
demand, the result would be chaotic markets. . . . Individual stocks would reach new highs one day and new
lows the next."

Yet stocks registered with the Stott and Wagner specialist unit do reach new highs one day and new lows
the next. Robert Stott is the specialist in Xerox, Schenley
and a number of other stocks. In 1967, Xerox's board of

directors paid for an hour of television time to plug the financial establishment and its specialists. As though they'd come down in tandem all the way from the ark to 11 Wall Street, Xerox's directors focused on their specialist; I would also like to focus on him, on behalf of the shareholders in Schenley.

The Schenley Book: March 13, 14, and 15, 1967

Over the long term, the activity at Post Sixteen, where Robert Stott has his unit, tends to concentrate on one stock at a time. Schenley has been one of their most active stocks, because rumors have so often permitted bull raids in the stock. Again, in February, 1967, rumors of a merger were circulated—this time with Lorillard—and Schenley began to move up from the mid-30s to the accompaniment of a large increase in volume. On March 3, another rumor was teletyped through the brokerage boardrooms of the country that the directors of Lorillard, in conjunction with the directors of Schenley, were "considering a possible consolidation."

Schenley had advanced on Friday, March 10, to 61½. On Monday, March 13, after the rumor, it rose to a 1966–67 high of 63. Big blocks moved across the ticker tape. It was the second most active stock that day: it had a turnover of 172,500 shares and closed at 61⅞, up ⅜ above Friday's close.

I wondered if this specialist had employed his trading account in the manner outlined by the SEC in its 1962 Staff Report on the conduct of members of the American Stock Exchange. Commenting on Gilligan, Will's use of a trading account, the Staff Report had this to say (p. 31): "Upon occasion, the specialist's trading account distributed large blocks of stock to the public by selling short. The account then covered by transferring stock from specialists' long-term investment accounts . . ." By mid-morning Tuesday, March 14, rumors had begun that the Lorillard-Schenley merger was now off. Schenley began to decline. Trading was halted at 58.

Now we come to the most bizarre aspect of that day's activities—the part played by a near-legendary figure named Meshulam Riklis. The Exchange loves him for his big-block fees, and he likes their big-block facilities. On Tuesday, March 14, although trading had been halted and the public had not been allowed to participate, Riklis picked up 200,000 shares of Schenley at 50—the price at which it had re-opened at the end of the market day. Schenley then opened Wednesday morning at 60¾, an overnight advance of 10¾ points. Meshulam Riklis was not only on target but once again he'd hit the bull's eye. According to the available evidence. Riklis then started selling his 200,000 shares at this opening for a net profit of $2.1 million.

This brief outline can convey no adequate impression of the substantial maneuvers that must have taken place on March 14 and 15. Now, in order to illustrate a phenomenon repeated without stint on the floors of the Stock Exchanges, I will present two accounts that purport to tell what occurred. One is by the *Wall Street Journal*, the other by Meshulam Riklis' biographer as he allegedly was told the story by Meshulam Riklis. It is a rare felicity that two such contrary points of view exist to shed their light over a subject of such rapacious interest.

First the *Journal's* story.[14] The facts are there, in abundance; indeed, age cannot wither nor custom stale their infinite monotony:

TRADER THAT SCORED SCHENLEY STOCK COUP EVEN AMAZED HIMSELF

Riklis, Seeking Control of Firm, Had Glen Alden Buy 200,000 Shares, for $2 Million Profit

The *Journal*'s reporter continues:

Meshulam Riklis' frustrated desire to buy control of Schenley Industries, Inc., the big distilling company, turned into a stock-trading profit of nearly $2.1 million last week, Mr. Riklis disclosed.

The Chairman and President of Rapid-American Corp. over the weekend confirmed that Glen Alden Corp., which Rapid-American controls, was the mysterious trader that bought volatile Schenley shares at the bottom of a price slump Tuesday and sold high the next day. The transaction involved 200,000 Schenley shares, and the outcome was something of a surprise to Mr. Riklis, he conceded.[15] The identity of the trader was almost as hot a topic for discussion on Wall Street last week as the latest sure-fire tip.

The 43-year-old Mr. Riklis, whose complex of companies consists mostly of retail stores, had long been known to have hopes of persuading Lewis S. Rosenstiel, chairman of Schenley, to agree to a merger. These hopes were dashed two weeks ago when Schenley and P. Lorillard Co., the tobacco concern, reported they were discussing a consolidation.

Early last week, however, rumors that the Schenley-Lorillard talks had hit a snag began to spread. The New York Stock Exchange halted trading in Schenley Tuesday morning, and it didn't resume until the closing bell, when blocks of 301,400 and 14,000 shares were sold at $50, off $11.875 from the prior day's close.

On the chance that he might get another crack at Schenley if the Lorillard move flopped, Mr. Riklis had Glen Alden buy 200,000 of those shares at $50, a $10 million investment.

Tuesday night, Schenley and Lorillard announced agreement in principle on merger terms that one estimate valued at about $70 for each of Schenley's slightly more than 5 million outstanding shares.

. . . Mr. Riklis, disappointed again, ordered the Glen Alden block of Schenley shares sold for cash. The opening of trading was delayed until after noon on

Wednesday, but the first sale was made at $60.75, up $10.75 from Tuesday's close. Schenley closed Wednesday at $61.25 . . .

The Glen Alden block of Schenley was sold at a price of more than $61 a share Wednesday, returning a gross cash profit of about $2.3 million, before commissions and other charges reduced that by about $230,000, Mr. Riklis said. The net profit of nearly $2.1 million is before Federal income taxes, but Mr. Riklis said he believed it wouldn't be subject to taxes because of credits due to Glen Alden.

. . . *He said he had no idea why Schenley's price had dropped so sharply Tuesday, nor who had sold the shares Glen Alden bought* . . .[16]

If the directors of Lorillard had not announced "an agreement in principle" *after* the close Tuesday and *before* the opening Wednesday—if, in other words, they had waited till after the opening in Schenley on Wednesday—the bottom would have dropped out of Schenley.

Obviously such an idea is inadmissible. Riklis was employing the funds of Glen Alden, and the laws governing a director's speculations in company money do not admit of such a possibility. A final question, therefore, suggests itself. Could this speculation have been guaranteed? With patience, but without comment, I am still waiting for an answer.

I came on Oscar Schisgall's *The Magic of Mergers— The Saga of Meshulam Riklis*. On the dust jacket we are told that Riklis consented to the biography as follows:

"You know," he said after a silence, and with a curious note of humbleness, "this is a wonderful country—far more wonderful than I dreamed it would be when I first came here. If your purpose is to show what people can accomplish in America, I'll be glad to go along. I owe the country that." [17]

According to Schisgall, on what must have been Tuesday, March 14, Riklis was in his car driving into New York:

> He turned to the stock market quotations. After checking several prices he glanced at the Schenley listing. It was at slightly more than 58¼ —a price to which it had leaped since the possibility of the Lorillard merger had been announced. [The stock had closed on March 13 at 61⅞, not 58¼.—R.N.]
>
> There is always a telephone in Rik's car. Shortly after nine he called his office. His secretary said, "Mr. Becker's been wanting to talk to you. He says it's urgent. I'll switch you over."
>
> Financial Vice-President Isidore Becker sounded tense. "Rik, there's a rumor that the Schenley-Lorillard deal *fell through!*"
>
> Rik said flatly, "I don't believe it. Has anybody checked?"
>
> "Everybody's checked. But nobody at Schenley's or Lorillard wants to talk."
>
> "Where's Mr. Rosenstiel?"
>
> "Somewhere off the coast of Florida on his boat. Can't be reached."
>
> Rik hung up the telephone and settled back to think. He considered the situation . . .[18]

He then had to interrupt his reflections to give a talk on mergers at the Waldorf Astoria:

> As soon as he had answered the last question from the audience he hurried to a telephone booth. He called investment banker Bernard Cantor in Los Angeles.
>
> "Bernie," he said, "I want you to put in a bid for 200,000 shares of Schenley at 50. Immediately. For our Glen Alden account."
>
> "Schenley closed at 58."
>
> "I know it. I still say 50." [19]

We know that Schenley did *not* close at 58; on Monday, it closed at 61⅞. On Tuesday, though, trading was *halted* at 58. How was Bernie Cantor able to have an order executed when trading in the stock had been halted? No mention is made of this.

Schisgall continues:

> Cantor said, "At 50 it could be a hell of a good buy—if it goes that low."
>
> "If it doesn't, I'm not buying and I'm not losing anything," Rik said. "On the other hand, if we do get the 200,000 shares and the Lorillard deal is off, we'll have a good piece of Schenley when we resume negotiations. And if the rumor *isn't* true, Schenley will go up again, and we'll make money. Buy the 200,000 shares." [20]

Heavy is the burden of this thought. Would a company director take such a gamble with his company's money? Other stocks, to the accompaniment of similar adverse news, have been known to decline more than 50 per cent from their highs.

> What neither Rik nor Cantor knew was that a Swiss syndicate—never identified—had just offered 250,000 shares of Schenley to be sold. Perhaps the rumor of the merger's failure had alarmed them; they wanted to take their profit while it could still be had. [21]

It seems implausible that a Swiss syndicate with 250,000 shares to sell would sell them at 50. Is it not more likely that the 200,000 shares Riklis picked up were stop orders entered in the Stott book by the market's trusting public? If a Swiss syndicate did sell its shares, they would have been sold at or nearer Schenley's high. [22]

Schisgall's recounting of the incident seems to be in error. For instance, Schisgall says:

> At any rate, with so much uncertainty about the Schenley-Lorillard future, the stock exchange suspended trading in the securities for a single day. When business resumed the next morning, the price was down, and Rik got his 200,000 shares at $50 a share! [23]

"Business resumed" not the following day but at the closing bell of the same day on which trading was halted.

The reader will recall the *Wall Street Journal* article stating "Tuesday night, Schenley and Lorillard announced agreement in principle on merger terms." This, as we pointed out, was *before* the stock opened the following morning at $60.75; the following quote from Schisgall's book indicates that it was the day after Riklis entered his order that the merger was confirmed:

> That same afternoon both Lewis Rosenstiel [President of Schenley] and Lorillard officers were reached by the press, by stockbrokers, by investors. Both sides indignantly denied the rumor of a collapse of negotiations. Both assured all questioners that the merger was indeed scheduled to go through; there was not even a hint of its failure.[24]

It's not difficult to guess why or how this rumor was circulated. "Instantly the price of Schenley stock skyrocketed. Within twenty-four hours it went up 11 points to $61. Meshulam Riklis was back on the telephone. '*Sell* our 200,000 shares,' he ordered." [25]

With Riklis' help, Schisgall muddles through to a harmonious finale. The whole affair is a mystery. Today, almost three years later, we still don't know what happened. Key transactions are unclear; there is no direct evidence; one is left with an unsettling feeling. On the face of things, it looks as though the public, once again, didn't have a chance. We have a right to know.

NOTES, chapter 2

---

¹ All unexecuted orders are automatically cancelled at the close of the trading day unless they are marked "GTC," "good till cancelled." This means the order is to remain in effect until it is either executed or cancelled.

² Special Study Report, Part 2, p. 76.

³ Special Study Report, Part 2, p. 154.

⁴ Emphasis added. As for the preferential treatment, accorded company insiders by specialists, the SSR (Part 2, p. 158) quotes an excerpt from a staff memorandum that is indicative of the NYSE floor department's views in this respect: "I told [the specialist] that he should get together with [the president of an issuer] and establish a friendly relationship with him. I emphasized that his company is one of the Exchange's customers, and that it is the responsibility of the specialist to conduct himself in such a way as to please and satisfy the officials of the company . . ." Such advice, of course, presupposes that somehow specialists and company officials will suddenly become disinterested enough to do what, in the face of human nature, they would not otherwise be able to do.

⁵ Special Study Report, Part 2, pp. 77–78.

⁶ P. 38.

⁷ Staff Report, p. 39.

⁸ Special Study Report, Part 2, p. 77.

⁹ Short sales will be discussed in Chapter 5. In brief, to sell short you arrange to borrow shares of a stock that you hope will drop in price, sell it at a high price, then buy the same number of shares ("cover") when the price is low, to return the shares to the lender. The profit is the difference in price.

¹⁰ You will always find a broker ready to tell you how to sell your stock when it starts to drop. He'd sell you a large barrel if he could, and after you'd worn it, suggest a smaller size.

¹¹ The figures on transactions by specialists and by other members are from the SEC *Statistical Bulletin,* December, 1969.

¹² Sometimes with the assurance that these trades will not be recorded on the ticker tape. The technique for such transactions is

39 Richard Ney

discussed in the NYSE brochure *Marketing Methods for Your Block of Stock*. See pp. 131 *ff*.

13 Yet the Stock Exchange boasts that, for a fee, it can unload big blocks (of 50,000 shares or more) and that "the big-block transaction would not affect the price structure in the auction market adversely." (See Chapter 10.)

14 *Wall Street Journal*, March 20, 1967.

15 It's legitimate to ask if the *Journal*'s editor wondered a moment over Riklis' commitment of $10 million of Glen Alden resources on speculation the outcome of which had presumably not been predetermined.

16 Emphasis added. As for the *Wall Street Journal*—if indeed its publisher and editors wish to excise the evils in the investment industry—such examinations of the existing evidence can only leave the evil to flourish and proliferate as never before.

17 Boston: Little, Brown, 1968.

18 P. 221.

19 P. 222.

20 P. 222.

21 P. 222.

22 Too, we can fairly assume that the timing of this sale made it a Swiss bank's transaction for a numbered account on behalf of a NYSE member, not on behalf of a Swiss syndicate. Stock Exchange members' secret accounts are examined in Chapter 4.

23 P. 222.

24 P. 223.

25 P. 223.

3

Mr. Smith Goes to Washington

**You have to work harder
when you're number two.**

If a consensus is wanted supporting the specialist, there
are those who are willing to provide it. However, this
consensus will not include the name of Don Smith, President of the Wolverine Aluminum Corporation. Smith is
one corporation president who is willing to fight the
Exchange when he finds that it poses a threat to his
stockholders' interests.

On July 9, 1965, Wolverine's stock was admitted to
trading on the American Stock Exchange. On that day,
as is the custom for officers of newly listed companies,
Smith went to visit the floor of the Exchange to be introduced to his specialist and to purchase the first 100 shares
of his company's stock to trade on the Exchange. As
Smith walked into the lobby, he was greeted by the Stock
Exchange uproar:

> The screaming and shouting which sounded like bedlam
> coming from the floor of the Exchange . . . more like
> a fish market than a sedate place of business . . . we
> watched the activity on the floor . . . it looked . . .
> like a bunch of grownups playing cowboys and Indians

40

. . . Many of the clerks up the slopes of the Exchange were extremely busy throwing paper wads at each other.[1]

Something told him he had made a mistake: "A little voice kept telling me, 'Don, get out of here. This is not the place.' There was no dignity . . . [it] was not at all conducive to a pleasant feeling of trust."[2]

The Exchange then showed him a movie:

Watching this movie, I was amazed . . . Early in the movie a handsome young man arrives on the floor of the Exchange apparently to start working there, and his first words were "Hello, Dad." Nothing more need be said about this. This answered one of the questions that came to my mind later about how you become a specialist.

At eleven o'clock in the morning, Smith purchased the first 100 shares of Wolverine at 12⅛.

After luncheon with Exchange officials, Smith returned to the floor, where he learned that his stock had just traded at 11¾. At home that night he found that the day's high was 12⅛, and that only 300 shares had traded in the day. It was Friday night, and what he refers to as "the beginning of the nightmare."

Monday morning, Smith called the Exchange. He was told that the market for Wolverine stock on Friday was 11¾ bid and 12¼ asked. He knew this was wrong. He had personally stood at the trading post before the opening, and the specialist had told him that the market was 12 bid and 12¼ asked, and he had bought the first 100 shares in the middle, at 12⅛. When he asked why the price had fallen off after his purchase, he was told that the market had dropped and that the specialist "had moved Wolverine Aluminum down in sympathy with other stocks." But Don Smith didn't want his stock moving up and down "in sympathy"—furthermore, the Dow Jones Industrial Average on the Big Board had finished higher by 1.64! [3]

Smith then learned that the specialist had had no inventory in his stock. Yet he had "supplied" him with 100 shares at 12⅛. Subsequently,

> during the day 200 shares were offered for sale, and 100 shares were purchased by a brokerage firm for one of their customers at 12. At this point the specialist made the market 11⅞ bid and 12 asked. There was no further activity for a while, so soon the specialist reduced the bid price to 11¾ and kept the asking price at 12. The specialist then purchased the second 100 shares for his own account at 11¾, and he was now even in his stock account but had made ⅜ of a point by buying 100 shares at 11¾ in order to pay me the 100 shares he owed me and had previously sold to me at 12⅛.

The drop in Wolverine stock that first day had nothing to do with management, earnings, or anything else. What had happened, Smith realized, was that this specialist had sold short at 12⅛ to supply him his 100 shares and had covered that short position at 11¾ for a profit to the specialist. Smith then got on the phone to the Exchange:

> Suddenly, near the end of the phone conversation offering me these answers, the dream had become a shambles and bitterness began to creep in. To realize suddenly that a distant disinterested specialist could so arrogantly and thoughtlessly, and with a complete lack of consideration for you or me or Wolverine, do what he had done on the first day of trading with our stock, shocked me almost beyond belief. It suddenly became crystal clear that those feelings of suspicion had been completely verified and that the finest thing we could do for Wolverine and for our shareholders was to get out of there as fast as we could.

An Exchange spokesman advised him that "the specialist had lowered the price of Wolverine because it had had a $2.00 per share run-up in the few weeks before the beginning of trading on the Exchange." Don Smith knew this wasn't true. If it had been, why would the specialist have opened it on the American Stock Exchange at 12⅛ on its first trade? It dawned on him

> that the specialist on the first day of trading had lowered the price of Wolverine Aluminum Corporation stock from 12⅛ to 11½ bid, and that if you multiply ⅝ of a point by the 492,000 shares of Wolverine stock outstanding, the specialist had, with the flick of his pencil and eraser, removed more than a quarter of a million dollars from the market value of the outstanding shares of Wolverine.[4]

Smith advised the Exchange official that he planned to delist and withdraw his stock from trading on the Exchange as soon as possible. The official apologized and admitted the explanation given him had been incorrect; he insisted, however, that Smith couldn't delist, that the Exchange provided him and his firm with a renowned pedigree, etc., etc. Obviously, the Exchange preferred the sign that said "Enter Here" to the one that said "Exit."

More than anything else, Don Smith was appalled at the power of the specialist. To give this power to "one person or a small group of people is an invitation to disaster. It is hard to believe that any human being could long resist using the information for personal gain." Smith's conclusion deserves the careful attention of his fellow capitalists:

> The specialist who arbitrarily lowered the bid price of our stock on the first day was a perfect example of the arrogance, the thoughtlessness and complete disregard for any persons except his own position, and this was a clear message. The specialist made ⅜ of a point on the stock he sold to me, and this amounts to $37.50 gross.

Certainly this does not concern me because I can spill that much Scotch, but the message became clear: the power, and what could be done, and the lack of controls.

Talking to an Exchange official, Smith was informed: "The only thing the specialists must report to the Exchange is the percentage of the purchases and sales that they made against the trend of the market." If the thoughts of the Exchange spokesman ran in circles, Smith's didn't:

This proves now to be the most meaningless figure in the world even though it makes them look like heroes. Why don't they publish the only figure that has any meaning whatsoever, and this is how much profit each specialist makes buying and selling stocks for his own account that he is assigned and in which he makes the market. No other figures háve any value.

The Exchange's spokesman reminded Smith that the system's formula of *caveat emptor* had worked well in the past and that "interference with these processes is dangerous." But Smith is not only a theorist but also a practical man. He regards the concept of "let the buyer beware" as just what it is, a special brand of nip reserved for the fat cat. He was told that "this must be an excellent method of operating a market because it has survived for so many years." But as Smith stated to Wolverine stockholders:

This, of course, did little to convince us. Many things have survived for many, many years that are not the best . . . We are firmly convinced that the small investor does not have any chance in a market of this type and repeat again and again, there must be a better way.

In his letter to Wolverine stockholders, Smith gave some of the conclusions he had gleaned from his unhappy encounter with the Stock Exchange:

We admit that there must of necessity be a marketplace where Wolverine stock can be bought and sold, but we say that this price should not vary during the day and should not vary from day to day and should move only occasionally and very gradually and only because of supply and demand caused by three things: earnings, dividends and future prospects of the company. Nothing else matters. Par value means nothing. Book value means nothing unless the company is going to liquidate. Past performance means very little except as a guide because there certainly is no guarantee that next year will be like last year. We feel that the ideal "better way" would be to have a market price set by a salaried expert running a computer and who would be expressly prohibited from buying or selling or owning or dealing in the stocks on which he is setting the price. This expert could analyze all of the facts pertaining to the stock and set a price, one price, and not a bid and asked price, and this would be the price at which stocks should be bought and sold, plus or minus a fair commission. Obviously, this would put all specialists and market makers out of business so there is very little chance of this occurring.

Don Smith thus became committed to the same basic convictions that caused me to fly to Washington in June, 1963, to present my testimony on the specialist system before the Senate Subcommittee on Banking and Currency. There, I stated: "There is no question but that the specialist does provide certain benefits, but they are nothing . . . a trained attendant could not perform."

Wolverine's specialist taught Smith that if you draw enough water you'll find mud at the bottom of the well:

Observing again on the only reporting done by specialists and the reason we find the figures they publish are meaningless is this (and an officer of the Exchange admitted this could be done. However, the specialist might get his wrist slapped). Hypothetically, "North Overshoe Manufacturing Company" could be selling at $12.00 per share. The specialist could, over a period of weeks or days, lower his price gradually down to about $10.00 and keep buying stock for his own account. Then he could stop buying and hold the stock in inventory and work the price back up to $12.00 and then work it gradually from $12.00 to $14.00 and sell his inventory of stock. Then he could smilingly send in an excellent report stating that he had made 100 per cent of his purchases and sales against the trend of the market and still he would have to work overtime to count his profits in large bills. We do not say that this is being done. We only say that it is possible and that no reports are required regarding this. If there is a better set-up, then we are not aware of it.

The specialist has immunity and exceptionally poor controls. He never has to meet or face an irate stockholder who has lost money in the market. Most investors probably don't even know what specialists are and certainly none of them ever know who the specialist is that handles the stocks that they deal in. This must breed indifference to the public among the specialists. If not, they would not be human.

Smith came away with some definite views on the SEC's permissiveness and partiality toward the Exchange:

We, as officers and directors of a corporation, and of course this now applies to many more corporations than in the past under recent Federal legislation, must report monthly to the Securities and Exchange Commission and to the Exchange if we buy or sell one share of stock in our own company, and if we make a profit buying and selling because of inside information, we could be held liable. We were informed by the Legal Department of the Exchange that the specialists who deal freely for their own account in the stocks that they handle need not report to any person, to the Exchange or to any agency the profits they might make dealing in their stocks.

Don Smith gained a valuable and all too rare insight into a kinship system that keeps wealth and power within a tightly knit and homogeneous circle. He saw the Exchange as part of a culture in which all conflicts are resolved by the specialist's big-money power plays with the aid of his political weapon—a bureaucracy that exists in order to protect and condition the public to accept and support the specialist system.

Two years later, the Exchange was still insisting that Smith pay his company's annual listing fee. Still refusing to pay the money, he concluded a letter to the American Stock Exchange in January, 1967, as follows: "Our complaint about this to you and the SEC got us nowhere, and we received a standard reply from the SEC that while the actions of the specialists might be questionable . . . nothing could be done."

In December, 1967, Don Smith went to Washington. He had decided his problem had not engaged the attention of the proper authorities. Shortly thereafter Wolverine Aluminum was delisted.

NOTES, chapter 3

---

[1] All quotes in this chapter are from Don Smith's July 22, 1965, letter to Wolverine shareholders, unless otherwise noted.

[2] Nor are matters any better on the NYSE. According to an article in the *Institutional Investor* (August, 1969), "An Anthropological View of the Floor," "People have used other metaphors to describe the floor. The most common was the one used in the SEC's special study: a private club. But one broker refers to it as a snake pit—'and you want to be a cobra.' And others compare it to a battlefield. 'You have to go to war too often down there,' says one wearily; 'it's a vicious environment.'

"Still others compare the floor to a nursery school, citing the somewhat youthful goings-on. Piles of shaving cream on Bob Meffert's shoes. Eddie Cohan's deadly aim with a water pistol. John Uzielli handcuffed to a post for two hours . . .

"The crowd at Post #3 treats specialist John 'Buddy' Conklin as a pack of teenagers might treat a Beatle. They are ripping off his shirt, starting with the collar. Conklin is beginning to get angry; after all, he bought the shirt at lunch because the one he wore in the morning had met a similar fate."

The same article states: "New chairman Bernard H. Lasker's first major policy directive, issued on June 6 of this year, noted that 'any sort of practical joke which causes water, powder, balloons, and the like to fall on the floor increases the chance that someone will be injured. This factor alone urges the discontinuance of such practices. However, in addition, water and powder can get into electric machinery and teletypewriters so they might not operate properly. Also . . . unbecoming conduct observed from the gallery lowers the image of the membership and the Exchange.' Any member acting in an unseemly fashion will now pay a $1,000 fine. A second memo was dispatched to the floor clerks."

[3] On July 14, 1965, in answer to a letter from me in which I took exception to the specialist's transaction in Jewel Tea, Keith Funston, the President of the NYSE, replied as follows:

"With respect to the decline in price in Jewel Tea on June 21, there were four transactions in this stock, each involving 100 shares, at the following prices: 65, 65, 64⅜ and 63⅞. The specialists who already had a long position, bought the last 200 of the 400 shares sold. The market on that day, as measured by the popular Dow Jones Industrial Average, was down 5.05 points."

We see here that it is the rationale provided by an advancing or declining Dow Jones Average that alibis the advance or decline of all other stocks. It can be said, therefore, that the 30 specialists determine the prices of the 30 stocks in the Dow Jones Industrial Average which, in turn, determine the economic health of the nation.

The fact is, specialists set the prices of stocks and determine the overall prices, therefore, at which these crosses will be made. Surprisingly enough, we learn that there are still large sections of contemporary Wall Street opinion that are either unaware or totally disregard the autonomy of the specialist to set prices—

and that it is this function that is all important since it is this function that makes possible the investment profits and big block fees of Wall Street's financial hierarchy. The practical conclusion to be drawn from this fact is that as long as the specialist system is allowed to exist there is no easy way out of this desperately complex situation. Conversations with the very gifted partners of large Wall Street investment banking firms revealed that even they are unaware of the grand strategies of the specialist system. In consequence, although my appraisal of this system finds a sympathetic audience among many on Wall Street, this audience still includes many among whom Wall Street's conditioned reflexes are still conspicuously stronger than the human spirit. Thus, even though we find the heads of many of the largest investment banking firms in overall agreement with my "basic premises about the specialist system," they feel obliged to make a generalized comment to the effect that I "tend to overstate the case." This must be expected because while they are partly creators, they are also the creatures of their total environment.

[4] On a larger scale, a 1-point drop in the price of GM—which has 285.3 million shares outstanding—lowers the market value by more than a quarter of a billion dollars.

4

Specialists' Investment Accounts
or
Sodom at the Bottom

**The money stolen from many
is divided among a few.**

A specialist's trading account, like his book, is a device that benefits a highly privileged few as they trade with the unprivileged many. According to Exchange public relations, however, the specialist's trading account is employed to service the market in his stock; his trades for this account are confined to those reasonably necessary to maintain a fair and orderly market. In an actively traded stock a substantial percentage of specialist income is derived not only from the trading account's commissions but also from the profits he makes for this account "trading with the book"—that is, trading in this account against orders sent in to brokers by customers and placed on the book. When he does this, he often "reaches" for a bid or offer, which then establishes a new price level. In other words, the "liquidity" he supposedly offers is of greater advantage to him than to the public. If he had to wait for members of the public to trade with the orders that are on his book, he would be less likely to effect transactions at prices that served to establish new highs or lows in his stock.

> For example the quote may be 50 bid, offered at 51, with the last sale at 50½ and with the specialist as broker bidding for 200 shares at 50 for the book. If the specialist sells 100 shares for his own account, to the book at 50, he creates a new price; if he "cleans up the book" by selling it 200 shares, the next bid may be at 49½, and thus he has widened the quote. The third proposal [which was not adopted—R.N.] would have prevented the specialist from trading with the book at prices that would establish new highs or lows for the day, thus preventing the specialist from stimulating public speculation by his own trades.[1]

Specialists do not confine their transactions to their trading accounts, however. In addition, they use two basic types of segregated accounts. One, called the "segregated investment account," and sometimes called "long-term investment account," is used by the specialist in a number of ways, but was essentially established for tax purposes. In another segregated account—called an "omnibus account"—all orders for buying or selling stock are placed in the name of a bank or a brokerage house. In both cases regulations provide for the keeping of records with the Exchange. The major point of these regulations, however, is less to protect the public than to enable the Exchange hierarchy to say "Members have abided by the rules."

The Exchange's rules are curiously silent regarding the use of omnibus accounts by specialists. In a related matter, the investigations of former U.S. Attorney Robert M. Morgenthau revealed that many brokerage firms conduct a large portion of their business for such accounts. According to Morgenthau, "Many New York brokers deal in such large volume for Swiss banks that they either maintain open Telex lines or talk on the telephone with them several times a day." [2]

There is a formidable conflict between the use of omnibus accounts by specialists on behalf of their own portfolios and those of their families and friends, and the whole stated scheme and purpose of the specialist system. Under the most favorable conditions there remains the question whether the omnibus account or any account other than his trading account can be reconciled with existing rules governing the specialist's participation in the market.

In the words of the Special Study Report:

Specialists' dealings may be motivated by considerations of tax planning rather than by the needs of the market. In the Amex report, certain observations were made with respect to the practice of some specialists on that exchange of segregating securities in which they were registered as specialists in long-term investment accounts:

"The primary motive behind the creation of these accounts is to turn profits which would otherwise be taxed as ordinary income into long-term capital gains. Section 1236 of the Internal Revenue Code is the key provision. It provides that a gain by a dealer in securities from the sale of a security shall not be considered as a capital gain unless: (a) the security was identified within 30 days of the acquisition as a security held for investment; and (b) the security was not, at any time after the expiration of such thirtieth day, held by such dealer primarily for sale to customers in the ordinary course of his trade or business . . .

"However, purchases made on the Exchange for the purpose of segregation into long-term investment accounts raise problems which go to the heart of the specialist system. The specialist is permitted to trade for his own account only when such trades affirmatively contribute to the maintenance of a fair and orderly market . . . Where the specialist goes into the market with the intention of segregating the securities purchased and not with the purpose of creating a fair and orderly market, the trading is clearly contrary to the statutory and regulatory standards. Beyond this, the specialist with a long-term position now has a stake in seeing that the security rises in price—he has become an 'investor' as well as a dealer . . .

"A further problem arises when the specialist who maintains such long-term accounts is required to sell stock to maintain a fair and orderly market and he has no stock in his specialist trading account . . . [if] the 6-month period of the tax statute is almost over, the specialist may well be tempted to keep his stock in the long-term account and neglect the needs of the market."

That this practice and attendant problems also relate to the NYSE is indicated by the fact that as of June 16, 1961, when total specialist inventory was 3,229,556 shares, 890,733 shares or 28 per cent of the total inventory were segregated into long-term investment accounts.[3]

Needless to say these figures do not include the specialists' omnibus accounts.

On page 165, Part 2, the SSR states: "Specialists frequently establish these [segregated] accounts by taking advantage of their exemption from Federal margin regulations, a purpose contrary to the purpose of the exemption."

Exercising his power to control prices, the specialist will keep the price of his stock up until he has sold his and his friends' investment portfolios. An alibi is then provided to rationalize a decline in stock prices. The ability to make this adjustment in the price of his stocks is part of every specialist's bag of tricks. And after this operation, he needs no extraordinary incentives to establish new investment accounts at prices anywhere from 50 to 75 per cent below the price level at which he sold out his portfolio.

Here is what could happen. At a time and a price of his own choosing, and with the approval of the Exchange, the SEC, and the Fed, the specialist can press the market's panic button. It is in the chaos of selling that ensues that he acquires his stock. His purchases have two distinctive features: they are made without risk, and their profitability is guaranteed. It's like shooting fish in a barrel. The legacy of privileges central to the segregated account exists within an economic tradition that nourishes the idea that privation and poverty are a cultural norm. No man of conscience can be indifferent to the impact of the segregated investment account.

Whether the stock is segregated into a "tax account" or a simple investment account depends on whether the specialist unit is a corporation, a partnership, or an arrangement in which all trading profits and losses are regarded as gains or losses to income. For example, if, within a partnership, the specialist must hold stock six months in order to declare a long-term capital gain, then he will segregate his investment portfolio into a "tax account." On the other hand, if the specialist regards all gains as ordinary income or if he is taxed as a corporation, then he may minimize taxes in other ways. If a specialist supervises 40 stocks, it is probable that he will, at one time or another, establish one or more segregated accounts in most of these stocks—and, more often than not, he can hold these stocks' prices down if he chooses, despite good earnings, until he has enough in his own accounts to take the edge off his appetite. Therefore, because of its built-in incentives, the segregated investment account is the key to an entire chain of the specialist's manipulative activities.

In a stock with only a small capitalization or floating supply, the segregation of large blocks into long-term investment accounts for the specialist further decreases the supply of stock available to the public. The specialist thus accelerates the advance of that stock far beyond the best interests of stockholders, who may be left holding the bag when his investment accounts are liquidated. Often the specialist has no stock in his trading or investment accounts. In this case, his short selling creates excessive participation, since he must drop the price of his stock, then, in order to cover this short position profitably.

The language employed by the Exchange to rationalize the effect that the specialist's segregated tax accounts have on the public is striking for its blurring of focus. The Exchange asserts that stock segregated by the specialist and placed in special tax accounts "must be made available to the market if necessary" and then adds, "or the specialist must sell short in an amount at least equal to the amount in the investment account" (Special Study Report, Part 2, p. 134). He is, to be sure, happy to supply as much stock as public demand can absorb by selling short, and even to sell stock from his segregated accounts, once the price has advanced to what he has decided will be its intermediate or major high.

Selling to the public the stock he has accumulated for himself in these accounts—selling at their highs—is the logical outcome of the existence of segregated accounts. At such times the Exchange, approaching reality with great care, can truthfully say that "the stock in the long-term investment account of the specialist has been made available to the market." The Exchange's practice of manipulating language to show its own operations in a favorable light is crucial.

The *Los Angeles Times* of December 10, 1968, ran an Associated Press story that included statements by Robert M. Morgenthau, then U.S. Attorney for the Southern District of New York—the Wall Street area— and Irving M. Pollack of the SEC concerning Stock Exchange members' use of "special omnibus accounts":

Morgenthau and Irving M. Pollack, director of trading and markets for SEC, also said foreign banks have been used as intermediaries by corporate officials dodging legal curbs on inside-information trading in their own stocks. Key to the use of Swiss banks in market operations, Pollack said, is the "special omnibus account," which an exchange member firm may carry for a foreign bank. Trading for the bank's customers [among whom are specialists and other members—R.N.] is done through this account.[4]

The New York Stock Exchange, in answer to a query by the Special Study group concerning the long-term investment account, stated its position as follows:

The Exchange also believes that it is perfectly proper for the specialist unit to carry stock in a long-term investment account. This is based on the following considerations:

1. The specialist acquires the position through transactions made to maintain a fair and orderly market;
[The position is acquired subsequent to the specialist's having sold an investment account at top prices. Contrary to all the principles of a fair and orderly market, he is then anxious to establish a new position for himself.—R.N.]

2. The stock in the long-term investment account of the specialist unit must be made available to the market, if necessary, or the specialist must sell short in an amount at least equal to the amount in the investment account;
[The investment account is then subsequently delivered over to the trading account to cover the short sales and a long-term capital gain is established!—R.N.]

3. The specialist does not cause price trends, since these are the result of public supply and demand;
[We know the specialist *does* establish price trends *contrary* to the laws of demand.—R.N.]

4. The Exchange polices [*sic*] its specialists to see that fair and orderly markets are maintained by them.
[No comment.—R.N.] [5]

The SSR commented that "In view of [the] regulatory background, the points numbered 1, 3, and 4 in the NYSE statement seem somewhat disingenuous."

James Gilligan of Gilligan, Will and Co. was one specialist whose use of segregated accounts became public. Elected to membership on the American Stock Exchange on June 25, 1919, he resigned on April 28, 1961. In the years 1959 and 1960, "the stocks in which Gilligan, Will specialized accounted for 10.31 per cent and 7.5 per cent of all [American] Exchange volume, respectively. In addition, the firm is an important source of financing to other specialists." [6] The firm—now headed by Gilligan's son, two sons of Will's, and three other men—carried on the business. It was quite a business: in 1962, the firm had 44 specialty stocks (17 of them newly listed securities acquired between July 1, 1956, and September 30, 1961—"more than any other specialist account [was allocated]" [7]), as well as those they handled in conjunction with other specialist units that were financed by Gilligan, Will:

> The joint accounts which Gilligan, Will finances currently specialize in 85 securities of 76 issuers. This gives Gilligan, Will participation in specialist trading accounts in 129 securities of 118 issuers, including those securities traded at Post 23 [the Gilligan, Will post].[8]

According to the SEC, "One of the features which often characterized securities listed at the Gilligan, Will post was that prior to listing the companies sold stock to the prospective specialists, partners of Gilligan, Will, and agency accounts maintained at Gilligan, Will, generally at prices below the current market." [9] One illustration of the operations of this specialist unit is their affair with

Occidental Petroleum. James Gilligan was personally involved in joint drilling operations with this company, and he spent $89,600 on them. As the SEC puts it:

> Such participation gave Gilligan information regarding the progress of the company's business affairs which was not available to the general public. Gilligan stated that he resigned from his firm rather than give up this joint venture interest. He still retains the interest and Gilligan, Will, the firm of which his son is now senior partner and in which Gilligan retains a substantial financial interest, remains registered as specialist . . .[10]
>
> A specialist's long-term account at Gilligan, Will purchased 25,000 shares of Occidental Petroleum stock from the brother of the company's president on November 24, 1959 at 3¼ and the same account purchased 30,000 shares on January 29, 1960 at 5½ from one of the largest stockholders of the company . . .[11]
>
> A specialist's long-term account at Gilligan, Will purchased a total of 85,000 shares in 1959 and early 1960 from the company and from individuals close to the company. All 85,000 shares were sold on the Exchange from February 29, 1960 through December 13, 1960 . . .[12]
>
> Another long-term account acquired 5,000 shares of the common stock of Howell Electric Motors from two of the officers of that company . . .
>
> In January 1959, the specialist long-term account acquired 100,000 [Guild Films] shares . . . This long-term account delivered out 100,000 shares for sale on the Exchange in 1960 . . . In addition [one of the Gilligan, Will joint-account specialist unit's] investment account acquired 68,768 shares in late 1958, which shares were placed in the specialist's trading account on December 23, 1959 and eventually distributed to the public.
>
> . . . All of the above transactions were off the Exchange and in many instances were followed by distribution on the Exchange.[13]

Gilligan used his trading account to distribute large blocks of stock to the public by selling short. The trading account then covered the short sales by transferring the stock from the long-term investment accounts into the trading account.

The Staff Report devotes many pages to Gilligan, Will's finagling and in the course of them says a number of harsh things about this specialist unit. We have the figures—some of them—on Gilligan, Will, but how do we know the specialist units on the New York Stock Exchange do less?

Nowhere in that Staff Report are figures given that would pinpoint the profit to the specialists and the loss to the public that result from the specialist's use of long-term investment accounts; nowhere is there even a mention of the specialist's omnibus accounts. The Report states that "Specialists have been shown to be the dominant group in the government of the Exchange." [14] Where, then, is the complete, uncompromising investigation of specialist activities—on *both* Exchanges—that the public is due? [15]

The lengthiest investigation we have had—which is not of course to say that it was sufficient or effective—is the SEC's Special Study. In a memorandum dated September 24, 1964, the New York Stock Exchange dispensed with the Special Study Report and the long-term investment account as follows:

SPECIALISTS' LONG–TERM INVESTMENT AC– COUNTS

Proposed Measures Adopted by the Board:
None at this time.

Discussion:
The SEC Special Study recommended that all securities in which a specialist is registered, which are owned by

that specialist or his unit, should be maintained in a single trading account and should not be segregated for tax purposes.

The Exchange believes strongly that specialists should have the right to maintain long-term investment accounts, since the favorable tax consideration involved —which are available to all other investors—help prevent erosion of specialists' capital invested in their specialty stocks.

Further discussion of this question between the Exchange and the SEC has been deferred.

Thus, the light was switched on, allowed to shine for a brief moment, then abruptly switched off.

NOTES, chapter 4

---

[1] Special Study Report, Part 2, p. 80.

[2] Testimony before the House Banking and Currency Committee, quoted in the *Wall Street Journal*, April 23, 1969.

[3] Special Study Report, Part 2, p. 133.

[4] Taken as a whole, Morgenthau's indictment of the broker's use of the numbered Swiss omnibus account is a marvelous achievement. Obviously Morgenthau is aware that the present Attorney General is closely allied to the Exchanges since his professional expertise was not on the bench but as a municipal bond expert. One can only applaud the felicity of purpose that inspired Morgenthau. As a political animal he must have known that his days would be numbered.

The Internal Revenue Service was just about to hand Congress a statement supporting legislation to enforce disclosure of transfers of money to foreign banks when pressure from "the nation's most respectable bankers" caused the IRS statement to be withdrawn, according to Jack Anderson's column in the January 29, 1970, *Washington Post*.

[5] Special Study Report, Part 2, p. 134.

[6] SEC, *Staff Report on the Organization, Management, and Regulation of Conduct of Members of the American Stock Exchange,* January 3, 1962, p. 23.

[7] Staff Report, p. 24.

[8] Staff Report, p. 25.

[9] Staff Report, p. 26.

[10] Staff Report, p. 28.

[11] Staff Report, p. 29.

[12] Staff Report, p. 32.

[13] Staff Report, p. 29.

[14] Staff Report, p. 19.

[15] Much is made of "specialist liquidity" and the need of specialists for more capital. Completely ignored is the fact that it is not specialist capital that is at issue, but the investment accounts and omnibus accounts of specialists which "are contrary to the statutory and regulatory standards" (see p. 53). Give specialists more capital, grant them greater exemptions from margin regulations (see William McChesney Martin letter p. 115 and p. 116) and the fact is specialists might well use this added capital to acquire larger investment and omnibus accounts for themselves. As for the "threat" presented by mutual funds and the necessity that they might force the specialist to absorb big blocks of stock—if such big blocks were, indeed, a threat—is it likely that specialists would go searching for them as they do? (See the brochure "Marketing Methods for your Block of Stock: An Investment Manager's Handbook," published by the NYSE, p. 131.)

5

The Short Sale
or
When His Cup Runneth Over Watcheth Out

If you can't stand the sting, don't reach for the honey.

One day your telephone rings. It's your broker. Boeing, he tells you, is about to get the SST contract—you can't miss. So you buy Boeing—and then you watch the price drop. No one had told you that public demand can send a stock's price down, that, in fact, demand is often the signal that sends the specialist to the barricades armed with his short sale.

In the hands of the specialist, the short sale is a device that begins by ignoring and ends by violating the laws of supply and demand. Commonly, the short sale is used by traders anticipating a decline in the price of a stock. Three actions are involved. First, the trader must arrange to borrow stock. Second, he must sell it. Third, he must go into the market—though it needn't be immediately— and complete the transaction by buying the same stock in order to replace the borrowed shares. After the first two steps, he has no alternative; ultimately, whether the price goes down or up he must buy that amount of the stock. This is called "covering" (covering his previous short sale). The difference between the price when he covers and the price he received for his short sale is the short seller's profit or loss.

Those who aren't specialists are more likely to end a short sale with a loss than with a profit. The main difference between specialist and nonmember short selling is timing: the specialists (and their friends) know *when* to sell short; the public doesn't. The converse of this is also true: the specialist knows *when* to cover his short sales; the public doesn't. There are three reasons for this: (1) the prediction value of the book, (2) the specialist's immediate access to the market, and (3) the specialist's control over prices.

In Chapter 2, the advantages the specialist derives from his book and the forecast of prices (including knowledge of ceilings and floors) the book can give him were discussed. His "immediacy advantage," also discussed in Chapter 2, is of enormous value in short selling —he is right there when the price is, for instance, 60; the public, on the other hand, can put in an order when the price is 60 but by the time the order is executed the price could be anything. The fact that the specialist is the one who sets his stock's prices, albeit within limits, is obviously beneficial to the specialist engaged in short selling.

Another basic difference between public and specialist short selling is the specialist's ready access to vast supplies of stock, enough to meet almost any demand—the result of his contacts with bankers and with brokers.[1] Brokers control a great deal of their customers' stock, which they hold "in street name," and according to the terms of their customers' margin agreements, can lend this stock out. In more than 99 out of 100 cases, a specialist can supply all the stock needed to meet demand.

Nonmembers who sell short will frequently do it at the market's bottom and just before the market is about to rise. The public is tricked into covering their short sales at the top of an advance or rally, just as prices are about to decline. The specialist always knows when a short sale has been made: the customer's order slip when handed to the specialist is marked "short sale." Once a nonmember has committed himself by selling short, the specialist can raise the price of his specialty stock one or more points on every 100 shares, if he chooses. Those who sold short watch the price climbing and are easily frightened into covering at a loss. No nonmember who sells short can have the vaguest idea when it is best to cover in a rising market: a 3-point rally and he is taking Alka-Seltzers, 5 points and he is an insomniac. A specialist can raise his stock's price 7 points or more in one transaction—before dropping it. For this, the specialist must obtain the approval of a floor governor, who himself may be another specialist.

According to the SSR (Part 2, p. 247):

In 1934 the Senate Banking and Currency Committee found that "few subjects relating to Exchange practices have been characterized by greater differences of opinion than that of short selling," and the matter was one of the central issues in controversy during the Congressional scrutiny of exchanges and their practices which led to enactment of the Securities Exchange Act of 1934.

Since the turn of the century major declines in the stock market have prompted public debates and arguments over the specialist's short selling practices. Congressional committees have responded to the uproar by conducting investigations for the benefit of the press. One of the reasons specialists still enjoy high esteem is that despite all the noise made by countless congressional committees that should have made specialists' short selling practices known to the public, these practices and their consequences have remained unknown. There are rules that purport to govern their practices, but the specialist does not need to be crude in order to violate their intent— he can, with finesse, weave his way through the rules.

If it is true that habits of work become habits of thought, then the ability to sell short must obviously foster habits and attitudes congenial to short selling. That is, the specialist's ways of thinking and his customary ways of reacting to public demand are determined to some extent by the discipline imposed on him by the existence of short selling as a practice. An examination of the use made by the specialist of the short selling instrument, of the opportunities for financial gain and price control it affords him, and of the imposing myths employed by the regulatory bodies, by Congress and the Exchanges to rationalize short selling, will show not only that the myths of the specialist system are the servants of its short selling techniques but that these techniques are the servants of the myths.

The impact on the economy of the specialist's use of short selling can be attributed to a failure on the part of government to regulate the Exchanges; with the tacit permission of the government, the financial interests of a few have taken precedence over the interests of all. No amount of rationalizing can mask the competitive advantage the short selling technology has placed at the specialist's disposal or the magnitude of the devastation it has caused. Yet the Special Study group failed to place this device in proper perspective. And because of this, the Special Study Report becomes little more than a piece of propaganda in code, dedicated to the greater glory of short selling:

In part, the objections to short selling seem grounded in a vague attitude that it is simply gambling, of no economic value. More particularly, it has been attacked with the claim that its banishment would remove a market force which serves only to accentuate the violence of periodic price swings. The crux of the argument in defense of short selling is that it helps to maintain an orderly market and to stabilize price fluctuations. The classic theory has held that short selling occurs when the market advances, thereby acting as a brake to the rise, and conversely, that the resulting covering transactions, which represent the only compulsory buying power in the market, take place as prices decline and thus act as a cushion breaking the force of the decline.[2]

Short selling does indeed brake advances and short covering does cushion declines—when they're done at the right times. Done at the wrong times, they do not have this effect on the market—but in either right or wrong times for the market, short sales are usually a source of profit for the specialist. If specialists didn't take prices down so they could cover their short sales at a profit, they wouldn't make money on short selling. An analysis of short selling during the May, 1962, break shows how well specialists use the short sale to profit from the market. On May 31, 1962, after a 36-point advance in the market, 40.2 per cent of all sales by specialists were short sales. At the close of the next trading day, the market, in terms of the Dow Jones Industrial Average, was off approximately 2 points and was headed lower. From May 31, where it closed at 613, it proceeded to a mid-June low of 524.6.

Specialists can sell short under nearly any conditions. They can sell short during the times the rules, supposedly, prevent it; the SSR commented on short selling during the May 28–31, 1962, market break that

in spite of the Commission rule limiting short selling to up-ticks, and without evasion of that rule, in six of the eight stocks [that the SSR studied] most or much of the selling occurred at times when these stocks were under the greatest pressure.[3]

Of necessity, specialist short selling can take place only when there is public demand. There must be a public for specialists to sell to. Conversely, specialists can only cover when, for one reason or another, the public is selling. In plainer words, public demand (which we're told sends prices up) makes it possible for specialists and other Exchange members to sell whatever stock they hold in inventory and borrow more and sell it short, then employ controls to force prices down. Thus, public demand, coupled with specialist short selling, sends prices down instead of up. It is legitimate to ask, therefore, if such short selling contributes to a free market.

To paraphrase a famous saying, there may be some doubt as to who are the best people to have in charge of a stock, but there can be no doubt that specialists are the worst. They can precipitate declines in their specialty stocks for any one of a variety of reasons. Taking a hypothetical example, let us say that rumors of a merger have enabled a specialist to take his stock to its all-time high of 63, at which price he sold out his investment account and the accounts of his fee-paying big-block customers. Knowing he has orders for several hundred thousand shares at 50, he will want to drop it to that price as expeditiously as possible. Let us now assume, therefore, that the stock, having declined a little from its high, is now selling at 60 bid and 61 offered with the last sale at 60½. All the specialist need do is obtain permission from the floor governor to "hit the bid" at 60. If he "cleans up the book" by selling stock for his own account to the book at 60, the next bid may be at 59½. Thus he has not only widened the quote but, assuming that there are a series of stop orders on his book under 60 (which is usually the case) and all the way down to 50, it becomes a simple matter for him to trigger these stop orders. If a rumor is circulated that the proposed merger has been called off, then it is certain that, without any effort whatsoever, he will be able not only to trigger the stop orders but to provide himself with an excellent alibi for halting trading at 58 and then reopening his stock at 50 at the close—having cleaned out his book on the way down. He can cover any short position he may have established in an omnibus account and establish a new investment account for himself, and, by virtue of his book's orders and the stock supplied by those who sold when they were told the merger had been called off, he is also able to supply his big-block orders.

A rule was created some years ago that, in the words of the *Wall Street Journal,* was "aimed at restricting the opportunity of speculators to drive down the price of stock by heavy short selling." [4] This rule, called the "uptick rule," states that a short sale can only be made after there has been a transaction one-eighth of a point or more above the last preceding price. Since it is very often easy enough for a specialist to take advantage of an "uptick," this rule hardly hampers him. As for the idea that short selling by the public drives prices down, this is only another of the myths that serve to confuse the public.

The uptick rule enables specialists to trap members of the public into selling short at the bottom. The specialist takes his stock down without an uptick, and nonmembers who have entered orders "to sell short at the market" find that their orders were executed at or near the stock's low price, when an uptick was allowed by the specialist. This is one of the devices employed by specialists to assist in covering their short sales at the bottom—and one of the reasons for what appears to be the public's persistent bad timing in short sales.

The short selling activities of the specialists in May,

1962, provide an example of the manner in which the impeccable timing of specialist short selling affects the whole market at important turning points.[5]

On May 28 there was a 35-point drop in the Dow Jones Industrial Average. In American Telephone and Telegraph (according to the SSR, Part 2, page 287), most of the short selling was by nonmembers, and a large part of nonmember short selling occurred as the market neared its low in the latter part of the day. The same is true for General Motors (SSR, Part 2, p. 288): "Short selling represented 3.8 per cent of total selling in the stock, most of it by nonmembers. About one-third of this selling occurred during the final half hour of trading, near the lowest price of the day."

Specialists, though, did not make their short sales "near the lowest price of the day." Commenting on the short selling of specialists in U.S. Steel, the SSR (Part 2, p. 286) asserted there had been "substantial short selling by the stock's specialists on May 28." The SSR further stated (Part 2, p. 286) that this short selling was accomplished *before* the stock declined that day, and that during the period of decline, "specialists did not use their short position to absorb selling pressures which is the usual reason offered by specialists for their building up a short position."

Of course not. That "classic theory" about braking advances and cushioning declines can only be made credible with trick mirrors. Furthermore, there is no particular reason why the specialist in U.S. Steel should have been singled out by the SSR. As we shall soon see, specialists in the most important stocks did not cover their short positions, did not use them to "absorb selling pressures," until the morning of May 29—prior to that day's 27-point advance.

Consider the consequences to investors of specialist short selling in stocks like General Motors, AT&T, U.S.

Summary of markets and short selling by members and nonmembers May 28, 29, and 31, 1962

	May 28	May 29	May 31
MARKET			
Dow Jones Industrial Average			
(close)	577	604	613
Net change from preceding day	−35	+27	+9
Total round-lot sales			
(thousand shares)	9,820	15,452	10,997
SHORT SELLING			
A. Shares sold short (thousands)			
All short sales	368	774	1,417
Members	214	611	1,202
Specialists	185	530	1,033
Floor traders	10	15	63
Members off floor	19	66	106
Nonmembers	154	163	215
B. As a per cent of total sales			
All short sales	3.7	5.0	12.9
Members	2.1	3.9	10.9
Nonmembers	1.6	1.1	2.0
C. As a per cent of all short sales			
All short sales	100.0	100.0	100.0
Members	58.2	79.0	84.8
Specialists	50.3	68.5	72.9
Floor traders	2.7	1.9	4.4
Members off floor	5.2	8.6	7.5
Nonmembers	41.8	21.0	15.2
D. As a per cent of their own total sales			
Members (excluding odd-lot			
dealers)	11.3	15.2	35.6
Specialists	12.8	15.9	40.2
Floor traders	5.8	7.2	31.8
Members off floor	7.0	13.8	17.2
Nonmembers	2.0	1.5	2.8

Source: Special Study Report, Part 2, p. 284.

Steel, and Standard Oil of New Jersey. The specialists who are charged with the "stability" and "liquidity" of these bellwether stocks are watched carefully by their fellow specialists, in order to determine their day-to-day trading patterns and objectives.

Concerning specialist activity in General Motors, the SSR had this to say (Part 4, p. 850): "On May 29 [prior to that day's 27-point advance] specialists bought heavily at the opening at 46, *down 2⅞ points*. Their purchases and sales for the day were about balanced . . . [emphasis added]." The short-covering transaction of specialists has produced and brought to excellence a genre of manipulation peculiarly its own. Prior to a major advance in the price of their stocks, specialists will often drop prices at the opening. This makes it possible for them not only to cover their short positions at pleasantly low price levels, but also to acquire a larger inventory of stock.

Concerning the specialist in American Telephone, the SSR states that, on May 29, he

purchased heavily—14,600 shares—as the stock *opened down 2⅛* . . . For the day as a whole, he had a purchase balance of 10,000 shares, so that he closed the day with a considerably larger position than he generally assumed in the stock. This was in marked contrast to trading on the previous day [when the Dow Jones declined 35 points—R.N.] when the specialist added only 900 shares to his inventory.[6]

According to the SSR, the same thing happened in Standard Oil of New Jersey:

After a *lower opening* on May 29, the stock moved steadily upward. Specialists sold on balance for the day. Forty per cent of their sales were short sales and were affected in the latter half of the day.[7]

In other words, the specialists in General Motors, Standard Oil of New Jersey, and American Telephone (and, we can assume, many other stocks) waited for an additional decline on May 29, the day after a 35-point decline in the Dow Industrials, to buy "heavily." It is logical to assume this buying made it possible for them to cover all their short sales and also add to the inventory of stock for their trading accounts.

In all its discussions of short selling during the May 28–31 period, the SSR, for some curious reason, fails to describe in detail the short selling activities of specialists and other members on May 31—the day when nonmembers (the public) sold short only 15.2 per cent of all short sales compared to members' short sales of 84.8 per cènt. It is also significant that on May 31, when overall trading volume had declined by nearly 50 per cent from the trading volume of May 29, the short sales of members had *doubled!* Why, then, in the avalanche of print provided by the SEC concerning the market break of May 28–31 was there no mention of this by these masters of the ancient craft of storytelling? Confronted with that day's pathetic climax, could anyone on the Commission have supposed that specialists would cover the shares· they sold short on May 31 at *higher* prices?

The SSR emphasizes the importance of short selling by nonmembers on May 28, though the evidence would seem to indicate that it had very little importance. But then, the SSR has a habit of getting hold of the right things by the wrong end. Nonmember short selling on May 28 doesn't matter; member short selling on May 31 does. The investigation raises questions at every point; however, it fails to answer them. Hence the SSR maintains that it uncovered no manipulation by members and that the disasters of the 1962 crash were attributable to the short selling activities of nonmembers.[8] With this astonishing conclusion, the SSR would seem to have at least compromised its investigations. Obviously the Special Study team does not contemplate the coming of revelation.

As for Ralph Saul, the man in charge of the Special Study group's investigating team, one can only wonder why he did not attempt a greater penetration of the monumental privacy of member short selling and covering transactions prior to and on May 28 and 29. With the air of a waiter anxious not to interrupt the conversation, he tactfully refrains from aligning member transactions with the 35-point decline on May 28 and the 36-point advance on May 29 and 31. Perhaps that is because the SEC didn't care what was said about member short selling, so long as it wasn't the truth.

NOTES, *chapter 5*

[1] Merrill Lynch, for instance, advertises that it holds $18 billion worth of customers' stock "in street name." The supply of stock that specialists can borrow from this firm alone can be appreciated when it is understood that many of these Merrill Lynch customers, as the "beneficiary owners," have signed "margin agreements" allowing Merrill Lynch (as the "owners of record") to borrow or lend the stock at their discretion.

[2] Special Study Report, Part 2, p. 247.

[3] SSR, Part 2, p. 286.

[4] May 20, 1969.

[5] The figures provided are for the May, 1962, break in the market. They are the only figures ever provided by the SEC or the Stock Exchanges that devote particular attention to the processes of change inherent in the practice of short selling and make it possible to discover the enduring principles of short selling.

[6] Special Study Report, Part 4, p. 849. Emphasis added.

[7] Special Study Report, Part 4, p. 851. Emphasis added.

[8] Part 4, p. 857, of the SSR states: "The detailed analysis of trading in individual stocks reveals . . . non-members characteristically dominated transactions in the stocks studied." On p. 859, the SSR states: "In view of the fact that the NYSE has published its own study (NYSE, "The Stock Market Under Stress," 1963) containing relevant aggregated data for the three particular days, the Special Study has sought to avoid duplication of that analysis. Neither this study nor that of the New York Stock Exchange was able to isolate and identify the 'causes' of the market events of May 28, 29 and 31. There was some speculation at the time that these events might be the result of some conspiracy or deliberate misconduct. Upon the basis of the study's inquiry, there is no evidence whatsoever that the break was deliberately precipitated by any person or group or that there was any manipulation or illegal conduct in the functioning of the market. The avalanche of orders which came into the market during this period [The SSR is presumably suggesting here that this "avalanche" of orders came from the public.—R.N.] subjected the market mechanisms to extraordinary strain, and in many respects they did not function in a normal way." The SSR then concluded its remarks with the following: "Neither the study, nor the NYSE has been able to ascertain the precipitating 'causes' of the May 1962 market break . . ."

6

A Telephone Call from Humpty-Dumpty
or
Mr. X of the SEC

It is difficult to get a man to say something when his income depends on his not saying it.

MR. X : This is Mr. X of the SEC— [1]

RICHARD NEY : Yes?

X : I'm just calling to apologize because we have all these letters here from you, and we haven't gotten around to really answering any one of them yet—

R.N. : Yes?

X : I just want to apologize for the delay and to just let you know that we're going to try to answer them in the next few weeks and get them all answered.

R.N. : Why haven't they been answered?

X : Well—I'm afraid that's been my fault primarily because we've been kind of short of people here, there are complications.

75

R.N. : But some of these letters go back for months and months.

x : Pardon me?

R.N. : Some of these letters go back for months.

x : Well—

R.N. : And I've only just had one answered after about a year.

x : Well—uh—I'm afraid I just can't say anything in addition to that—you spoke to Mr. Birnbaum in the past?

R.N. : Yes.

x : He's been out ill over a month now.

R.N. : I'm sorry.

x : So—I just thought—you know—that I was going to try and get around to—working on this and— try to get around to answering all of it and I just wanted to let you know.

R.N. : I appreciate that.

x : I—I—hope you can figure it out all right—and that you know what I'm saying—

R.N. : On the one hand I'm enormously appreciative, on the other I am considerably disturbed by the nature of the exchange that I have had with the Commission—my request for comments about the Douglas situation, about the United Aircraft situation in which the Commission told me they were making an investigation but couldn't reveal the results of the investigation to me—the fact that on that order of United Aircraft, as pointed out in the letter that Mr. Funston [2] sent to me, which I sent to the Commission—

x : Yes, I know—

R.N. : —there was a difference in the offer and the bid on the United Aircraft of *one full point*—

x : Yes—

R.N. : —and this subsequent to my having my block on there for 3,000-odd shares. This is unusual in a stock as active as United Aircraft, with that much capitalization, and in view of the Exchange's printed publicity that the difference between offer and bid prices is minimal, about one-eighth of a point in situations like that . . .

x : Well, as far as that goes—well, I think—I don't want to comment right now on this, because it's—

R.N. : Why don't you want to comment?

x : Well, the facts aren't that fresh in my mind right now and besides it's—well, I just wanted to say —to say off the rec—

R.N. : Don't say anything off the record to me.

x : Pardon me?

R.N. : Don't say anything off the record to me.

x : Well, I—I just wanted to comment that—you mentioned a point—a point spread—and—it would seem unusual to have a point spread in a stock, even in a stock—as active as Douglas—

R.N. : United Aircraft!

x : Yes—yes—United Aircraft. Even in the absence of the—of the specialist's participation—I don't

> know if a specialist—that is, I can't determine
> right now—I don't have the facts in front of me—
> if a specialist was in there one-quarter of a point
> below.

R.N. : Well, he was. I have the letter from Funston
which I sent you.

x : Yes, well, I don't—

R.N. : Well I would suggest—candidly—

x : Yes?

R.N. : Candidly, I'm making use of all this material—

x : Yes, I believe you expressed that—

R.N. : To Mr. Birnbaum.

x : In another letter—

R.N. : Yes, and I'm really shocked that the Commission
has not taken any stand in any of these matters . . .

x : Well, I just wanted to tell you that it's part of the
inquiry. I just wanted to point out that when you
inquire about a specific trade—there isn't time
just now to look into these trades.

R.N. : I know, but it takes very little time and the Commission presumably has all the facts right there
at hand to make an investigation immediately and
to determine on the basis of black and white.
There shouldn't be any delay in determining
whether this is equitable or inequitable. There's
a matter here of over several hundred thousand
dollars of clients' money involved in United Aircraft and no statement by the Commission has
been forthcoming for the protection of these non-

member participants in the market, and the Commission exists, not for the sake of the Exchange, or the banks, or the brokerage fraternity, but for the public . . . Now, what is it doing to protect my clients? This is what I want to know.

x : Well, uh—well Mr. Ney—I—I—just—I—

R.N. : Well, you see, if they're putting you on this matter now and you're not familiar with it—

x : Pardon me? No, I'm just—I—

R.N. : Well, someone by now should have all the facts and be able to make a categorical statement of opinion.

x : If I can—if I can just finish what I was going to say—that—that about these situations—I just don't happen—to have on tap right now that comment about what you said because my sole purpose—my purpose of my call right now is primarily to let you know that we're—to apologize for the delay and to let you know—that we're going to answer all this as soon as possible but we have about—we have quite a few letters here and —and—I just wanted to assure you that—that we haven't forgotten about them and—and whatever comments we'll have to make will be in the letters—but I just didn't—I just didn't want to comment on the situations right now.

R.N. : Well, can I have a comment on the United Aircraft incident as soon as possible?

x : Why—why—I—I—I'm going to try. We're going to try here. I just wanted to let you know that —that—the people we've—

R.N. : Well this is a matter of the—

x : They've been reading them—and I just wanted to—to—let you know—that—that you can expect those replies shortly.

R.N. : Well, believe me, this is a matter that involves the Commission and which I would certainly hope the Commission would devote some attention to now. Months have gone by since April when this happened, and it doesn't make it any easier for my clients, for me, or for the Commission to postpone making a statement on this problem. As I say, it's a matter not just of an opinion, there's a matter of several hundred thousand dollars involved . . . you know yourself in the matter of Gilligan, Will that twenty years, according to Gilligan's statement, went by before he was reprimanded at all.

x : Uh-huh—

R.N. : And then, he was only given a five-day suspension by the Commission. There is nothing being done to correct the problems that exist at the very center and heart of the market, and that's the specialist and this is what we're contending with even today in Douglas Aircraft. The probability is that the specialist established his long-term segregated tax account or another tax account at the fifty-nine level by taking the stock down there under considerable volume . . . now I'm curious to know if he is in fact establishing a segregated account and getting off-limit orders . . .[3]

x : Well, I'm sorry—I didn't understand as far as establishing an account and getting off-limit orders? . . .

R.N. : He's allowed to get off-limit orders for pensions, pension funds, and other funds—

x : Yes, but he doesn't know for whom these other orders are.

R.N. : How can we be sure of that? The brochure put out by the NYSE states that the broker goes to the specialist and, in confidence, discusses the problems with him, and then, that the specialist will then execute these orders, and there's no print on the ticker, no record kept in the specialist's book, that these things are done privately, and they enumerate the fees that are charged for these limit orders.

x : Well, this is—this—this is not what—I thought you were talking about the new orders on the specialist's book.

R.N. : Well, they know—these are orders which are not included in the specialist's book.

x : Pardon me?

R.N. : These are orders which are not even placed on the specialist's book.

x : Well—I—I think you're talking about what a broker comes up with when he's handling this.

R.N. : No, when a broker goes to the specialist and asks him to—

x : Yes?

R.N. : I sent the Commission, some time ago, a brochure put out by the NYSE called—I think it's *Marketing Methods for Handling Your Large Block of Stock for the Portfolio Manager*. On page 9 of that brochure they indicate the whole methodology behind a large block transaction. There are several, about seven block offerings indicated in this book—

x : There are several, yeah—

R.N. : And this is one of them . . . I don't know what the Commission is going to do about it, but from year to year they take the attitude that they will postpone any action about the specialist system in this regard or that regard "pending further study of the problem." This has been going on year after year. Now I'm not going to take any more of your time about this.

x : I—uh—I—as I said, we're going to try to get back to you again very shortly.[4]

R.N. : All right; thank you very much.

x : This is—this is something that has been bothering me—and we'll try to get back to you as soon as possible—that's why I wanted to call you rather than—send you a letter you know—let you know firsthand that we haven't forgotten your letters. We just wanted to get back to you.

R.N. : Well, thank you very much.

x : Okay, bye-bye.

NOTES, chapter 6

[1] From a telephone call received in July, 1966.

[2] Keith Funston, President of the NYSE.

[3] I was wrong. In my wildest imaginings I had not considered the possibility that the decline would not halt at 59, but would continue to 30.

[4] He never has.

7

The Financial Elite
or
Measuring the Stock Exchange's Economic Power

**Listen to the Stock Exchange when it shouts
"Long Live America."
Under its breath you'll hear it add
"It belongs to me."**

The New York Stock Exchange provides its specialists with abundant support in pamphlets, testimony, and public relations, for the specialists are a part of an intricate system of interlocking interests in which the most powerful men in America participate. The New York Stock Exchange, as the center of activity for this interlock, determines the distribution of American money. The liaison between the Exchange and the managers of the companies listed on the Exchange—the most powerful group of companies in the world—is a matter of the most urgent social interest.[1]

It is probable that one of the most important single problems in the thinking of the management teams of

83

most major corporations is not how to increase their companies' sales and earnings but rather how to increase their personal profits from the fluctuations in the price of their companies' stocks. They share this interest in the stock fluctuations not with the stockholders in their companies but with the New York Stock Exchange: earnings and prospects are allotted a distant second and third place, and management allies itself with the Exchange in opposition to the interests of the companies' stockholders.

Unfortunately, the easiest way for management to profit from price fluctuations is by the exploitation of stockholders. By not revealing how price fluctuations are brought about, management is sparing the investors' feelings at the expense of their purses, for the fact is that, in order to profit from such fluctuations, management must surrender its company control to the specialist and his system. And of this fact and its alarming implications, management finds it best to keep the public ignorant.

It is interesting and most instructive to examine the way in which the Exchange, without contradiction or conflict, achieved this control. Doing so gives one a clear perception of the Exchange's processes and points up the all-important fact that the Exchange members possess the right to vote or are able to control the votes of the proxies of the stock left in their custody by their customers in "street name" (this is stock that is registered in the broker's name as the "owner of record" but supposedly held in a segregated account for the customer, who is known as "the beneficial owner").

Employing half-truths and evasions, the Exchange's sleight-of-hand gains for it the power to vote the proxies left with brokerage firms in street name—when it wants this power. The most obvious way it can do this is through the broker's advice to his customers on how to vote. But the rules give the brokerage house, *not* the customer, the right to vote this stock. In the following excerpts from its rules, note how the Exchange can make it impossible for the customer as the beneficial owner to vote his stock. Note too that the customer is obliged to receive the proxy from the broker, examine it, and then return it to the broker so that he shall have it back within a five-day period—all this "by first class mail."

Stock Exchange rules 450 to 460 govern the regulations and policies of the NYSE concerning proxies. Thus we have rule no. 450 stating that, as to matters which may be voted without instructions under rule 452 (2452), *if such instructions are not received by the tenth day before the meeting,* the proxy may be given at discretion by the owner of record of the stock *when the proxy soliciting material is transmitted to the beneficial owner of the stock at least fifteen days before the meeting.*

The Exchange is careful to provide its brokers with the proper form letter. Here is rule 451.20:

When Broker May Vote on All Proposals Without Instructions

To our Clients:
   We have been requested to forward to you the enclosed proxy material relative to shares carried by us in your account but not registered in your name. Such shares can be voted only by the holder of record.
   We shall be pleased to vote your shares in accordance with your wishes, if you will execute the enclosed proxy form and return it to us promptly in the self-addressed, stamped envelope, also enclosed. It is understood that, if you sign without otherwise marking the form, the shares will be voted as recommended by the management on all matters to be considered at the meeting.
   Should you wish to have a proxy covering your shares issued to yourself or others, we shall be pleased to issue the same.
   The rules of the New York Stock Exchange provide

that if instructions are not received by the tenth day before the meeting, the proxy may be given at discretion by the holder of record of the shares.

If the proxy is stamped (metered) by the broker and there is a delay in mailing, the customer can't possibly receive it in time. If it is mailed as soon as it is metered, and, with mail (and customers) as slow as they are, even if the customer is in New York and the proxies are mailed from the city, it is doubtful that five days allows enough time to receive the proxy, consider it, and see that it's back in the broker's hand within five days. Who is to say that it didn't take *six* days? How many customers realize the urgency involved? If the customer is out of town it would of course be impossible for him to return his instructions within the five-day period. The Exchange will of course maintain it will not vote such proxies when they "affect substantially the rights or privileges of such stock." But this is a value judgment. For example, the Exchange would maintain it does not "substantially" affect the stockholder's rights to have a broker on the company's board of directors, yet nothing can more adversely affect the stockholder's interests.

It's an ideal situation. When you control a corporation's proxies, everyone is sympathetic to your point of view and your choice of directors. This is the other reason why nearly every major corporation listed with the Exchange has a broker or a broker's banker on its board. It gives the Exchange a pipeline to that corporation. It is like having a syndicate man on the FBI payroll. The cash value of a two- to six-months' tip on earnings and other corporate announcements is obvious. So too are the advantages of having someone on the board under strict orders to provide at least two of the six rumors printed each quarter by one of the Jones boys' news services. More than that, this system gives the broker an excellent way of keeping tabs on the insurgents on any board of directors. In the end, management looks to the broker on its board for counsel and direction; this broker, then, helps the firm keep up not only with the Joneses (and the DuPonts, Lehmans, and Loebs) but with the habits and thinking of the boards of most other companies in the same industry.

In many companies, corporate management now selects itself and its successors from year to year. Nevertheless, management has a free hand only when its decisions conform to the will of the Exchange and provided the Exchange doesn't decide it can effect a merger more profitable to its interests. In all of this, of course, Exchange control is disguised. The charade of stockholder power is advertised, since it provides the Exchange and management with the external signs and seals of legitimacy. All matters of dress, morals, and the make-up of annual reports are left to the corporation's board of directors. The Exchange, however, has a heavy hand in the determination of such matters as the nature and the timing of earnings announcements, write-offs, depreciation schedules, rumors of mergers, and so on. Certainly standards should be determined concerning the nature and timing of company announcements, earnings, and so on. These, however, should conform to governmental standards for such matters—along with inflexible accounting procedures. These all-important matters should not be left to the whims of an uncontrollable specialist system or to the caprice of an unscrupulous company official.

One of the prime functions and objectives of the Exchange's system is to see to it that the plans for its speculations materialize. It would be naive not to realize that in order to make these multibillion-dollar speculations pay off, the Exchange will see to it that its members are able to sell their stock at peak prices to the market's conditioned illiterates and that to do this, the nation's entire apparatus of persuasion will be employed so that at exactly the right season, there will be buyers for the merchandise that specialists and other members wish to liquidate. That members are able to consummate these sales year after year, with a minimum of risk, both raises and answers questions of the first importance.

The Exchange's control of proxies enables it to control an economy it would have you believe it merely serves. And there is no means of putting a limit on what the Exchange, using as its instrument its control over the nation's industrial complex, shall desire or seek to acquire. Certainly, this control has given it a species of all-embracing power that goes far beyond anything Congress originally intended.

Not only does the Exchange's interlocking directorate of brokers provide it with the most intricate and powerful Politburo in the world but the existence of this directorate makes it possible for the Exchange to punish any infractions by a company's board of directors on the spot—by either a raid on the insurgent slate or a takeover in the form of a proxy battle, tender offer, or merely the threat or rumor of one of these. Is this any way to run a nation's industrial complex? Ask any specialist on the floor of the Exchange.

In this connection, the following excerpt from an April 8, 1968, article by Stanley Penn in the *Wall Street Journal* is revealing:

AVCO BELIEVED BIDDING FOR FOX FILM'S HAND WITH LEHMAN BROTHERS AS MARRIAGE BROKER

NEW YORK—Avco Corp. would like to acquire Twentieth Century-Fox Film Corp., but Fox, for the time being at least, would prefer to go its own way.

That's the chief impression one is left with after interviews with a number of people who are familiar with the thinking of the top managements of both concerns.

Friday, rumors recurred that widely diversified Avco was holding merger talks with the big film producing and distributing company. Avco promptly denied these rumors, but withheld comment on whether the two sides might not sit down for talks in the future. Fox officials weren't available for any comment.

Adding fuel to the merger rumors is the fact that Lehman Brothers, the large investment banking house, is represented on the boards of directors of the two companies. Robert Lehman, a partner of the banking house, is a director of Twentieth Century-Fox; Herman H. Kahn, another partner of Lehman Brothers, is on the Avco board.

Apparently, if one Wall Street source can be believed, Lehman Brothers may serve as the go-between. It's being speculated that Avco and Lehman Brothers have talked over the possibility of Avco's acquiring the film company, but that Fox hasn't entered the discussions . . .

Not to question the motives or the imposing achievements of Lehman Brothers, it seems logical, considering the broker mentality, that a broker on the board of one company will conduct discussions with a broker on the board of another company, when they belong to the same brokerage firm, in order to effect a merger—which is legal—or create a rumor that may be profitable to them and their partners—which is wholly illegal.

It is of interest, therefore, that neither Zanuck nor any of the other directors on the board of Twentieth—with one exception—had apparently been consulted. The exception was Robert Lehman, senior partner in Lehman Brothers. According to the *Wall Street Journal,* he discussed it with Herman Kahn, another partner of Lehman Brothers and a director on the board of Avco. According to the *Journal* rumor, "Avco and Lehman Brothers have talked over the possibility of acquiring the film company, but . . . Fox hasn't entered the discussions." Like

Cain, the Exchange long ago discovered that dead victims can't protest. Nor does the spirit of fair play cloud the Exchange's analytic processes. Self-interest being the controlling criterion, the Exchange is aware that, while it may appear more politic, it is often unnecessary to bring together the directors of the companies it wishes to merge or take over. Thus it approaches such matters very much like an imperial nation bent on colonizing a weaker nation with exploitable potential. In the present instance, the rumor of a merger between Avco and Twentieth made it possible for members to launch a bull raid on the stock of Twentieth Century. The stock was raised to price levels at which it was profitable to distribute it to the public, preliminary to establishing important short positions. As is often the case, the rumor of this merger engendered the expectation of great deeds, which was ultimately accepted as a substitute for the deeds.

By August, 1969, there were 890,000 margin accounts, representing a New York Stock Exchange customers' debit of $5.2 billion.[2] Add to this the fact that the market value of all shares listed on the New York Stock Exchange then amounted to $611 billion [3] and that the Exchange probably controls the proxies of at least 50 per cent of all these shares, and you will begin to see the nature and extent of the establishment's control over the nation's corporate hierarchy.[4] On June 24, 1969, Merrill Lynch placed an ad in the *Wall Street Journal* in order to bring to the attention of institutional-portfolio managers the fact that Merrill Lynch had the facilities to dump as much stock as any manager wanted to get rid of—to dump it into the auction market customer's portfolio. Few things in the market rival Merrill Lynch's blatant ad copy. Its headline stated:

BULL BEAR OR MIXED:
MERRILL LYNCH CAN RETAIL BIG BLOCKS
OF STOCK IN ALL MARKETS

Walking on thin ice, Merrill Lynch's advertising department nonetheless gets its message across:

> When the market looks sunny, a fund manager can find plenty of brokers eager to sell his big block of stock.
>
> But let a cloud appear, and the picture changes. That's where Merrill Lynch has something to offer. We're always there, always ready to talk business.
>
> Why? Because we have certain built-in advantages that help us retail big blocks of stock no matter what the market's doing.
>
> *Customer confidence*
>
> When we call our customers with an offer, they're usually ready to listen. Reason: They know we never handle a block unless our Research Department thinks it's a good buy for one or more investment objectives.
>
> Another advantage is our huge number of customers: over 1,500,000 individual and 3,000 institutional. That's more people than the total population of Cincinnati, Ohio.
>
> To give you some idea of their buying power, we hold over $17 billion worth of customer securities in street name. (U.S. gold reserves at the end of 1968 were only $10.4 billion.)
>
> It's because of this huge buying power that we were able to sell—in a single offering—over $100 million worth of stock entirely to our own customers.

How marvelous for Merrill Lynch that their research department makes it possible for them to employ their customers' portfolios whenever they want to dispose of a big block.

Of even greater interest, however, is the fact that this one brokerage firm controls more than $17 billion worth of customers' stock—as "the owners of record."

It should not be difficult for stockholders to understand not only that the Exchange is *not* "representing" stockholder interests, but that the Exchange's interests run in a direction quite contrary to those of stockholders.

While specialists are prohibited by the rules from obtaining inside information concerning the stocks in which they are registered, there is precedence to indicate that they have, on occasion, obtained such information; and there is precedence to indicate that specialists have abused their position to affect stock action to their advantage. If he is privy to inside news, a specialist can take a stock's price down with the assurance that the company's chairman will be announcing, one month later, that "earnings for the rest of this year should not be much, if anything, better than last year, due to a reduction in sales." The stock's decline is then rationalized. In all this the Exchange is able to demonstrate to the officers of a company how easy it is for the knowledgeable insider to sell his shares at top prices and to buy them back at bottom prices, thereby making a healthy profit.

A casual examination of just a few of the corporations that have brokers or investment bankers on their boards of directors should haunt any establishment apologist:

BROKERAGE AND INVESTMENT BANKING FIRMS	NAME OF PARTNER	DIRECTOR IN COMPANY
Adler & Coleman	John Coleman	Chrysler Corporation
E. F. Hutton & Company	Sylvan Coleman	General Dynamics
E. F. Hutton & Company	Sylvan Coleman	Continental Telephone
Buckner & Company	Walter G. Buckner	IBM
Kuhn, Loeb & Company	Robert F. Brown	Polaroid
Morgan, Stanley, & Company	Henry S. Morgan	General Electric

BROKERAGE AND INVESTMENT BANKING FIRMS	NAME OF PARTNER	DIRECTOR IN COMPANY
Brown Brothers Harriman & Company	E. Roland Harriman	Anaconda Company
Mallgarten & Company	Maurice Newton	Anaconda Company
Eastman Dillon	Joseph H. King	Sperry Rand
Eastman Dillon	Dwight Baum	United Cities Gas Company
Eastman Dillon	Dwight Baum	Southwest Gas Corporation
Eastman Dillon	Burch Williams	H. & R. Block & Company
Eastman Dillon	W. S. Boothby	Commonwealth Telephone
Dempsey Tegeler	Jerome Tegeler	Mississippi River Transmission Corporation
Hornblower & Weeks— Hemphill Noyes	John J. Markham	National Terminals
Hornblower & Weeks— Hemphill Noyes	John J. Markham	Penn Controls
Hornblower & Weeks— Hemphill Noyes	Ben Regan	21 Brands
Hornblower & Weeks— Hemphill Noyes	Clifton P. Walker	Bunker-Ramo
Lehman Brothers	William H. Osborn, Jr.	Ling-Temco-Vought, Inc.

BROKERAGE AND INVESTMENT BANKING FIRMS	NAME OF PARTNER	DIRECTOR IN COMPANY
Lehman Brothers	Lucius D. Clay	Allied Chemical
Lehman Brothers	Lucius D. Clay	American Express
Goldman Sachs & Company	H. Krimendahl	Lane Company
Goldman Sachs & Company	Alan Stein	Hi-Shear Corporation
Goldman Sachs & Company	John C. Whitehead	Compton Company
Goldman Sachs & Company	Gustave Levy (former Chairman of the Board, New York Stock Exchange)	Utilities and Industries
Goldman Sachs & Company	Gustave Levy	Foster Grant Company

The thoughts of the Stock Exchange member who sits o
a company's board of directors are, like the forces of
hurricane, more orderly than they might seem: they r
volve about their centers in obedience to the quite ca
culable impulses of profits, on behalf of their own or the
brokerage firm's trading accounts. For example, brok
Gus Levy, Chairman of the New York Stock Exchang
(as of January, 1969) and senior partner of the Goldma
Sachs brokerage firm, sits on the board of the Foste
Grant Company. His brokerage firm has a trading a
count in the stock of Foster Grant.[5] It is legitimate to as
what Levy does when, for instance, he knows before th
company's stockholders do that the next Foster Gra

arnings report will contain bad news—what about the
Goldman Sachs trading account as it buys and sells these
shares? Gus Levy is an honorable man; how many others
of the many brokers in comparable positions are? The
company's interests are not always parallel with the
shareholders', especially if the shareholder is a trader.[6]
The Exchange long ago made the amiable discovery that
a brokerage firm's trading accounts were the most profitable aspects of that firm's business—when the firm had at
least one of its partners sitting on a company's board of
directors. The outer world of the auction market is all
the more ghostly because the inner world of insider
member trading on behalf of their own speculations is so
live.

Perched on the crumbling citadel of reason we have
broker Howard Butcher III of the Philadelphia brokerage
firm of Butcher & Sherrerd. According to the *Wall Street
Journal* (September 26, 1968), Butcher resigned from
the board of directors of the Penn Central Railroad, subsequent to the filing of a suit by a stockholder who
charged that Butcher's firm acted on "secret information"
in selling Penn Central stock.

On October 1, 1968, a *Wall Street Journal* story stated
that the partners of the Butcher & Sherrerd brokerage
firm were "quitting boards of public firms to bar interest
conflict." What was interesting about this was that when
the disguising drapery had been pulled back we saw the
picked bones of the auction market's skeleton. The firm
of Butcher & Sherrerd has only six partners. Its managing
partner said:

Although we feel absolutely that the presence of an investment banker on a board of directors results in important benefits to the company and all its shareholders,
we will relinquish all 36 of our directorships to put an
end to any concern that there may be conflicts of interest.[7]

According to *Time* magazine (October 18, 1968) Butcher himself "quit all of his directorships in close to 70 outside firms."[8]

But does this "put an end to any concern that there may be conflicts of interest," when literally thousands of brokers sit on the boards of thousands of similar companies and provide a direct pipeline to specialists on the floor of the Exchanges?

More to the point, while most brokerage firm "trading accounts" (including those of Butcher & Sherrerd) are for the stocks of unlisted companies in which the broker will say they "maintain a market," one has only to examine the profits attributable to these routine trading accounts to determine their essential function.

It seems likely that many of these partners maintain as well what are called omnibus or secret accounts with banks in which they trade in the stock of the listed company on which they sit as directors. As the reader will recall, when members employ an omnibus account, all orders are placed in the name of a bank. The bank then proceeds to conduct transactions on behalf of its customers. It is not surprising that members have opened such omnibus accounts utilizing the secrecy provided by numbered accounts in Swiss banks.

Obviously, when a broker acts as a director, his goal affect the stock's price. His inside information, regardless of any SEC ruling, is a gross contribution to his power. Moreover, the potential for gambling on behalf of his own account engenders a careless view of the stockholders' interests. And no SEC ruling limits the specialist's potentials for profit as insider information is relayed to him by broker-directors prior to being made public. Trading-account and omnibus-account speculating, having skimmed off the thick cream of most of the profits in most stocks, leaves little for the stockholder. It is not surprising that the legal speculations of thousands of such trad

ng accounts should cause so many bankruptcies among
he investing public.

Do these brokers and bankers do anything for the corporations which they serve? Are they concerned about
he well-being of their stockholders? Or are they more in-
erested in serving their own and their brokerage firm's
nterests?

OTES, chapter 7

The New York Stock Exchange's pamphlet *The Specialist on
e New York Stock Exchange: An Explanation Primarily for
orporate Officials* starts with "A Note on the Relationship Be-
ween Specialists and Company Officials. The specialist is
narged with doing all that is in his power to give the company
nd its stockholders the fair and orderly market that is expected
om a listing on the Exchange. To do this effectively, he must
aintain proper liaison with the company's officials. Properly
nducted, such liaison should foster a mutually beneficial un-
erstanding of the problems encountered by both. Company offi-
als should be kept informed of any unusual market problems
nd are free to call on the specialist for information if a question
ises about the market in the stock. The specialist, for his part,
ains from a greater familiarity with the company and its
fairs."

New York Stock Exchange, *Monthly Review,* August 22, 1969.

Compared to the market value of $87.98 billion for all shares
sted on the Exchange in September, 1929, and $34.55 billion in
ay, 1935.

According to the *Wall Street Journal* of August 27, 1969, "one
urce at E. F. Hutton & Co. estimates that major firms now do
per cent of their business in street name—up from 50 per cent
e years ago."

⁵ Brokerage firms' trading accounts are listed in the SEC monthly *Official Summary of Security Transactions and Hold ings.*

⁶ According to the *Wall Street Journal* of October 7, 1969, "th SEC charged Goldman Sachs with violating the margin or cred requirements of Federal securities law and the Federal Reserv System . ." The *Journal* stated: "According to the complai Madison Square Garden and Goldman Sachs entered into a f nancing arrangement whereby Goldman Sachs on behalf of i self and institutional clients would purchase up to 120,000 Roose velt Raceway shares. The agreement gave Goldman Sachs th right to sell the shares back to Madison Square Garden at th end of one year at 120% of the shares' original cost to Goldma Sachs."

In other words, Goldman Sachs was purchasing the stock o behalf of Madison Square Garden by putting up 100 per cent c the capital needed to finance the stock purchase and was *gua anteed* a long-term profit of 20 per cent.

What this maneuver did, of course, was to block the tend offer of Gulf and Western Land Development Corp. for th shares of Roosevelt Raceway stock. By guaranteeing Goldma Sachs a 20 per cent profit regardless of the price of the share the *Journal* said, "The SEC charged that the agreement 'serve artificially to inflate' the price of Roosevelt Raceway commo stock because they induced large purchases by Goldman Sac . . . without providing an incentive to buy at the lowest possib price." What is interesting about this particular case is that might never have come to light, Goldman Sachs being the pow it is in the financial establishment, if Goldman Sachs hadn't o posed itself to the interests of Gulf and Western Industries, t company that controls Gulf and Western Land Development and as revealed by the House Anti-Trust Subcommittee staff c August 6, 1969 (according to *The New York Times* of August 1969), "House anti-trust investigators sketched a picture today close cooperation by the Chase Manhattan Bank in the efforts Gulf and Western Industries, Inc., to grow into a giant conglor erate." The business relationship between Chase and G&W r vealed not only the powerful influence played by Chase in G&W takeovers but "a broker service in which the bank introduc G&W to companies seeking to be acquired." In other word Goldman Sachs had tangled with Gulf and Western, and whi Goldman Sachs is one of the high priests of the nation's financi establishment, Chase Bank is one of the establishment's gods.

The outcome of this battle was inevitable. Thus, on November 11, 1969, the *Wall Street Journal* headlined the following news: "Madison Square Garden Corp., G & W in Truce. Firms Battling for Control of Raceway Turn to Talk on Plan for Joint Venture. Neither Gained Upper Hand." The article had nothing to say about the SEC's earlier charges. Perhaps that's because on Wall Street it's one thing to be moved by the SEC, it's another thing to be mastered by it.

⁷ *Wall Street Journal,* October 1, 1968.

⁸ On July 28, 1969, the former president of Philadelphia Pharmaceuticals filed an $838,000 damage suit against Butcher & Sherrerd alleging fraud.

8

The Paradox of the
Federal Reserve System

**Don't lose your sense of humor;
it doesn't belong to you any more.**

Billions of dollars' worth of stock—it is impossible to determine how many billions—are left with banks as collateral for nonpurpose loans. This is an enormously dangerous situation. Stocks are too volatile to be used as collateral; and using them as collateral makes them even more volatile.

"Nonpurpose loans" are made by a bank with the understanding that they are to be used for tax payments, house repairs, or some other such unspecified expense— they are not supposed to be used for the purchase of stock. Nevertheless, they often are.[1] (Credit for the express purpose of buying stock is regulated by the Federal Reserve Board.)

When a bank makes a nonpurpose loan and the collateral used is stock, the stock is put in the bank's custody. Although banks are obliged, technically, to contact their borrowers, before they sell this stock, they often sell it without notice when the price falls below a certain level. Therefore, banks often enter stop orders in the spe-

100

cialist's book if they think the market might drop. For example, if 1,000 shares of General Motors are serving as collateral for a loan when General Motors is selling at 100, the bank may enter an order with a broker, who enters it with the specialist, with instructions to sell if he sees the stock going down to 80.

Then, too, there are unregulated lenders—lenders other than brokers or domestic banks—who take stocks as collateral but aren't subject to Federal Reserve Board controls. Since they lend a very high percentage of the stock left with them as collateral, and thus have less of a cushion than regulated lenders do, unregulated lenders tend to enter stop orders frequently; and the specialists react to finding a number of stop orders on their books. With regulated lenders, the amount of collateral must be a certain percentage of the amount of money borrowed; the percentage is set continuously by the Federal Reserve Board. Unregulated lenders decide for themselves what percentage of the loan they want in collateral. The Special Study Report comments:

> The existence of a large amount of nonpurpose loans principally collateralized by stocks which could be carried at low margin and are readily subject to call during deteriorating markets must be regarded as a potential threat to market stability . . . the great increase in bank margin calls with respect to unregulated loans contrasted sharply with the virtual immunity of regulated loans at the same banks during the 1962 market break.[2]

On an earlier page, the SSR notes,

> it is . . . liquidity that enables, and price volatility that causes, the lender to demand the right to "sell out" the collateral if the maintenance limit is passed when prices decline. Thus, wholly apart from public or self-regulatory controls, the unique nature of securities as economic assets and the private economic interests of bor-

rower and lender cause both an initial margin and margin maintenance requirement at some level to be a characteristic feature of most security credit transactions. Public concern is with the wholesale effect of the private arrangements just described.[3]

A clear and unprejudiced view of this arrangement is difficult to develop, since most people have been conditioned to think of the "Fed" as a nonprofit governmental agency operating on behalf of the nation's majority. Nothing could be further from the truth. The wishes of the financial establishment provide an implicit bias in the decisions of the Federal Reserve, because the policy makers in the Fed are members of that establishment. The Federal Reserve System has unprecedented control over the currency and credit of the nation.

The stated original purposes for the passage of the Federal Reserve Act in 1913 were to give the country an elastic currency, to see to it that the money supply expanded with more business and contracted with less, to provide facilities for discounting commercial paper, and to improve the supervision of banking. The bankers' man, Senator Carter Glass, who had steered the Federal Reserve Act through Congress in 1913, had maintained that the Federal Reserve banks would be merely "lenders of money." The only collateral they were to accept was notes that could be paid when, in the course of business, goods and services had been manufactured and distributed. However, almost from the day of its inception, the Federal Reserve System set about making loans on common stocks.

Banks monetize—in effect, make into money—whatever they accept as security; all such deposits can be regarded as printing-press money. Accepting a deposit is no different from printing new money. The Constitution assigned to Congress the power *and* duty "to coin money and regulate the value thereof"; Congress has abdicated in favor of the Federal Reserve Board.

Not only has the Fed monetized common stocks and similar assets—which can, of course, be used to purchase additional common stocks and bonds—but each time the stock market coughs, the banks have a different volume of deposit currency. That is, when the price of a stock goes up, the value of the bank's cache of that stock grows; when the price on the market goes down, the bank's cache diminishes in value. Obviously, a major collapse of the stock market could lead to another collapse of the banking system.

The full list of the directors of the Federal Reserve Banks and branches can be found in the *Annual Report of the Board of Governors of the Federal Reserve System*. The Federal Reserve Bank of New York—the most important unit of the Federal Reserve System and quite possibly the most important financial instrument in the world—had as its Board of Directors in 1968:

		Term Expires December 31
Class A		
Robert G. Cowan	Chairman of the Board, National Newark & Essex Bank, Newark, N.J.	1968
Eugene H. Morrison	President, Orange County Trust Company, Middletown, N.Y.	1969
R. E. McNeill, Jr.	Chairman of the Board, Manufacturers Hanover Trust Company, New York, N.Y.	1970
Class B		
Milton C. Mumford	Chairman of the Board, Lever Brothers Company, New York, N.Y.	1968
Maurice R. Forman	President, B. Forman Co., Inc., Rochester, N.Y.	1969

		Term Expires December 31
Class B		
Arthur K. Watson	Chairman of the Board, International Business Machines Corporation, Armonk, N.Y.	1970
Class C		
Kenneth H. Hannan	Executive Vice-President, Union Carbide Corporation, New York, N.Y.	1968
Everett N. Case	President, Alfred P. Sloan Foundation, New York, N.Y.	1969
James M. Hester	President, New York University, New York, N.Y.	1970

We take the Federal Reserve System for granted, as if its principles were settled and beyond discussion. Are its policies in the public interest or in the interest of the financial establishment? The men who issue and control the nation's money, who are in charge of the nation's credit and decree the level of its interest rates, are a group each member of which is either involved with an institution or foundation that is in the business of lending money or of obtaining money from foundations or he is interested on behalf of his company in the government's subsidy program or in restricting the sources of credit available to competing businesses. By allowing these men a position in which they may have conflicting interests, are we not demanding more than human nature would allow? When a change in rates is planned, is it conceivable that not one of these men, even inadvertently, relays his inside information?

Clear back in 1912 the House Banking and Currency

Committee, investigating "the concentration of control of money and credit," said:

> It is a fair deduction from the testimony that the most active agents in forwarding and bringing about the concentration of control of money and credit . . . have been and are—
> J. P. Morgan & Co.
> First National Bank of New York
> National City Bank of New York
> Lee, Higginson & Co., of Boston and New York
> Kidder, Peabody & Co., of Boston and New York
> Kuhn, Loeb & Co.[4]

The evidence is that the changes made in the past fifty-eight years have not made a meaningful difference.

The same committee said, further, that "from what we have learned of existing conditions in finance and of the vast ramifications of this group throughout the country and in foreign countries we are satisfied that their influence is sufficiently potent to prevent the financing of any enterprise in any part of the country requiring $10,000,-000 or over, of which for reasons satisfactory to themselves they do not approve. Therein lies the peril of this money power to our progress, far greater than the combined danger of all existing combinations." [5]

Discussing Wall Street, and the banking system's permissive credit policies toward the financial establishment, one of Kuhn, Loeb's senior partners had this to say to me in June, 1968:

> I am not one of those who thinks that the gospel was written down here in Wall Street, by any means. I think some of the things that are going on down here are absolutely unconscionable and I haven't minced any words on the subject and I think the amount of money that is being loaned for takeovers is a complete abuse and misuse of credit and I think that's what has this market churning worse almost than it was in 1929.

I think banks' loans are a case in point. Take one example: Ling-Temco-Vought borrowed a very substantial portion of $600 million to take over Jones and Laughlin. Now that's just like your Joe Doaks borrowing money for a margin account and not having to put up any substantial part of the total. They borrowed it from a group of banks, part of it being Euro-dollars, and dollars are dollars. There are lots of takeovers. I think this is what makes money scarce for constructive loans, loans to companies that want to expand and have every right to, or where there should be plant additions or new equipment purchased. Because of these takeovers the interest rate is enormously high since the law of supply and demand works with credit and money just the same as it does with peanuts, popcorn, or vegetables. And this is where I think the trouble is in our present economy.

The Exchange has obtained comprehensive controls over the nation's credit resources not only for the reasons stated above but in order to finance gambling on margin and on behalf of member firms' segregated accounts and trading accounts. Specialists employing their special credit exemptions are intent on accumulating enormous quantities of stock for themselves and their institutional accounts. To do this they have pursued a high-interest-rate policy. When New York banks raise interest rates, a condition is created that makes it too costly for members of the public to borrow in order to finance stock purchases. This then leaves the stock that is being sold at the bottom of the market for the benefit of the Stock Exchanges—and the banks. Another important aspect of the rise in interest rates as stocks move toward their lows is that it preserves a buying reserve. When stocks move toward their highs, interest rates will be lowered in order to attract this potential reserve of buyers into the market. Stock Exchange members and the bankers themselves will no longer need so much credit since they once again will be liquidating their portfolios and their credit carrying charges.

Because the Fed is part of the "financial community" under the aegis of the Stock Exchange (see Chapter 9), the values and ideology of the Exchange have become absolute and now impose themselves on the credit policies of the nation. The Fed's wisdom in raising interest rates is now revealed as no more than a myth; in the words of Congressman Wright Patman, "for the Fed to raise interest rates in order to cure inflation is like pouring gasoline on a fire to put it out." [6]

Also relevant to the Fed's high-interest-rate policy is the fact that the NYSE in its *Monthly Review* of July, 1969, listed customers' margin debt in May, 1969, at $5.6 billion. That averages out to approximately half a billion dollars a year in interest paid by its customers! This is another reason why gamblers in the stock market are dying beyond their means.

We have a monetary system in which banks, because they keep themselves liquid by lending on stocks, commit the entire banking system to the stock market's speculative gyrations. When the inevitable day of reckoning arrives, the call of loans by banks always exceeds the availability of new funds being offered. Under these circumstances, conditions are perfect for the Fed, working in harness with the specialist system, to precipitate wholesale deflations of stock prices. The Federal Reserve System, using these monetary techniques, sealed the fate of the stock market in 1929. But that was only one episode. The Fed's policies have also served to undermine the foundations of the entire banking system. [7]

In all this, it is not only the speculator who is injured by these reprehensible practices. Productive business enterprises that have had nothing to do with bank-created money also suffer. In fact, it can be said that with the help of Congress, the financial establishment had contrived to put out nets that caught everyone except the sharks. Yet, according to the charter of the Federal Reserve System, loans on stocks and bonds were specifically excluded from the privileges of being rediscounted as follows:

> Such definitions shall not include notes, drafts, or bills covering merely investments or issued or drawn for the purpose of carrying or trading in stocks, bonds, or other investment securities, except bonds and notes of the Government of the United States.

There is a stereophonic silence in government and big business concerning the Federal Reserve System; it is because the system is controlled by the heads of big business. Whether politicians get their slice of the pie depends on how willingly they cooperate with and support the Fed's policies on behalf of commercial bankers, the Stock Exchange's special credit arrangements, and governmental monetary, tax, and subsidy programs that serve the interests of those who control and siphon off the major profits from the growth of the American industrial complex.

William McChesney Martin, when he was Chairman of the Federal Reserve System, admitted that "sharp expansion in the credit usage of both brokers and their customers could, of course, contribute importantly to the inflation of prices in stock markets and if carried to excess could conceivably lead to a disorderly stock market condition." [8] Not only has the expansion of credit usage by brokers, their customers, and specialists led to a sharp inflation of stock prices and the persistent chaos of booms and busts, but the Exchange's use of credit has played the most important role in causing the pressures now being suffered by the social structure. This is a crucial point, for it is the fragmenting impact of the Stock Exchange's use of credit that is the major cause of today's desperately spiraling inflation. Nothing could be more obvious than the disintegration of the framework of society that this inflation is now causing.

The history of governments is also the history of great myths. At present the principal danger to our government lies not in the violence of the street and campus riots but in the myths masking organized money's purposeful exploitation of the social structure. The interests of the Federal Reserve and of the Stock Exchanges are not compatible with the interests of the nation's majority. This exploitation and the negation of the fundamental principles of government it embodies have shaped the pattern of American politics. It is the illogic of this situation and its indefensible consequences that now assert themselves on our campuses and on our streets.

NOTES, chapter 8

---

[1] However, there are no iron compulsions or holy negatives in existence to prevent the illegal use of nonpurpose loans for the purchase of stock. Thus, with the full knowledge of many bankers, such loans are made to brokers and others. In fact the extent to which this is carried on by New York banks suggests the existence of what might be termed a broker-aid program. In this connection mention should also be made of the loans made by banks like Chase to companies like Gulf and Western for the purchase of stock. According to *The New York Times* of August 7, 1969, the House Anti-Trust Subcommittee focused on G&W "bank borrowings to 'take a stock position' in a company in order to examine the merits of possible acquisition. Representative William M. McColloch . . . questioned the legality of such loans under Securities and Exchange Commission regulations. According to subcommittee documents, G&W obtained such loans from the Chase Manhattan Bank."

[2] Part 4, p. 18.

[3] Part 4, p. 9.

[4] *Report of the Committee Appointed Pursuant to House Resolutions 429 and 504 to Investigate the Concentration of Control of Money and Credit,* February 28, 1913, p. 56.

[5] P. 160.

[6] Congressman Patman made this statement July 10, 1969, on NBC's *Today* program. The inflation-control theory Patman refers to is in contradiction to the Federal Reserve System's inflation-control programs—which are not notably successful.

[7] In his autobiography, Herbert Hoover points out that he had tried, as a lame-duck President, to reach FDR to consult with him about closing the banks. He was surprised when FDR didn't respond to his messages. Only later, after leaving office, did he realize that FDR had failed to return his calls because he wanted to be able to close the banks during his own Administration.

[8] In a November 13, 1967, letter. It is quoted in full in Chapter 9.

9

America Shall Rise Again
or
The Role of Stock Exchange Credit and the Morning After

Those for whom you go to war always have the best credit ratings.

In 1949 the New York Stock Exchange completed its control over the nation's credit. With a mastering grip on credit, specialists and other members of the exchange could now acquire huge investment portfolios and the secret accumulations of stock for special numbered accounts in Swiss and other banks. The NYSE asserted that the Federal Reserve Board should exempt specialists from its margin requirements. The Special Study Report says:

> In 1940, at the time of the NYSE's unsuccessful attempt, and again in 1949 in its successful endeavor, to have specialists exempted from the margin requirements of regulations T and U, the Exchange strongly argued that the needs of the market made such an exemption a proper and wise one. In 1940 it argued that

the exemption was necessary because declining markets could tie up "all or a substantial part of the capital available to many specialists." In 1949 it was urged by specialists that an exemption from regulations T and U would make available "such financing [that] would permit specialists to deal in their stock more frequently, enabling them to narrow the spread between bids and offers, and generally to improve the liquidity and continuity of the market." [1]

The Fed granted their request. By lowering the credit requirements it raised Exchange morale. Not only were specialists exempted from the old margin requirements but all members were included under the following ruling (rule 325) from the New York Stock Exchange Constitution and Rules:

No member or member organization doing any business with other than members or member organizations or doing a general business with the public, except a member or member organization subject to supervision by State or Federal banking authorities, shall permit, in the ordinary course of business as a broker, his or its Aggregate Indebtedness to exceed 2,000 per centum of his or its Net Capital . . .

In other words, the member can leverage his capital at a rate of 20 to 1, whereas the nonmember is granted credit of only 20 per cent according to the rules laid down by the Fed.[2] Specialists, on the other hand, are able to seek credit on any "mutually satisfactory" terms. Thanks, therefore, to the credit exemptions granted specialists and other members, the longest and biggest bull raid in stock market history was begun by Stock Exchange members in 1949. It lasted twelve years.

The implications of these exemptions tell us more about those who granted them than they do about those who use them. With $8,000, *you* can buy $10,000 worth of stock, but with $8,000 in stock, any Stock Exchange member can buy $160,000 worth of stock for his own segregated investment account. Concerning these investment accounts, the Special Study group of the SEC had this to say, in 1963:

> . . . it seems clear that the segregation of specialty securities into long-term investment accounts is subject to strong possibilities of abuse without any corresponding public benefit or reason of effective regulation, and in addition represents an unfair use of the specialist's exemption from margin requirements. On both grounds, the practice should be prohibited.[3]

The SSR also pointed out (pp. 133–134) that although specialists are allowed to participate as dealers only when necessary to maintain a fair and orderly market, this practice proves that "specialists' dealings may be motivated by considerations of tax planning rather than by the needs of the market" and

> the primary motive behind the creation of these accounts is to turn profits which would otherwise be taxed as ordinary income into long term capital gains . . . However, purchases made on the Exchange for the purpose of segregation into long-term investment accounts raise problems which go to the heart of the specialist system. The specialist is permitted to trade for his own account only when such trades affirmatively contribute to the maintenance of a fair and orderly market . . . Where the specialist goes into the market with the intention of segregating the securities purchased and not with the purpose of creating a fair and orderly market, the trading is clearly contrary to the regulatory and statutory standards.[4] Beyond this, the specialist with a long-term position now has a stake in seeing that the security rises in price . . .

In other words the specialist will, now more than ever, be interested in having a bull raid conducted in his stock.

An interesting statistic was then provided by the SSR showing that as of June 16, 1961 (and prior to the bull raid that was about to be conducted on the market by specialists), "890,733 shares or 28 per cent of the [NYSE specialists'] total inventory were segregated into long-term investment accounts." [5] It is interesting to speculate about what the SSR would have said about this percentage if the stock segregated into omnibus accounts had also been included in this percentage.

The measure of SEC integrity is what it did *not* do about these practices when its Special Study group told it what to do. Clearly, there was a profound divergence in bias between the SEC investigator and the SEC Commissioner. The reasons for the contradiction become clear as SEC Commissioners leave the Commission to become presidents and vice-presidents of the Stock Exchanges.

William McChesney Martin was born on September 17, 1906. He was, from 1937 to 1938, Secretary of the Conway Committee to reorganize the Exchange. Martin was hardly less impressive in his accomplishments on behalf of the Exchange then than as head of the Fed, and the Exchange hierarchy saw that Martin dedicated his efforts to further implementing its powers. For this he was made Chairman of the Board and President pro-tem of the New York Stock Exchange in May, 1938. In July, 1938, at the age of 32, he was appointed President of the New York Stock Exchange. In 1941 he was drafted, and after the war he received further training in the Export-Import Bank. In 1949, he was appointed Assistant Secretary of the Treasury. In 1951 President Truman was prodded into appointing him Chairman of the Federal Reserve Board, which post he held for twenty years. [6]

In the following letter, Martin put his hand to an explanation of the privileges of credit:

BOARD OF GOVERNORS
OF THE
FEDERAL RESERVE SYSTEM
WASHINGTON, D.C. 20551

OFFICE OF THE CHAIRMAN

November 13, 1967.

Mr. Richard Ney,
Richard Ney & Associates,
170 North Canon Drive,
Beverly Hills, California.

Dear Mr. Ney:

This is in reply to your letter of September 22, 1967, which arrived during my absence. While we have not located your earlier letter, I hope that this response will offer you helpful information and clarification in the areas concerning stock market credit about which you have inquired.

First, let me clear up a misconception that seems to underlie several statements in your letter. Contrary to your assumption, brokers and dealers do not have any special borrowing advantage when trading for their own account; they are subject to the same margin requirements as their customers. It is true that when brokers and dealers borrow from banks in order to fulfill certain other functions they perform as financial intermediaries their loans are excepted from margin requirements. But the Board's margin regulations do not contemplate that credit obtained for these other professional purposes shall be used to support speculative transactions for a broker's own account.

For example, when brokers and dealers make margin loans to their customers, the customers' collateral can be used as security for broker borrowing from banks and such loans are not required to meet the margin set by Regulation U. In this case, however, under rules of the Securities and Exchange Commission, the total amount borrowed is limited to what the broker has actually lent to his customers. In effect, the broker serves as an intermediary borrowing the funds he relends; he is not allowed to use his customer's collateral to obtain credit in his own right for financing his own speculative trading.

Of course brokers also have access to any cash —free credit balances—left on deposit with them by their margin customers. While some firms pay interest on these balances, most such deposits are available to the firm free of interest costs. Since the same margin rules apply to these funds as to purpose loans, the balances offer brokers no opportunities for highly leveraged speculation on their own account. Rather, the funds are generally used in lieu of bank borrowing to finance margin loans to customers.

Other types of broker borrowing that are excepted from margin requirements include credit used to finance the distribution of securities to customers outside the medium of a national securities exchange (including primary underwriting of new issues as well as secondary distributions); loans used to finance bona fide arbitrage transactions in securities; and loans made in exceptional circumstances in good faith to meet the broker's emergency needs. Exceptions of the latter type are carefully reviewed by stock exchange officers to determine that they are in good faith before being granted. All of these forms of credit represent loans made in the performance of professional functions that promote the effective operation of the stock market and hence the public interest. The basis for their exception from margin requirements is therefore clear.

Loans to specialists are also excepted from margin regulation for much the same reason. Credit extended to the specialist supplements his own capital and makes it possible for him to take offsetting positions designed to moderate price fluctuations arising from the speculative activity of others. Since this helps to maintain a broad and continuous secondary market in stocks, ready access of the specialist to credit sources is also in the public interest.

While no data are published on the total volume of credit used by specialists on the nation's stock exchanges, this information is maintained in detail by the exchanges themselves and is available to the Federal Reserve. It shows that credit used by the specialists is a minor fraction of total stock market credit outstanding.

Going on to the other data you requested, no published information is available on the exact size of broker and dealer borrowing for their own account, although their total borrowings for all purposes are reported in the Federal Reserve *Bulletin* table on "Commercial Banks: Loans and Investments by Class of Bank" (p. 1772 in the October 1967 *Bulletin*). The annual reports of New York Stock Exchange firms carrying margin accounts (summarized in the table on page 1647 of the September 1967 Federal Reserve *Bulletin*) suggest that the magnitude of credit borrowed by brokers and dealers for speculation in their own accounts is not of the massive significance your letter implies. Thus, while total money borrowed by NYSE firms with margin accounts was $3,690 million in June 1967, $2,300 million of this total was borrowed on customers' collateral to fulfill the intermediary function of relending to finance the margin purchases of customers. Of the remaining $1,390 million borrowed on firm, general partners', or voting stockholders' collateral, $463 million was borrowed on exempt securities—i.e. debt of Federal, State, and local government units. Most of this undoubtedly represented the financing of underwriting operations and positions held by dealers to fulfill their function of making secondary markets. Probably a sizeable portion of the remaining $926 million borrowed on non-exempt (corporate stock and bond) collateral was also for the purpose of financing underwriting and other security distributions. In short, these data suggest that at most no more than $500 million, and probably less, was being borrowed to finance brokers' and dealers' own investment positions.

This approximate figure of less than $500 million in outstanding loans to brokers and dealers for financing their own accounts may be as much as $200–300 million larger than the comparable mid-year total that prevailed twelve months before. But your statement that "nothing has a greater impact on the credit of this country and the flow of money than the specifics of New York Stock Exchange member borrowings" is clearly not supported by the evidence. When one compares the $200–$300 million growth figure for brokers credit with the roughly $70 billion growth in total credit that occurred in the economy over the same mid-year to mid-year period, brokers borrowing does not appear to have been the "enormous drain on the credit facilities of the country" that you indicate.

Sharp expansion in the credit usage of both brokers and their customers could, of course, contribute importantly to the inflation of prices in stock markets and if carried to excess could conceivably lead to a disorderly stock market condition. As you know, the Federal Reserve has been given the regulatory responsibility to check this type of credit development and our staff along with those of the SEC and the stock exchanges follow stock market developments closely in order to be alert to unfavorable developments of this and other types when they occur.

Sincerely yours,

/s/ Wm. McC. Martin, Jr.

By employing the Fed's power on behalf of higher interest rates and taxes, Martin has curtailed the power, profits, and production of the public—and the beneficiaries of this policy are Stock Exchange members.

He not only chooses to dismiss the continuing, daily derangements caused by customers leaving their capital assets under broker control "in street name" or as "free credit balances" [7] but is so prejudiced on behalf of members' special interests that he chooses to reinforce the role of the Fed as a financial instrument belonging to the Exchange. The ultimate value of his argument lies in its rhetoric of persuasion:

> . . . Loans to specialists are also excepted from margin regulations for much the same reason. Credit extended to the specialist supplements his own capital and makes it possible for him to take offsetting positions designed to moderate price fluctuations arising from the speculative activity of others . . .

Disbelief darkens into certitude. Of all the reeds his argument leans upon, this one is the frailest. According to the Special Study Report (Part 2, p. 135):

> If, as the Exchange asserts, most specialists have acquired the positions carried in long-term investment accounts through the normal course of their business, they are utilizing credit made available by their exemption from current Federal Reserve Board requirements not to maintain continuity and liquidity but to realize an investor's gain. This also raises a question of fairness. In 1949 the Director of the Trading and Exchanges Division [of the SEC] opposed the proposed exemption on the ground that "specialists should not be given an advantage over members of the public generally": i.e., an ability to speculate with less equity than the public.

It makes a world of difference if control of credit is in the hands of a government interested in the growth of creative capitalism or in the hands of men concerned solely with brute speculation. It is not surprising that the golden age of perfect competition is largely imaginary when Martin can assert: "Contrary to your assumption, brokers and dealers do not have any special borrowing advantage when trading for their own account . . ." And as pointed out earlier, if existing credit exemptions are not adequate to satisfy the specialist's objectives, he is also empowered by the Fed to solicit credit arrangements that are "mutually satisfactory." [8]

Not once does William McChesney Martin acknowledge the fact that the Fed's exemptions have enabled specialists and other members to employ billions of dollars of credit to finance their own investment portfolios and omnibus accounts.

In 1938, Richard Whitney, then President of the New York Stock Exchange, was convicted of using customer collateral as part of his capital—a violation of laws then in force. The Federal Reserve System, instead of proposing more stringent laws, proceeded to give brokers the right to use customer cash and stocks as if they were their own, thereby making legal what for Whitney had been a crime.

Brokers will tell you this is not so—that they do not use customers' cash and stock to finance their own purchases. Let the words of William McChesney Martin confound them:

> Of course brokers also have access to any cash—free credit balances—left on deposit with them by their margin customers . . . the balances offer brokers no opportunities for *highly* leveraged speculation on their own account. Rather, the funds are *generally* used in lieu of bank borrowing to finance margin loans to customers.[9]

The letter demands attention—it marks the end of classic naïveté. There is no more stringent test of integrity than the use one man makes of the money left in his safekeeping by another, yet here we have Martin confessing what the Exchange and its members have always denied. And how important is his use of the euphemism "highly leveraged speculation" when we see that the chain of events involving customer cash concludes with brokers financing their own highly leveraged speculations, or the stock speculations of other gamblers—very, very rarely are they caught doing this, and even more rarely are they brought to justice!

A broker can borrow cash from his customer's cash account without any trouble. But he can't borrow stock from it unless the customer has signed a margin agreement; therefore, many investors, when they receive their statement, find that their account was without their knowledge or consent switched from a cash to a margin account in the course of a month. When for one reason or another there is a small debit balance in a customer's cash account, instead of requesting payment the broker will use the opportunity to lend his customer money. He will lend whatever is required, placing the necessary funds in the customer's account. He then turns the customer's cash account into a margin account. Then, after a few minutes' doubletalk in which he explains to the customer how small the amount of money is that's involved, and why he didn't wish to trouble him, and so on, he has the customer sign a margin agreement. Salesmen are offered a bonus for opening margin accounts. In signing the margin agreement, the customer allows the broker to borrow "any securities which you [the broker] may be carrying for the account of the undersigned . . . and *all* accounts carried by you for me" [emphasis added].

The broker's art does not end here. What many brokerage firms do—although it is unethical and should long ago have been prohibited by Congress, the SEC, and the Fed—is to take all the cash they can out of the customer's margin account and transfer it to his cash account. They then charge the going rate of interest on the debit balance in the margin account but pay no interest on the credit balance in the cash account. In other words, the customer pays interest on his own money, as well as granting borrowing privileges to the broker, who then employs the cash in the manner described by Martin.

Yet how many customers who leave their stock or cash balance with the broker and sign a margin agreement allowing the broker to borrow realize there is an Exchange regulation that states "any securities or other property loaned to the broker or dealer . . . may be used and dealt with by the broker or dealer as part of his capital and shall be subject to the risks of the business" or that when an investor signs a margin agreement he is signing a form that reads:

CUSTOMER'S CONSENT TO LOAN OF SECURITIES

The undersigned hereby authorizes you to lend, to yourselves as brokers, or to others, any securities which you may be carrying for the account (other than in a Regulated Commodity Account) of the undersigned or under his control on margin.

This authorization shall apply to any and all accounts carried by you for me or under my control either individually or jointly or in common with others, and shall remain in force until revoked by me by written notice addressed to you and delivered at your main office.

This authorization also allows the broker to borrow and use all monies and securities or other collateral belonging to him "as collateral for [the brokers'] loans, without limitation as to amount and without . . . retaining possession or control of property of like kind and amount." In other words, any money or stock in any other cash account investors may have with this brokerage firm can also be borrowed by it and used as part of its net capital, once the customer signs a margin agreement.

In view of these authorizations allowing brokers to use customer "securities or other property" as part of their capital, it is absurd for the chairman of the Fed to argue that the broker "is not allowed to use his customer's collateral to obtain credit in his own right for financing his own speculative trading."

Another brokerage procedure that mines a rich and unsuspected vein of profits (though not for the customers, of course) is the interest brokers charge on monies lent to margin customers when the brokerage firms have had the monies fully paid back to them. The broker will borrow the stock one customer has bought on margin—without the knowledge of this customer—and then lend it to another customer who had sold short. Although the brokerage firm was paid back in full with the cash proceeds from the sale of what was in reality the margin customer's stock, the margin customer not only receives nothing for the use of his stock but continues to pay interest on his debit balance. Legal, perhaps; but hardly ethical. The brute facts of this practice have been carefully kept under wraps; yet it is this use of customer collateral that has caused many instances of the complex and often bewildering phenomenon referred to as "failure to deliver" by important brokerage firms. For when the margin customer sells his stock—which has already been sold by the short seller—the brokerage firm does not have the stock to deliver.

The need for restrictions on the Stock Exchange's monopoly over credit and for withdrawal of authority for its use of customer collateral is greater than ever. These economic powers can have consequences that go far beyond the confines of Wall Street. The dislocations caused by a major financial breakdown in a more primitive financial community, such as in the Soviet Union, would be felt far less than those that could be caused by a comparatively minor financial collapse in this country.

The unexpected failure of one of the most respected brokerage houses in the country is a case in point.

In November, 1963, because it was duped by one of its customers, the Ira Haupt brokerage firm was unwittingly implicated in a fraud involving the manipulation of millions of gallons of nonexistent salad oil. Haupt's financial collapse affected its almost 21,000 customers— they'd left close to $500 million in stocks and cash with the firm in street name. About $90 million of this amount was in margin accounts and, according to the conditions stipulated in the margin agreements, pledged to banks for loans. Not only were all the firm's partners wiped out but when the warehouse receipts for the nonexistent salad oils proved to be worthless, the firm itself was left with $37 million in debts.

To compound Haupt's and the New York Stock Exchange's problems, it was impossible to return the stock to customers because the stock had been pledged to banks by Haupt.

In the realm of values the use of customer collateral has an invisible autonomy over the thinking of those who understand its implications. When the problem of Haupt's customers was brought to the attention of the nation, great concern was expressed by the editors of almost every major newspaper. The questions raised by the inability of these customers to obtain their shares could be seen to have a deep pertinence to the investor's and the community's well-being. The *Washington Post* of January 2, 1964, carried an indignant editorial demanding the protection of investors:

One aspect of the great vegetable oil swindle that has been accorded scant attention is the inadequacy of the laws and regulations drawn to protect the cash balances and securities which brokerage houses hold in custody for their customers.

When Ira Haupt & Co. failed after it became hopelessly enmeshed in the futures speculations of Anthony

De Angelis, many of the firm's customers were unable to withdraw their cash balances or take possession of paid up securities that were held in "street" name (registered in the name of Haupt). The members of the New York Stock Exchange worked out a plan under which $12 million were made available in order to free the assets of Haupt's customers, and to date it has paid out more than $6.7 million. But in spite of this prompt action, many of Haupt's customers have suffered losses for which they will not be reimbursed. The dividends on securities held in street name were immobilized for periods of a week and upwards, and many investors were unable to trade during a period in which there were opportunities to make considerable profits.

Haupt's bankruptcy underscores two weaknesses in the provisions of the Securities and Exchange Act. As a consequence of the custodial functions which the Nation's brokerage houses perform, they currently hold about $1.2 billion in "net free credit balances"—the funds from the sales of securities, dividends, and interest which are in excess of debts due from customers. These free balances are an important source of working capital, and there is little doubt that brokerage fees would be much higher in their absence.[10]

But the law makes no provision for protection of free balances in the event of bankruptcy. Consequently the *Report of the Special Study of Securities Markets* recommended that brokerage houses be required to maintain cash reserves of 15 percent against customers' free balances, a principle which has worked well in the commercial banking industry. And the *Study* also urges that customers be fully informed that their balances are being used by the firms holding them and that they are vulnerable in the event of insolvency.

There is also a danger because the law is not clear as to whether a broker may hypothecate—pledge against a loan—a fully paid security without the consent of his customer. And where a blanket consent is obtained, hypothecations can be made without informing the customer.

Although the organized exchanges have done a credit-

able job in protecting the public when their members
have been bankrupted, the SEC Act should nonetheless
be amended to provide adequate reserve against customers' free balances and tighten rules governing the
hypothecation of securities by brokers.

It is to Keith Funston's everlasting credit that he w
ultimately able to demonstrate to the Exchange membe
ship the importance to them of committing the financi
resources of the Exchange to the aid of the Haupt fir
Had he not been able to focus their attention on the lon
term advantages accruing to the Exchange, bankrupt
proceedings would have been instituted against the Hau
firm and many of Haupt's customers might have lost the
stock while others might not have had their shares r
turned to them for years to come.

But even as Funston sought to solve the complex a
bewildering problems precipitated by the Haupt failu
he was confronted—three days later—by the financ
panic that followed the assassination of President Ke
nedy. It was apparent to him and to others that wh
then happened on the floor of the Stock Exchanges cou
affect the economy at its most critical points. For mo
the tragedy of November 22, 1963, obscured the signi
cance of the Haupt debacle, but at the same time
magnified the consequences of the crisis situation th
preceded it.

It was also apparent to some that the governmen
financial controls over the Stock Exchanges were inad
quate to counteract the psychological effectiveness
those who are specialists in the cultivation of chaos. O
financial crisis coming on the heels of the other cou
have combined in a thousand ways to create disord
that could have disrupted the entire fabric of the natio
community.

Today, more than ever, we are at the mercy of t
uncontrolled operation of the specialist system's use

credit. Geared as it is to the monopoly of this instrument on behalf of its gambling in stocks, the immediate gains as well as the losses are capable of tearing apart the financial foundations of the economy—as they have, indeed, already begun· to demonstrate. The amount of credit being employed for such gambling was, in 1963, many billions of dollars less than it is today, and more than ever the future well-being of the nation is profoundly affected by the manner in which the Exchanges control their sources and supply of credit.

How human nature, on the floor of the Stock Exchanges, is willing to risk this well-being for the sake of immediate gains—how, indeed, tragedy is exploited to achieve these gains—is part of history.[11] At present, the machinery of government is geared to the Exchange's control over the sources and supply of credit. Because this monopoly makes the nation as a whole the servant of the Exchange's myths, these myths and the control of credit they sanction have become a source of continuing menace. As a matter not of ideology but of economic engineering, as a matter of economic necessity nations now attempt to control their currencies. Yet nowhere is this control more threatened than in the United States, where the threat is from the New York Stock Exchange's control over credit.

The economic prosperity of mankind depends on the proper use of credit, its availability, and its cost. More than oil or electricity, credit provides motive power to the world's economic engine. Yet in the United States, credit has become the captive of special interests.

NOTES, chapter 9

1 Special Study Report, Part 2, p. 135.

2 In other words, the Stock Exchange has seen to it that its members are allowed to legally leverage their capital 100 times more than are nonmembers—on behalf of their gambling in stocks.

3 Special Study Report, Part 2, p. 135. Another reason the practice should be prohibited is that, while the law places specific limitations on the public's right to borrow at banks in order to speculate in stocks, for practical purposes these restrictions are lifted for Stock Exchange members—thereby further implementing their monopoly over credit.

4 And, contrary to the Internal Revenue codes.

5 SSR, Part 2, p. 134.

6 Concerning the appointment of Arthur F. Burns to succeed Martin as head of the Federal Reserve, Albert Kraus said, in *The New York Times* of October 19, 1969: "Both Mr. Martin and Dr. Burns are considered conservatives, strongly dedicated to the market system."

7 Infringements of the statutes concerning brokers' use of customer securities left "in street name" are an almost daily occurrence.

8 More than thirty-five years ago, in *The New Republic* of October 17, 1934, John Flynn expressed his premonition of what would happen (and has happened) to Stock Exchange credit once control over the margin rules had been handed to the Fed: ". . . The Exchange Commission, of course, had nothing to do with the margin rules. These were promulgated by the Federal Reserve Board. They represent a total loss. Of course they were to be expected. Control of margins was taken from the Commission and put into the hands of the Federal Reserve Board at the demand of the Treasury and the Stock Exchange. It was done for the purpose of weakening the Act."

9 Emphasis added.

10 In May, 1969, these "free credit balances" totaled in excess of $4 billion.

11 See Chapter 12.

The Department of the Treasury has as its secretaries and undersecretaries brokers like William McChesney Martin and C. Douglas Dillon of the brokerage firm of Dillon, Read & Co. A former Secretary of the Treasury left Washington to join the brokerage firm of Goldman Sachs. If these men condone by habit and foster on principle the interests of the Stock Exchanges—including the credit instruments—we should not be very surprised.

On July 18, 1969, Congressman Wright Patman was quoted by the *Los Angeles Times* to the effect that the Justice Department's anti-trust division is investigating to determine whether the commercial banks are engaged in some type of conspiracy to set the prime rate. He then added, "It now appears that the conspiracy may well lead right to the front door of the Treasury Department."

10

Gluttony on the Bounty
or
The Big-Block Myth in
Exchange Folklore

Justice can wait. She's used to it.

Exploitation could never have kept pace with privilege without the Exchanges' big-block merchandising techniques.

The big block has turned the Exchanges into a mass consumer market for stocks that are retailed on a production-line basis. Big blocks—2,500 to 250,000 or more shares—are now sold for the sake of the underwriting profits, the special fees, the special incentive bonuses, and the commissions. Such distributions have no importance or urgency because of any relationship to economic security; they do not exist for the sake of facilitating plant or equipment expansion or for securing the requirements of industry; society enjoys no particular advantage from their existence. Indeed, the reverse is most certainly the case.

In order to sell their big blocks the Exchanges employ

techniques that have gained the seal of SEC approval. Judge Robert Healy, one of the first Commissioners on the SEC, dissented strongly from the Commission's majority opinion on this matter. In his dissent he raised the most challenging questions about the relationship of regulators with those they regulate. His language was, occasionally, strong:

> Clearly defined manipulation is a planned effort by an individual or group of individuals to make the market price of a security behave in some manner in which it would not behave if left to adjust itself to uncontrolled or uninspired supply and demand.[1]

But it was not strong enough, unfortunately, to keep big blocks from being marketed as they are, for the benefit of the financial establishment and to the detriment of the investing public. In the course of big-block underwritings, underwriters are allowed by law to stabilize, peg, or fix prices until their stock has been distributed by the specialist or the underwriting firm. This also means, in effect, that investors are obliged to pay higher prices for stock than would have been necessary had the big-block customer been forced to use the facilities of the auction market in the same manner as other investors.

> The Commission's statement accepts the premise advanced by underwriters that they must always dispose of an issue within a few hours after the offering . . . I do not for one moment question the value of stabilizing to the underwriter . . .
> Against the principle that underwriters should not be permitted to take the public's money by any means other than those strictly honest, no considerations of the paucity of underwriting capital or the needs of industry for capital should be permitted to prevail. I for one am convinced that all the needs of legitimate industry for capital can be met without resort to decep-

tion. To contend otherwise is no compliment to our industries . . .

I think our primary consideration must be the interests of the investors, for if the investor is driven from the market by unethical practices our whole system will collapse. Moreover, the investor is not the only one who is immediately affected by stabilizing. During the stabilizing period bank loans which are collateralled by the securities being stabilized will be affected and margin calculations will be based upon artificial prices. So too, the proper appraisal of the value of securities necessary for a fair calculation of taxes owed federal and state governments will be hindered. Only by giving controlling consideration to the interests of underwriters can it be said that stabilizing is in the public interest. The statute [however] throughout speaks of public interest and the protection of investors as one and the same thing and I am convinced they are. In my opinion stabilizing is not in the interest of investors and thereby is against the public interest.[2]

The Exchanges' big-block merchandising techniques are set forth in a brochure printed by the NYSE for the benefit of managers of mutual fund and other similar portfolios. The brochure describes the bargaining power that may be obtained by allowing specialists and other members of the system to retail these big blocks. The brochure is called *Marketing Methods for Your Block of Stock— an Investment Manager's Handbook from the New York Stock Exchange.* Beginning on page 8 of this brochure, the Exchange describes the problems faced by portfolio managers and the measures they can use to increase their profits by exploiting the auction market. The Exchange makes it clear to them that it possesses the antidote for the auction market's poisons:

Consider the case of the investment manager who must quickly buy or sell a block which clearly exceeds the immediate supply or demand in the current auction market.

For this, too, the Stock Exchange has provided the answer. It has developed special block procedures which supplement the regular-way market, and yet make use of all the resources of the exchange community. These special block procedures include the following as they usually occur in ascending order of size:

ON THE BUY SIDE
Specialist Block Sale
Exchange Acquisition
Special Bid

ON THE SELL SIDE
Specialist Block Purchase
Exchange Distribution
Special Offering
Secondary Distribution

These seven special block methods are available to you through your member firm in teamwork with members working on the Stock Exchange floor . . .

While prior Exchange approval is required each time a special block procedure is used, authorization usually is given within a matter of minutes, unless Exchange officials determine that the order indeed can be accommodated in the auction market—and would cost the customer less there.

The brochure goes on:

Your broker will probably start at the hub of the auction market itself—with the specialist. . . .

A CASE IN POINT
. . . a pension fund manager gave his Member Firm broker an order to sell 5,000 shares of an issue then priced at 58. In the auction market, the stock was trading in orderly 100-share lots. But there did not appear to be depth enough in the auction market to absorb the block, short of selling the stock down perhaps 5 or 6 points. Speed was required, and, obviously, the situation called for special measures. A Specialist Block Purchase was explored and decided upon. Step by step, here's what happened:

NEGOTIATION

Following discussions between the client and the Member Firm, the floor broker disclosed the details of the order to the specialist—told him *privately* how much stock was involved and stressed the need for speed. By thus confiding in the specialist, the floor broker enlisted a strong ally. The specialist, after weighing the current market picture (57⅞ bid—58⅛ offered) and assessing his own dealer position, decided he could make a net bid of 57 for the entire block. The broker reported the specialist's bid to his firm. The customer was satisfied that he could do no better, and instructed his Member Firm to accept the specialist's block bid.

APPROVAL

At this point, the proposed Specialist Block Purchase was reviewed on the spot by a Floor Governor of the Stock Exchange. He quickly agreed that the block could not flow into the auction market, within the existing framework of volume, and in an orderly sequence of prices. On the other hand, the block transaction [that is, handled secretly by the specialist, as planned] would not affect the price structure in the auction market adversely. Stock Exchange approval thus was forthcoming in a matter of minutes.

TRANSACTION

The trade was made privately. There was *no* print on the ticker . . . no announcement of any kind, before or after . . . *no* entry in the specialist's book. The Specialist Block Purchase developed as a logical outcome of assessing the auction market *first*.

Concerning "the range of costs" for these retailing services, the brochure states that "costs to the seller" for one type of distribution have gone as high as "7.32, 9.33 and 8.62 times the average minimum commission"; in other distributions, costs have gone as high as "29 times the average minimum commission."

Were big-block customers not permitted to dispose of

their big blocks in privileged ways, they would be less anxious to swing in and out of the market. Consequently, they would be obliged to conduct themselves more like investors, instead of boardroom traders. The implications for constructive reform of the auction market are obvious. None of these special techniques and privileges would be necessary if the big blocks to be sold were of great and urgent interest to investors—as Judge Healy's dissent suggested. In that case investors themselves would create enough demand to maintain or increase existing price levels without having to submit to the subterfuge of the Exchange's "special brokerage efforts." What the brochure indicates is that the fund manager and the Exchange have a common enemy—you—and for a fee, the fund manager can have one free shot at you via the big-block offering. The half-truth is held up to obscure the whole lie: "On the other hand, the block transaction would not affect the price structure of the auction market adversely." This is true in the sense that prices do not drop immediately. The specialist sees to it that the price remains at peak levels until he has distributed the stock from inventory. Then, having exhausted demand (and perhaps having sold out his own inventory at slightly higher prices and going short), he lets the stock drop in price.

On page 11 of this brochure, Exchange distributions or acquisitions are discussed:

Assume now that the investment manager and his Member Firm have a good-sized block to sell or buy— ranging perhaps from 10,000 to as many as 80,000 shares. They have explored and assessed the auction market and find that, at the moment, it cannot absorb the block. To the institution, time is important. They may turn to the Exchange Distribution or Acquisition —perhaps the most flexible and adaptable of the special block procedures. These techniques involve a carefully charted search for offsetting orders to take up the block amount, with the block seller or buyer paying all brokerage costs. Through the private communications system of your Member Firm—without public announcement—offsetting buy or sell orders are accumulated.

These orders are crossed with the block order on the floor, within the current auction market "bid-and-asked" range.

Only after a "cross" has been executed does the Stock Exchange ticker disclose that a distribution or acquisition has been accomplished, as illustrated by this ticker message reporting an Exchange Distribution of a sizable block of an equipment manufacturing stock.

> . . . DIST. XYZ
> 10.900. s. 435½ . . .

Let's follow this case step by step:

The portfolio manager of an insurance company consults his Member Firm on how to sell a block of 10,900 shares of the stock—market value upwards of $4,700,-000. Currently, the stock is selling at close to 437 in the Stock Exchange auction market. It is a high-priced issue, enjoying widespread investor interest. But, once again, the investment manager's specifications call for speed beyond the immediate capacity of the regular-way market. The Member Firm recommends an Exchange Distribution.

ARRANGEMENTS

This offering was conducted by the originating Member Firm alone, relying on its own partners, branch managers and representatives to generate offsetting buy orders among their customers. The Firm, however, could have enlisted one or more additional Member Firms. No prior public announcement of a forthcoming Exchange Distribution is made.

APPROVAL

As in the case of all special block procedures, Stock Exchange approval was required. Governors of the

Stock Exchange reviewed the current auction market situation and, since it was clear that the block required special marketing effort, approval was forthcoming within a few minutes—as is usually the case.

TRANSACTION
In an Exchange Distribution, the Member Firm employs its private communications system to generate buy orders. Buyers are attracted to the offering, of course, because the seller pays all brokerage costs. These offsetting buy orders are crossed on the Exchange floor with the block sale order. For example, from the time the Firm advised its customers privately that the stock was available, it took but four hours and nine minutes to complete the transaction.

PRICE
An Exchange Distribution is accomplished at a price within the prevailing bid and offer in the auction market. When the block was sold, for example, the Exchange market was 434 bid—436 offered. The price to the buyers participating in the Exchange Distribution was 435½ net.

When the investment manager, through his Member Firm, wants to acquire a block of stock, the same procedure is available. It is called an Exchange Acquisition.

The chief importance to the Exchange of an influx of 50 million more investors—the little old ladies, the truck drivers, clerks, and steamfitters whose participation in the market is so often cited as proof of democratic methods— is not the additional brokerage commissions these provide, but that there are more fish for the fishhooks. That's why the biggest brokerage firms want every buyer they can get—from 10 shares to 10,000. An increase in the volume of small investment means that:

1. The auction market is better able to absorb big-block distributions.

2. There are additional sources of supply for big-block accumulations.
3. Big-block fees are greater.
4. Nonmember use of credit is greater, making it possible for members to increase their net capital and, in consequence, their own investment portfolios. The other side of this coin is that an increase in the use of credit by the public means greater profits to members of the Federal Reserve System, particularly the directors on the boards of the twelve central banks who, as the heads of IBM, Lever Brothers, and so on, are anxious for the largest possible market to facilitate the distributions of their company's shares.

Presuming the Exchange sold 50 million shares to nonmembers at low prices, who would then be available to buy stock from specialists and their big-block customers at the top? It's the *selling* done at the bottom by nonmembers that builds up customers'—that is, nonmembers'—credit balances,[3] and provides members with additions to their net capital.

Although these monies must one day be returned to customers, when better than at the top of a dramatic rise in the market? Not only are members then able to get out with a profit and liquidate their loans and carrying charges, but they are able to return the monies to their customers at the top, which they borrowed from customers at the bottom, so that—to the accompaniment of a propaganda barrage—their customers can now buy at the top.

In order to distribute continuing inventories of big blocks efficiently, the system requires the existence of brokerage houses that can absorb and supply stock on demand. Therefore, each brokerage firm has as many branch offices in important population centers as possible. During the formative periods of the market (that is, at critical market peaks and bottoms) the New York offices of these firms can issue directives to their branches throughout the country to go down their list of clients and find buyers or sellers for the main office's big-block boys. Even if the branch-office commission income can't pay for the office's upkeep, the office is necessary if the parent firm's partners are to harvest the fees available from big-block transactions.

Because of the need to distribute these big blocks the seals of legitimacy are lacking in many of the recommendations brokerage houses make to their public customers. Often not even the branch managers realize their function. In an article in the April, 1966, issue of *Fortune* the broker and his underwriting activities were brought into sharp perspective.

> Several of the big firms that did poorly on commission operations in 1964 trace this in part at least to the start-up costs of the new branches and digestion of acquisitions . . . In many cases these new retail-office facilities have been designed in part to support firms' underwriting activities. It is important to observe, in this connection, a long-term shift in the character of the underwriting business. When capital was relatively scarce, the main function of underwriters was to assume the risk of floating a new issue. Now the emphasis in investment banking increasingly is on distributing the securities directly to investors; what matters is not so much the underwriter's vast capital resources as his retail distribution system. As a result, firms that used to confine themselves largely to brokerage—e.g., Bache, duPont, and Hornblower & Weeks–Hemphill, Noyes— have increased their participation in underwriting syndicates; many have even become syndicate managers. Meanwhile, some of the older generation of underwriters—White, Weld & Co., for example—have shown a greater interest in retailing.[4]

Whether you are being persuaded to buy a big-block offering at retail price levels or to sell your stock at wholesale price levels, your main link with the Exchange and its specialist is, of necessity, your broker. By accident or design, he is more the specialist's ally than he is yours. If he is to become a successful commission man, he must align himself with the Exchange. Since he is your link with the Exchange, it is imperative you understand these "special brokerage efforts" and your broker's relation to them.

In this connection I might mention the Exchange blackjack, called "the incentive commission." This is the essential part of the "special brokerage efforts," and one reads with amazement the Exchange's announcement of its employment despite the laws governing "the dissemination of accurate information to investors." Many investors who leave their power of attorney with their brokers are sold into secondary offerings and other big-block distributions because the broker is able to earn an incentive bonus of $2 or more a share for every share of a big-block distribution that he sells. Many investors have seen their savings evaporate because the Exchange employs its "private communications system to generate buy orders" by investors in secondary-stock distributions.

Some firms prohibit discretionary accounts (accounts in which the broker has the power to buy and sell whatever stocks he chooses for a customer's portfolio without consultation with the customer). But, according to an article in the *Los Angeles Times* on July 7, 1968, by Arelo Sederberg, there is a growing trend toward them.

As far as the individual investor and most certainly the small investor are concerned, the trend so far is limited. Some brokerage firms, indeed, won't let their brokers operate that way. Few encourage it. Despite this, the managed account is gaining ground on the traditional client-broker relationship.

Partly, the reason for this is that some brokers foresee a change in the commission structure, which is set by the New York Stock Exchange. Sederberg notes that the SEC has begun hearings "to consider such commission items as volume discounts," and quotes the Executive Vice-President of Donaldson, Lufkin, and Jenrette:

> "With volume discounts coming, brokerage firms are looking to get a foothold in something else," he says. "If they're going to lose 20 per cent or so on their large volume transactions, they'll want to recapture it in something like management fees."

The Exchange describes the techniques with which it can sell or *acquire* big blocks from the public on behalf of the institutional customer:

> Good sized blocks—made up of as many as 65,000 shares, with market values as high as $2,439,000—can be distributed or acquired effectively by the simple procedure of announcing an attractive, fixed net price over the Exchange's nationwide ticker system—and then relying on the widespread resources of the entire Stock Exchange community to bring in, buy, or sell orders quickly and in volume. This method is called A Special Offering or Bid. Its success lies in letting interested investors in more than 700 cities know that a Special Offering or Bid is open to them.
>
> . . . A fixed price was determined by the customer in consultation with his Member Firm. They also fixed the incentive commission to be paid to brokers producing buy orders. The offering price was 54⅜ . . . and the seller offered an incentive commission of $1.00 a share to induce brokerage interest throughout the Exchange community. The regular commission would be about 45 per cent of this figure. (The amount of stock offered must be at least 1,000 shares with a market value of $25,000 or more.)
>
> In sum then . . . :
> Buyers . . . are attracted by the net price offering.

The incentive commission invites special brokerage efforts on the part of Member Firms.

To acquire a large block, the reverse procedure, known as a Special Bid, is also available. Sellers, in this case, find the net price offering attractive, and the special commission invites Member Firm brokerage efforts.[5]

"Flash" big-block distributions are often sold within minutes of their announcement. Inspired only by the bonus they receive for each share of stock, brokers help distribute these big blocks without informing themselves about their possible drawbacks and without disclosing the fact that they are receiving a special bonus—or "concession."

In 80 big-block secondary distributions reported to the SEC by the Exchange in 1961, 9 were completed in less than fifteen minutes, another 22 in less than one hour, 12 in one to four hours, and 32 by the close of the following day.[6]

In the February 28, 1968, *Wall Street Journal,* another full-page ad by Merrill Lynch was addressed to the portfolio managers of big blocks. Here, with a minimum of pious generalities, we have a typical brokerage firm advertising its ability to sell big money's big blocks to little money with no questions asked.

Institutions:

Merrill Lynch has 1,432,000 potential buyers for your next exchange distribution or unregistered secondary

Last year, we sold 1,453,136 shares in exchange distributions. That's tops in the field. We also sold 1,158,215 shares in unregistered secondaries. Quite a record. Scan the full list of shares we distributed—entirely to our own customers—and read why our exceptional distribution power can benefit both customers who sell through us and customers who buy from us. Then jot down Linton F. Murdock, Merrill Lynch, WH. 4–1212, against the day when you want to sell a sizable block with minimum fuss and maximum speed.

Our customers could probably buy Fort Knox— for cash

Merrill Lynch is blessed with 1,432,000 *individual* customers. (And new ones have been coming in at the rate of 1,800 per week.) Their buying and selling of securities has made us No. 1 in brokerage transactions by a wide margin.

We also get business from 3,000 *institutional* customers, including varying amounts of business from over 90 percent of the institutions whose accounts we believe to be the biggest in America.

Result: we have been able to sell, on a single offering, more than $100,000-000 worth of shares—*to our own customers*.

The potential purchasing power of our customers is an important asset to institutional sellers. We can save sellers the trouble of shopping around for buyers—and thus running the risk of depressing the price of their stock.

310,000 miles of private wire, and 3,000 account executives

When Merrill Lynch accepts a block for exchange or secondary distribution, we get the news to potential customers fast.

A wire flashes the news to our 170 offices. Our 3,000 account executives get the message. They can pass it on in minutes to those of our customers (individual and institutional) who may find the stock attractive. Sample times for Merrill Lynch distributions:

• Exchange distribution of *Eaton Yale & Towne:* 100,-000 shares retailed through 907 transactions. Time approved by the N.Y.S.E.: five minutes after close of market (3:35 P.M.) January 23, 1967. *Time completed: two minutes after market opening (10:02 A.M.) the following day.*

• Exchange distribution of *Radio Corporation of America:* 180,000 shares retailed through 2,060 transactions. Time approved: 12:25 P.M., December 19, 1967. *Time completed: six minutes after market opening (10:06 A.M.) the following day.*

• Secondary of *Campbell Soup:* out of a total offering of 320,500 shares, we retailed 145,069 shares through 783 transactions. Time approved: 10:58 A.M., June 9, 1967. *Time completed: 11:49 A.M. the same day.*

When an institution needs to sell a block fast, our combination of electronics and manpower can save hours, even days.

Cheaper for buyers, quicker for sellers

Our volume of secondary and exchange distributions benefits the customers who buy from us *as well as* those who sell through us.

Buyers benefit for two reasons:

1. They get stock commission free (since the *sellers* pay the commissions), and they pay no odd-lot differentials.

2. Merrill Lynch does not accept shares for distribu-

tion unless our Research Department approves the stock for one or more stated investment objectives. (Over the years we have turned down far more offerings than we have accepted.) Thus, our customers can be sure that when we offer a stock, we feel it is *worth* suggesting to them.

Sellers benefit because, when we do accept a stock for distribution, our potential purchasers usually have the confidence to make buy decisions *fast*.

Result: when Merrill Lynch offers a block, either as an exchange distribution or secondary, we expect the stock to be sold quickly and with minimum disturbance to price—before, during and after the sale.

If you'd like to take advantage of Merrill Lynch's exceptional selling power for your next exchange distribution or unregistered secondary, get in touch with Lynn Murdock at 70 Pine. The number: (212) WH. 4–1212.

Merrill Lynch's 1967 Exchange Distributions and Unregistered Secondaries

Merrill Lynch, wholly through its own organization, sold 2,611,351 shares in *exchange distributions* and *unregistered secondaries* last year. (We also sold 3,444,297 shares in secondary offerings that were *registered* with the S.E.C.)

ISSUE	AMOUNT RETAILED	TRANS-ACTIONS
Crown Cork & Seal	14,010	149
*Eagle-Picher	30,000	173
Mack Truck	40,152	372
So. Carolina Elect. & Gas	12,652	101
Deere & Co.	19,459	224
*Eaton Yale & Towne	100,000	907

ISSUE	AMOUNT RETAILED	TRANS-ACTIONS
Beech-Nut Life Savers	43,000	345
General Cinema	60,229	394
Cutler-Hammer	24,016	193
*Union Camp	21,000	77
Beech-Nut Life Savers	23,402	306
Woodward & Lothrop	8,629	73
Allied Chemical	101,001	916
*Amer. Air Filter	21,484	348
*Continental Baking	19,000	58
Cutler-Hammer	10,720	92
Minn. Mining & Mfg.	108,815	1,212
*General Tele. & Elect.	45,000	585
Pabst Brewing Co.	10,000	60
Minn. Mining & Mfg.	29,437	450
Northwest Natural Gas	5,000	20
Scott Foresman	50,325	310
Pepsico Inc.	141,832	1,377
*Texaco Inc.	35,244	190
*Amer. Electric Power	32,500	202
*Kendall Co.	64,500	379
*Gimbel Bros.	71,500	224
*Babcock & Wilcox	55,000	383
*International Harvester	25,000	220
Union Oil Calif.	25,000	235
*United Gas Improvement	20,000	129
Union Oil Calif.	16,075	124
*General Signal	9,100	53
Charter of New York	39,697	365
Cenco Instruments	50,466	317
*Shell Oil	21,107	171
*Revlon	94,900	845
Communication Satellite	15,000	64
W. R. Grace	25,226	219
Union Bank of L.A.	12,000	103
*Stauffer Chem.	44,800	460
*Hammermill Paper Co.	28,846	222
Alum. Co. of Amer.	20,000	222

ISSUE	AMOUNT RETAILED	TRANS-ACTIONS
Smith Industrial International	12,448	130
*Macke Co.	15,000	55
Campbell Soup	145,069	783
*Briggs & Stratton	15,900	153
*McGraw-Hill	22,100	73
Kaiser Alum. & Chem.	36,000	325
Gerber Products	13,400	84
*Mobil Oil	32,500	325
Marsh & McLennan	1,760	18
*Household Finance Corp.	405,090	2,692
*South Carolina Elect. & Gas	8,565	70
*Tri-Continental Corp.	35,000	171
Charter of New York	43,395	329
*Radio Corp. of America	180,000	2,060

* Exchange distribution: This is a method of distributing a large block of a listed stock—usually entirely within our own organization, but occasionally with one or more other brokers. The exchange is handled at a price based on the market for the stock at the time that the "cross" is made.

IMPORTANT:

Seller's costs in exchange distributions are usually lower than seller's costs in unregistered secondaries.

According to N.Y.S.E. averages, the cost of exchange distributions normally ranges between 2.31 and 3.16 times average minimum commission. The cost of secondaries runs from 3.98 to 6.45 times average minimum commission.

Thanks to the purchasing power of our customers, Merrill Lynch can often take on large blocks that would normally be handled as secondaries, and sell them as commission-saving exchange distributions.

Since 1965, we have sold, in the aggregate, more shares in exchange distributions than *all other brokers combined.*

On Tuesday, August 27, 1968, almost as a footnote to the ad, the rhetoric of regulatory public relations again was exercised; a complaint was filed against Merrill Lynch. It was theoretically possible to suppose that the Stock Exchanges were becoming more egalitarian and that the status of investor authority was advancing. However, appearance and actuality were grotesquely at variance. The SEC was merely making another creaking curtsey to the myth of its authority on the floor of the New York Stock Exchange.

The *Wall Street Journal* devoted almost a full page on August 28 to the story, beginning with a headline:

MERRILL LYNCH DISCLOSED INSIDE INFORMATION ON EARNINGS OF DOUGLAS AIRCRAFT TO 14 INSTITUTIONS, SEC STAFF SAYS

In part, it had this to say:

WASHINGTON—The Securities and Exchange Commission ordered administrative proceedings on staff charges that Merrill Lynch, Pierce, Fenner & Smith Inc.—the nation's largest securities firm—14 of its officers and salesmen and 14 institutional investors violated antifraud provisions of Federal securities law in 1966.

The order stunned the brokerage community.

According to the charges, Merrill Lynch in early 1966 supplied the institutions with "non-public information" about the declining earnings of Douglas Aircraft Co.

At the time, Merrill Lynch was a prospective managing underwriter of a $75 million offering of Douglas convertible debentures. The institutional investors, according to the SEC staff charges, on receiving the information either sold existing holdings of Douglas stock or sold the stock short.

While making the non-public information available to the favored institutional customers, the SEC staff charged, Merrill Lynch continued to transact purchases of Douglas stock for other customers without disclosing the information to them.

Yet two years earlier, on July 6, 1966, I had sent the following letter to the SEC:

July 6, 1966

Mr. Irving Pollack
Securities Exchange Commission
Washington, D. C. 20549

Dear Mr. Pollack:

I must ask the Commissioner to investigate for me the recent decline in Douglas Aircraft. I do not believe the decline in Douglas Aircraft of 29 points from 90 to 61 can be attributed solely to Douglas management's bad cost accounting practices. Granted these are incomprehensible, and deserving of scrutiny by the Commissioner. I have reason to believe that the extent of the decline was precipitated in order to deal more profitably for the specialist's own account and for the accounts of favored customers.

As the Commissioner well knows, a specialist with experience is encouraged by virtue of the ability to deal for his own account, for the special fees that are obtainable for obtaining limit orders at wholesale price levels, and for the benefits to be derived for his own long term segregated tax account, to employ principles and practices that are incompatible with the best interests of the public by "encouraging" a price decline in his specialty stock—once he has sold short . . .

It would therefore seem to be in the interest of investors for the Commissioner to determine what the short position was that was assumed by the specialist in Douglas Aircraft and the levels at which he covered this short position and the profitability of this short position to him.

If in the present instance, my presumptions are correct, and the specialist did, in fact:

1. Cover a large short position at the 61–62 level and;
2. Also established a segregated tax account at these levels and;
3. Executed limited orders between 61 through 65 for the high fees established for such executions;

then I maintain that the ethics and practices involved are inimical to the interests of investors in Douglas Aircraft, among whom I number many of my clients.

If indeed Douglas Aircraft has moved into the portfolios of funds and institutions in the course of the recent decline, then the floating supply of this stock has been materially reduced. Since it is now in strong hands, for the specialist in Douglas to segregate stock for his own account will therefore aggravate an already existing problem of supply. If he has kept stock for himself in his tax account and there is the kind of demand I anticipate for this stock, then he will be obliged to enter the market more often than would otherwise be necessary in order to sell this stock short, in order to supply this demand. This will cause increased fluctuations in Douglas stock further adding to investor problems and the specialist's profits for his trading account.

May I hear from the Commissioner concerning this matter.

Sincerely,

/s/ Richard Ney

P. S. It will be interesting to learn if Douglas insiders and Merrill Lynch bought on this drop.

It must be noted in passing that despite the receipt of my letter by the SEC their "investigation" accomplished nothing; there was no interference in the swindle then under way. Instead, during the months ahead the public was about to be handled with increasing violence. For although a period of stabilization then appeared to be under way, it subsequently became clear that what indeed one had every right to think were major accumulations going on in Douglas, after more than a 50 per cent decline in the price of the stock, were, in fact, further distributions. Word had been passed to big-block portfolio managers that Douglas was again about to be dropped in price and their big blocks were again being dumped at what precedent suggested should have been major buying levels. Shortly thereafter the public was again summarily blackjacked as Douglas stock declined to the 30 level.

There is an even more important consideration—the persistent intransigence of the SEC in the face of my repeated telephone calls and letters has many conjectural aspects. It remains for a higher authority to pass on the reasons behind the SEC's delay in pressing charges against Merrill Lynch and others involved.

It is said, by their fruits you shall know them:

SECURITIES AND EXCHANGE COMMISSION

WASHINGTON, D.C. 20549

July 29, 1966

AIR MAIL

Mr. Richard Ney
Richard Ney & Associates
170 North Canon Drive
Beverly Hills, California

Dear Mr. Ney:

Mr. Pollack has asked me to reply to your letter of July 6, 1966 in which you request an investigation into the recent market activity in Douglas Aircraft Co., Inc. common stock.

We appreciate receiving the information and comments contained in your letter and you may be assured that they will be carefully considered from the standpoint of the Commission's regulatory and enforcement responsibilities. In the discharge of these responsibilities, we keep securities markets under surveillance and make investigations when warranted. As you know, in the interest of effective enforcement and to protect innocent companies and persons, the Commission's rules provide that its investigations shall be conducted privately. Accordingly, the fact that an investigation may be undertaken in a given case is generally not revealed; nor does the Commission reveal the results of an investigation, except in those cases in which some public enforcement action is taken, either before the Commission or in the courts.

We hope that you will continue to bring to our attention any matters which you feel will be of interest to us.

Sincerely yours,

/s/ Peter A. Fried
Branch Chief

The curve of probability suggested that the charges against Merrill Lynch would be no more than a Salvation Army barrage. And why not? Why, it is legitimate to ask, would the SEC seek to clean up the Exchanges when it has a vital interest in maintaining the system's *status quo* and operates on the assumption that chaos and crisis must be accepted by investors as natural conditions?

A footnote to the whole affair is that the specialist's role in the swindle was completely ignored, so far as the public can tell. If the specialist was investigated and cleared of any charge of wrongdoing, we have a right to this knowledge. We should be told whether he was or was not exonerated—or at least if he was investigated. In a situation like this, a specialist could have known Merrill Lynch's selling plans before anyone else, and acted upon them. It is impossible to give a brief yet adequate account of the implications to the specialist in Douglas of this information and what it would have been possible for him to do on behalf of his own investment and trading accounts and the trading of his friends. The Commission should have focused its attention on the profit picture of the specialists registered in Douglas Aircraft, if necessary going to the Internal Revenue Service for this information.

This was an enterprise in which, according to "SEC sources," [7] $4.5 million was lost by investors; yet here is the extent of the penalty the SEC saw fit to impose: two Merrill Lynch offices were closed for 21 and 15 days respectively; not one Merrill Lynch member of the NYSE was implicated by name. Indeed, not one top member of the Merrill Lynch hierarchy was implicated, only lower-echelon vice-presidents and employees ("ten individual respondents were censured: in addition, one was dissociated from Merrill Lynch for 60 days and six others for 21 days" [8])—this was the Commission's conception of discipline. No other punishment was meted out because, as the SEC stated, "none of the respondents had previously been the subject of disciplinary action." [9]

Perhaps the most remarkable thing about the SEC's achievement is that for practical purposes a new rule is now operative, forbidding a broker sitting on a company's board of directors to use his inside information for the benefit of his brokerage firm's institutional accounts. By making its complaint against Merrill Lynch, the SEC added enormously to the decision-making potential of the specialist system as it competes with other members of the financial establishment for big-block fees and commissions. Obviously, it is not the investor's protection that is wanted so much as it is the investor's cash.

Business Week, in its issue for August 31, 1968, headlined its version of the story NEW BLAST ON INSIDE INFORMATION. Repeating most of the *Wall Street Journal*'s assertions, it added this:

> The SEC says that Merrill Lynch received "compensation" from the institutions for its Douglas tip in the form of give-ups, as well as through straight brokerage commissions. In Washington, an SEC spokesman described the give-up aspect of the Merrill Lynch case as "tangential." But the SEC has long objected to give-ups, and it has been holding hearings this summer at which the subject has come up over and over again. Indeed, the New York Stock Exchange has been obliged to propose an immediate end to give-ups—a highly controversial proposal that must still win approval from the Big Board's membership . . .

Give-ups are those portions of the commissions received by the broker that he is asked (by fund managers, for example) to "give up" to other brokerage firms that may have helped the fund obtain customers for its shares. The *Business Week* story would have been more complete had it stated that, in addition to its special fees for facilitating the big-block distributions of its institutional accounts, Merrill Lynch also received commissions as the broker for these sales and that often part of Merrill Lynch's commissions went to other brokerage houses as give-ups. When the SEC passed its rule forbidding give-ups, it made it possible for specialists and other underwriters (such as Merrill Lynch) to keep all the commissions as well as their big-block fees.[10]

The upshot of the whole thing is that insiders and institutions will continue, with the SEC's permission, to dump their big blocks into the auction-market investor's portfolio. The SEC should have prohibited big-block distributions by institutions that are able to handle them only because they can afford to pay the big-block fees entitling them to enlist the services of the specialist system in the distribution of their stocks.

The peculiarity of the non-fee-paying investor's situation is that, unlike the specialist's big-block customer, the small investor is compelled to make a painful adjustment to the realities of the specialist's existence. The Exchange asserts that the specialist (or another member of the specialist system) can buy big blocks of stock and then sell them in a way that "would not affect the auction market adversely." Does this not raise important questions concerning the validity of the specialist's most important function—stabilization of prices? Is there not something seriously wrong with this function when the specialist's best efforts can only be had on payment of a special fee? And, is there anything in the regulations that states a specialist must be paid a fee before he sees to it that the sale of *small* blocks does not "affect the auction market adversely"?

Does this not point the finger at a radical displacement of the specialist's supposedly most essential function? If it is possible for specialists to prevent price declines when blocks of 50,000 or more shares are being sold, why do they not prevent price declines when blocks of only 100 shares are being sold? The answer is simple. They don't have to.

Soon brokerage firms will go public. This is a goal dear to the heart of every member of the NYSE. The financial press will react to this by filling page after page with the explanations they have learned to accept from the Stock Exchange. Either by accident or design they will perform in the future as they have in the past—as neutral mechanisms devoted to the greater glory of the Exchange's speculations.

The enormous additions to broker capital because of the influx of public funds will have an impact on economic conditions and economic relationships at all levels. Vertiginous swings in the market will occur as members, now able to acquire far greater credit (at 20 to 1) with far greater capital resources, seek to shake loose the public's share of American business. It will not be unusual to see stocks dropping 75 per cent from their highs. In order to limit the influx of nonmember buying at these low prices, and to monopolize the available reserves of credit for themselves, the Fed—on behalf of the Exchange and its banker satellites—will attempt to raise the ceiling on interest rates; indeed, it has already begun to do so. Ultimately men will fight in the streets, not because they cherish a different ideology but because they need bread.[11]

NOTES, chapter 10

[1] SEC Release No. 2446, 1940. Healy also said: "The worst possible situation in which to permit stabilizing is when the offering price is represented to be 'at the market' . . . The investor, observing the Exchange price or (as often happens) having had his attention called to it by salesmen, believes, as he has a right to, that the price is one made by the free play of supply and demand in a fair and unmanipulated market. But when the offering price is 'at the market,' the possibilities of deception and injury to investors are immeasurably increased . . . Yet the regulation by permitting stabilizing of such securities permits an interference with the free forces of supply and demand and thereby tolerates the creation of a price mirage . . ."

Books are still being written by ill-used investors describing how they were "wiped out." As Healy phrased it, "The greatest injury done the investing public through the manipulation or control of stock exchange prices, was the pervasive, destructive and seemingly irresistible power of the print on the ticker tape to promote the distribution and sale of securities over the counter and by off-the-Exchange solicitations—securities many of which were overpriced, some of which were worthless, and others of which were issued from unworthy motives."

[2] SEC Release No. 2446, 1940.

[3] By "nonmembers," here as elsewhere in this book, I mean non-members who are outside the financial establishment, not just nonholders of Stock Exchange seats. That a particular Federal Reserve Director or institutional fund manager is not the owner of a seat does not mean he is in the same category as an individual investor—and it is the latter to whom I refer as a non-member.

[4] Stanley H. Brown, "Wall Street's Precious Margin," *Fortune* (April, 1966). Brown also says: "The volume in the stockbrokerage business is tremendous these days, but a lot of firms are still having trouble making money on commissions. Fortunately for them, they have other ways of extracting money from customers."

[5] *Marketing Methods . . .*

[6] Here are a few instances of the price declines that can be expected after distributions. The August, 1969, issue of the SEC's *Statistical Bulletin* listed four secondary distributions of common stock for the month of May, 1969: Cleveland Electric Illuminating Company, Olin Mathieson Chemical Corporation, Pennwalt Corporation, and Mobil Oil Corporation. Their prices per share have declined, since the offerings, as follows: Cleveland, offered at $39.875, declined to $31 by October; Olin, offered at $30, declined to $22 by October; Pennwalt, offered at $44.75, declined to $34 by July; Mobil, offered at $68.375, declined to $51 by July.

[7] According to the *Los Angeles Times*, November 27, 1968.

[8] *Wall Street Journal*, November 27, 1968.

[9] Richard Halloran of the *Washington Post* stated (in the *Los Angeles Times*, November 27, 1968): "The Securities and Exchange Commission imposed severe penalties on the nation's largest investment brokerage [firm] for violating antifraud provisions of the securities laws." Just how severe these penalties

were can be judged from the statements quoted by the *Wall Street Journal* of October 10, 1969, in an article concerning a suit by the SEC against others associated with Merrill Lynch in the transactions in Douglas stock. The headline was THREE CUSTOMERS OF MERRILL LYNCH FACE LICENSE LOSS: "The Securities and Exchange Commission's staff recommended revoking the investment adviser registrations of three institutional investors accused of trading unlawfully on so-called 'inside' information provided by Merrill Lynch, Pierce, Fenner, and Smith . . . the staff also recommended that the remaining 12 customers be permanently barred from any association with broker-dealers . . ." The lawyer for one of the defendants took exception to what seemed to be bias in the attitude of the SEC favoring Merrill Lynch. According to *The New York Times* of October 11, 1969, the lawyer maintained that "The comparative slap on the wrist which Merrill Lynch, the major respondent, received when it settled with the SEC means that the staff cannot be seriously urging these recommended sanctions which are the business equivalent of the death penalty." This of course makes sense. What the lawyer was in essence saying was that it really wasn't fair for the SEC to distinguish between Merrill Lynch and the small fry; when the law raids a house, it's customary for the madam to accompany the girls to the clink.

[10] In this connection it is interesting that in none of the stories covering the SEC's charges against Merrill Lynch and others was anything mentioned about the existence of the big-block fees paid by Merrill Lynch's institutional sellers.

[11] From *The Web of Government* by R. M. MacIver (New York: Macmillan, 1947), pp. 212–213: "When certain favoring conditions are present and when under these conditions oligarchical government inflexibly resists the demands of the subjected —or exploited—classes revolution is the method to which such classes resort. The drive that animates it is the rankling sense of the oppressiveness of social inequality . . . Social inequality generally brings with it economic exploitation, and the removal of economic burdens becomes most frequently the objective in the name of which the leaders of the revolution can most effectively rally their followers." P. 216: "Established power is so tenacious of its prerogatives that rather than part with any of them it will often by blind resistance invite the loss of them all." From *Eldridge Cleaver: Post Prison Writings and Speeches*, by Eldridge Cleaver (New York: Random House, 1969), p. 143: "I want to say 'all power to the people. Black power to black peo-

ple, white power to white people.' And do you get uptight about that, because you haven't had white [power], you've had pig power? You haven't had any white power. We say, power to the people, all people should have the power to control their own destiny." P. 173: ". . . time is running out. It may still be possible, barely possible, to revolutionize this society—to get fundamental structural changes—without resorting to civil war, but only if we get enough power before it's too late . . . Works on guerrilla warfare have been widely circulated, and a lot of people understand that it doesn't take millions of people to undermine the stability of the American economic system in that way. That's what's at stake—the stability of the system."

11

A Case in Point

There is only this difference between the New York Stock Exchange and a dictatorship— the dictator confiscates your money outright while the Stock Exchange conditions you to think you made a bad investment.

In March, 1966, it seemed clear that United Aircraft stock was undergoing distribution. There was heavy activity on the tape, but the price was not going up. There remained only the problem of extricating clients as near the high as possible. Experience suggested that its specialist would probably be selling out his investment accounts at the 100 level. As the stock moved into the 80s, I stupidly entered an order with a New York broker to sell all, or as many shares as possible, of a block of 5,000 shares of United Aircraft at 99. Only later did I learn that limit orders of that size should never be entered in the auction market.[1]

Later in the day the broker telephoned; his firm's floor partner had said that the block was so large that the specialist, seeing it on his book, would take the price structure of United Aircraft up to a price just *under* 99 and then sell stock all day long without executing the sale of my client's block—knowing where and at what price he could obtain more stock if he needed it. The firm's floor partner had suggested he be allowed to "feed out" the stock once the price reached 99—in other words, to supply it in smaller lots so that the specialist wouldn't see the big block. This, then, was the order: the broker was to tell his floor partner to withdraw the block and feed it out, as he had suggested, at 99. Since it was a block to be sold on behalf of clients and since it would undoubtedly be sold at different prices above 99, it was even decided that the different prices that different clients would receive for their portion of the big block would have to be subsequently determined.

The stock then moved into the 90 level. On April 14 it closed at 96⅛. The following morning when I arrived at my office, United Aircraft had opened at 99¾. I called the broker in New York to ask him about the sale. He told me that nothing had been sold; that, in accordance with my instructions, he had been trying to sell it as a block. I corrected him on this, and he stammered an apology, but, by accident or design, the specialist had carried the day. I wiped the pie off my face.

Another order was entered on April 18 to sell 3,000-odd shares of United Aircraft at varying prices from 99¼ to 99½. My indicators suggested I could count on the stock again approaching these levels. It did—on April 21. But Ben Jacobson & Sons, the specialist unit, entered the market ¼ of a point below my clients' orders on their book. Their book supplied "1,100 shares and the specialists as dealers, the remaining 1,600 shares . . . a transaction involving 2,700 shares." In other words, the specialists sold 1,600 shares of stock from their own account instead of executing the public orders existing on their book, orders that could have supplied the needs of a legitimate "auction market." The public orders on their book made it sure that the specialists' move was safe. I wrote to the President of the New York Stock Exchange and in his reply Funston asserted:

> On April 21, United Aircraft stock opened at 97⅝, up one-quarter of a point from the previous day's closing price, on a reported volume of 1,700 shares. This transaction appeared on the ticker tape at 10:02 A.M. During about the next fifteen minutes, the stock traded in a range of 97¾–98 on seven transactions involving a total reported volume of 1,600 shares.
>
> After 1,000 shares sold at 98, the quotation became 97¾ bid, offered at 98½. The specialists had on the book the following orders to sell: 100 at 98½, 100 at 98⅞, and 900 at 99. There were two competing buy orders in the Crowd, one for 1,100 shares and the other for 1,600 shares.
>
> At 10:17 A.M. a quotation of 98 bid, offered at 99 appeared on the system. It was agreed that both buy orders would be completed at 99 with the book supplying 1,100 shares and the specialists, as dealers, the remaining 1,600 shares. Accordingly, a transaction involving 2,700 shares occurred at a price of 99, up one point from the previous transaction. Through a clerical error, 2,800 shares were printed on the tape at 10:18 A.M. The quotation after the sale was 98¾ bid, offered at 99—both the bid and offer being on behalf of the specialists' dealer account.
>
> Subsequently, an order reached the Post to sell 100 shares. This order was effected against the bid price of 98¾ and appeared on the tape at 10:22 A.M. During the remainder of the day, the stock traded in a range of 98⅞–95¾ on 94 transactions involving a total reported volume of 18,000 shares.
>
> In reviewing the facts in hindsight, we find no basis for criticizing the specialists' supplying 1,600 shares of United Aircraft at 99 to complete both buy orders. In fact, we consider that they were properly performing their function as specialists in so doing.

In 1969 I came upon NYSE Rule 107 (a) and (b) in the NYSE's rules and regulations and I understood for the first time the manner in which major distributions of stock could occur at a stock's high without any indication of this being provided by the published volume statistics. How, I wondered, could the SEC tolerate the existence of so patent a legalized larceny? More than anything else, Rule 107 illuminated the gross injustice and rationalized anarchy of the specialist system.[2]

Certainly the existence of Rule 107 runs contrary to the assumptions and unformulated valuations of the investing public:

Specialist's Transactions off the Exchange

Rule 107. (a) A specialist may, with the prior approval of a Floor Governor, purchase off the Floor of the Exchange, for an account in which he is directly or indirectly interested, a block of stock in which he is registered, without executing the purchase orders on his book at prices at or above the per share price paid by the specialist for such block . . .

Rule 107. (b) A specialist may, with the prior approval of a Floor Governor, sell off the Floor of the Exchange, for an account in which he is directly or indirectly interested, a block of a stock in which he is registered, without executing the selling orders on his book at prices at or below the per share price received by the specialist for such block . . .

It is not surprising that the existence of such a rule has not previously been mentioned or its purposes been made accessible to careful thought. Let those sympathetic to Exchange power argue to the contrary, we are nonetheless able to perceive that the market's destiny is in the hands of those in a position to control it.

The malign infantilism of Rule 107 (a) and its particular commitment to the interests of special interests helps us toward a better understanding of the grand strategy of the specialist system—and we see here that the specialists' preoccupations are directed to consummating transactions off the tape for accounts "in which he is directly or indirectly interested." It is this role that he practices with sober diligence. Thus, according to Rule 107 (a), when his stock has reached its high (say, at 99½), the specialist can leave "unexecuted" the sell orders entered into his book by the public at that price while he makes it possible for "intimate friends" and mutual funds (for a fee) to sell their stock to him. This, then, is the stock he can "purchase off the Floor" (at 99½). Rule 107 (b), on the other hand, allows the specialist to eclipse with a certain deftness those who have entered purchase orders on his book at what hindsight reveals was the market's bottom.

It is not merely a question of whether the rule conforms to the principles that are supposed to govern the auction market, but also what its existence implies about the entire nature and being of the specialist system. For we see that the specialists' purposes never really lend themselves to the auction market investor's purposes or expectations. Indeed, this rule and its perquisites and privileges—to paraphrase Keats—"is the teat from which [his] mind or intelligence sucks identity."

And when the transaction is effected for the mutual fund manager he is assured (in "Marketing Methods for your Block of Stock," published by NYSE, p. 132) "The trade was made private. There was *no* print on the ticker . . . *no* announcement of any kind before or after . . . *no* entry in the specialist's book . . ."

It should also be pointed out that in the same letter to me, Funston stated, "Our definition of stabilization is set forth in Rule 112. We consider purchases at prices below and sales at prices above the last different price to be stabilizing." No consideration is given here to the existence of the specialist's different investment accounts or omnibus accounts and that if the specialist sells short ("at prices above the last different price") in response to rumors broadcast by the Dow Jones News Service, or when he is also maintaining investment or omnibus accounts that could have been employed to supply stock in response to public demands, then he is *not* stabilizing the market since he will want to subsequently see to it that his stock's price declines in order to cover his short positions at a profit. In addition to this, it cannot be considered stabilizing if he conducts a bull raid in his stock (as would seem to be the case in United Aircraft) in order to sell out his investment accounts for long-term capital gains.

UNITED AIRCRAFT TRANSACTIONS OF THURSDAY, APRIL 21, 1966

Sales of stocks between 10 A.M. and 1 P.M.

1700	97⅝	100	98⅜	300	98⅛
100	97¾	100	98¼	100	98⅛
200	97¾	200	98⅜	100	98⅜
300	97¾	400	98¼	100	98⅛
200	98	100	98⅜	100	98⅛
300	98	600	98¼	100	98⅜
300	98	100	98¼	200	98½
200	98	100	98¼	100	98½
2800	99	100	98¼	100	98¼
100	98¾	400	98¼	200	98½
200	98½	300	98¼	100	98¾
300	98¼	100	98	200	98⅞
300	98⅜	500	98¼	100	98½
100	98⅜	100	98	100	98½
100	98¼	100	98¼	200	98⅜

Sales of stocks between 1 P.M. and close

200	98⅛	400	98¾	100	98⅞
100	98½	100	98¾	100	98½
100	98¼	400	98⅞	200	98⅜
100	98¼	200	98⅝	100	98½
100	98¼	100	98½	100	98¼
400	98½	200	98⅞	100	98⅜
100	98⅝	100	98½	100	98¼

Sales of stocks between 1 P.M. and close (*continued*)

200	98	100	96¾	100	96
100	97⅝	100	96¾	100	96
100	98½	300	96½	100	96
300	97½	100	96½	100	96
200	97½	200	96½	100	96
100	97¼	100	96½	100	96
100	96⅞	100	96⅛	500	96
300	97	1000	96¼	100	95¾
800	97¼	100	96	100	95¾
200	97⅛	100	96	100	95¾
200	97	100	96	100	95⅞
100	97	100	96	100	95¾
300	96¾	200	96	200	95¾
				200	95¾

Some of the United Aircraft order was on the tape; there may well have been a big block that was not. All we know about is what was on the tape. (See table above.)

Clearly, between the rules and regulations, Funston's pronouncements, and the average investor's conception of the auction market, there is a profound divergence in point of view. In the performance of his role as NYSE spokesman, Funston asserts that the specialist supports the market, stabilizes it, makes a market for his stock (that is, supplies a buyer or seller when there is none about), and above all, maintains the liquidity of his stock.

How small the value of these functions is to the investor can be seen in the case of the United Aircraft stock. There was an offer already on the book at 99¼. The offerings on the specialist's book represented the auction market; the specialist's offerings for his own account did not.

Funston had no alternative. His function was to defend the specialist, to reconcile integrity with the specialist's militant partisanship on behalf of his own account. Funston argues that specialists supplied 2,700 shares, but he is careful to avoid indicating whether:

1. The block for 1,600 was a short sale by the specialist;

2. The block was a short sale or straight sale to an omnibus account in which the specialist had a "direct or indirect interest," the purpose of the sale possibly being to enable the specialist's omnibus account to now purchase 1,000 shares of stock from the specialist's trading account and 1,600 shares from the specialist's investment account in order to cover the omnibus account's short position;

3. The two competing orders in the crowd were "at the market" or at limit prices;

4. If the competing orders were "market orders," then specialists should not have "participated," since they were acting as agents for public sellers and buyers who, in an auction market, as sellers, could have elected either to lower their selling price or to cause the buyers to raise their purchase prices;

5. The specialist was entering the market in order to undersell his customers, not "in order to narrow the spread." This is obvious since his sale price was not at 98½—which would have narrowed the spread—but at a full point from the last transaction, a one-point gap on 1,500 or more shares being a typical specialist transaction as he sells short prior to dropping his stock's price.

Funston's note, "and the specialists, as dealers, [supply] the remaining 1,600 shares" gives away the game. It is legal, but is it right for the specialist to act as principal for himself and as agent for an auction-market customer and then use his advantageous position to:

1. Charge one customer (for whom he is acting as agent) one point more so that he can make more money for himself?

2. Move into the market, having raised the price one full point, ¼ point *under* his auction-market customers (for whom he is acting as agent) in order to sell his own stock? It was only his position as a specialist that gave him knowledge of the price at which he could undersell those customers for whom, under law, he was acting as agent.[3]

Possibly the most important point of all is that two big blocks—one for 5,000 and the second for 3,000 shares—had been entered with the same specialist to be sold in the auction market at a limit price. Neither order was executed. The lesson here is simple: the "auction market" may satisfy the buy-and-sell orders of the average investor for a few hundred shares of stock, but it is not meant to be used by the public for the sale of big blocks. Big blocks are only to be sold in the auction market by the specialist and then only when the appropriate fees are paid. The auction market, then, is reserved exclusively for the specialist's fee-paying big-block customers. It would be perfectly simple to sell these big blocks if one paid the specialist his "protection money."

Funston has tried to justify the specialist's behavior in this affair, but the attempt is unsuccessful. It looks—although, as usual, we do not have access to full essential details—as though the specialist acted without regard for the interests of his customer.

NOTES, chapter 11

---

[1] Blocks of this size should be sold in the "third market"; there are brokerage firms that specialize in such transactions. Members of the NYSE must, according to the rules, execute all NYSE-

listed stocks on the NYSE; nonmembers, however, can trade over the counter in NYSE-listed stocks, and this trading operation is called the third market.

2 On the other hand, the NYSE puts out a brochure for the public's reading called, whimsically, *Now, About the Specialist.* On p. 10 it says: "Therefore, an investor who wishes to buy or sell a substantial amount of stock should let his Broker know what he wishes to do, so that the Broker may seek to determine the depth of the market on the Floor and enlist the services of the Specialist, if he so desires. In such a case, the investor should not hesitate to 'show his hand,' since the market usually has greater depth than the nominal quote indicates.

"The Specialist is prohibited by rule from buying for his own account at a given price while he holds an order to buy at that price for someone else. And the Specialist must not buy stock at *any* price for his own account while holding an order to buy that stock 'at the market' (the best available price). The same holds true with respect to a Specialist selling for his own account while holding a sell order for someone else. He can't compete at the same price, for his own account, with orders he holds as a Broker's Broker.

"If an investor 'feeds' parts of a large order to his Broker on a piecemeal basis without advising his Broker of his full intentions, he may well be eliminating the Specialist's help, thus contributing to price pressure in the stock as successive portions of the block are executed . . ." And so on.

3 From *Hearings Before a Subcommittee on Interstate and Foreign Commerce,* p. 1119, in the testimony of Walter Frank, then Vice Chairman (and later Chairman) of the NYSE:

CONGRESSMAN [JOHN D.] DINGELL: Now, let's understand one thing. Under a market which is going through very radical swings, it is a fact that liquidation by a specialist is not in the interests of the investors; isn't this a fact?

MR. FRANK: No, sir.

12

He Lived Apathy Ever After
or
Commissioner Saul's Analysis of Specialist Activities Subsequent to President Kennedy's Assassination

Those who seek status seldom make the mistake of calling things by their right names.

The stock market is an environment that is subject to all the forces that operate in or concern themselves with the community. Having examined the specialists and how they operate within the market complex, we can turn our attention to the political activities and controls that are supposed to regulate specialist activity and the market complex and safeguard investors. Rarely do investors reflect on the background and personalities of the government officials who implement the regulations that govern the Stock Exchanges. Aside from Ralph Nader, no one has conducted a major examination of the permissiveness of our regulatory bureaucracies and the effect on the public of this permissiveness. It is this prevailing attitude of permissiveness that has enabled the SEC to complacently keep from dealing with the Stock Exchanges' systematic exploitation of the public. The time has come. Investigation of our investigators is imperative.

This chapter, therefore, has several purposes: it is meant to show not only how specialists respond to an instance of national emergency, but, more important, how an SEC official saw fit to dispose of the questions put to him by a member of Congress. It is important to consider why the Congressman accepted the face-saving explanation of the SEC concerning the financial gains of specialists on the day in question.

The main function of the chapter, however, is to direct attention to the SEC's failure to prevent damage to the economy.

On Friday, November 22, 1963, President John F. Kennedy was assassinated. For a few hours, the nation was virtually paralyzed. But this paralysis did not affect the Exchanges. The moment the news of the assassination was confirmed, there were specialists who set about milking investors—to such an extent that the investors all across the nation began telephoning and telegraphing their Congressmen. An investigation of the Stock Exchanges was demanded, and one was finally conducted —but *behind closed doors*.

The nation heard the first rumors of the assassination about 1:40 P.M., E.S.T. According to a memorandum prepared by Commissioner Ralph Saul, then Director of Trading and Markets of the SEC, prices on the New York Stock Exchange started to decline within six minutes. For what it is worth, my records indicate that prices began to decline earlier.

The volume for the abbreviated period from 1:40 until the close at 2:07 P.M. was quite heavy: 2,400,-000 shares were traded. At the close, the Dow Jones

Industrial Average was off 21.16 points from the previous day's close. The ticker tape was almost an hour behind. Specialists have been known to drop prices on any news or rumor that might enable them to rationalize a swing in their stocks, but a rumor is one thing, a fact is another. Investors who had entered buy and sell orders a few minutes before the news of the assassination found that their sell orders were executed at the bottom, while their buy orders were not executed.

According to the *Los Angeles Times* staff writer Arelo Sederberg,

> The assassination of President Kennedy occurred while my plane was flying from Atlanta to New York. Hurrying to my office in Wall Street I caught the bus just as it was leaving for Manhattan. Two brokers seated in front of me were unemotionally discussing the market's reaction to the just announced assassination. One turned to the other and said, "When the market opens again we ought to have a good buying opportunity." [1]

At the opening on Tuesday, November 26, 9,320,000 shares were traded; American Telephone and Telegraph opened 10 points higher, RCA almost 5 points higher, United Airlines almost 5, and Polaroid 10. Countless other stocks opened at even higher prices. In almost all stocks the decline in prices that had occurred on Friday past was matched by an equal gain in prices at the opening on Tuesday. Because of this, Ralph Saul had asserted that "in many cases the losses of November 22 were wiped out at the opening." This, of course, was not so. The stocks themselves may have recovered their previous price levels, but the investors who had been frightened into selling on Friday had not had their losses wiped out.

At the close, the Dow Jones Industrial Average had gained 32.03 points from Friday's close and stood at 743.52. In 10 of the 25 stocks Saul examined, price increases on Tuesday equaled or exceeded Friday's decline.

On December 2, 1963, Congressman Harley O. Staggers, Chairman of the House Subcommittee on Commerce and Finance, addressed himself to the conduct of specialists on Friday, November 22, 1963, and on the next day of trading, Tuesday, November 26. The investigation was headed by Ralph Saul, who had been a staff member of the SEC since 1958. The popular theory about the SEC is that its commissioners have all the information they require and from this information create the rules and regulations they then administer. But the letter sent to Congressman Staggers, accompanying the "results of a study . . . of specialist and floor trader activity on the New York Stock Exchange on November 22 and 26, 1963," says:

> One point should be emphasized about the reconstruction of the market for individual stocks contained in the attached study. It was based entirely on reports filed by individual specialists and floor traders with the New York Stock Exchange and the Commission. Thus, the accuracy of the present study is necessarily limited by the reliabiltiy of the underlying documents. As the Report of the Special Study noted, under present procedures and techniques this type of market reconstruction is a difficult and complex task involving the use of disparate and sometimes conflicting records.[2]

The SEC's sole sources of information for this investigation of specialists and floor traders were the reports filed by specialists and floor traders. This is like supposing that the killer caught with a smoking gun in his hand is the man most likely to tell the police who fired it—or that an asylum is best run by its inmates.

Out of 1,400 stocks, the SEC investigated 25. On December 31, 1963, Commissioner Saul wrote to the presidents of the two Exchanges:

> In connection with a study the Commission is making of the activities of specialists on November 22 and 26, 1963, we would appreciate receiving certain informa-

tion from your exchange. Specifically we are interested in the following items:

 a. The closing time of the Exchange on November 22, 1963;

 b. The name of the official or group directing the closing on November 22, 1963:

 c. Was trading halted in certain stocks prior to the close on November 22, 1963? If so, the name of the official or group halting such trading.

 d. During the period between November 22 and 26, 1963, did the Exchange review the financial condition of each specialist unit? If such a review was undertaken and the need for additional capital by some specialist units was shown, did the Exchange take any action to assure that adequate financing would be available upon resumption of trading?

Since the Commission is attempting to complete its study as soon as possible, your earliest response would be appreciated.

Was it too much to expect Commissioner Saul to have included a query about specialist short selling and covering transactions and the profits from them, along with a query about the profits from the sales from their investment accounts and the investment accounts of their friends and financing firms? Instead, all he provided Congressman Staggers with was a highly inadequate report: *Profiles of Specialist and Floor Trader Activity in Twenty-five Selected Stocks on November 22 and November 26, 1963*. Herewith, the section on AT&T:

AMERICAN TELEPHONE & TELEGRAPH

November 22

Reported Volume	189,200
Open	137⅛
High	138½
Low	130
Close	130
Change	−7(5.1%)

The specialist in American Telephone & Telegraph was long 1,800 shares at the opening. From the opening until 1:41 he purchased 3,800 and sold 4,800 shares, resulting in a position of 800 shares long. During this period the stock traded approximately 72,000 shares at prices ranging from 136¾ to 138½.

At 1:41 American Telephone & Telegraph was at 138⅜; from then until trading was suspended at 2:00 the price declined to the low and close of 130 on approximately 117,000 shares. During this interval the specialist purchased 13,700 and sold 2,500 shares.

As American Telephone & Telegraph declined from 138¼ to 135 on approximately 54,500 shares, the specialist purchased 1,000 and sold 1,300 shares. The bulk of this buying appears to have come from orders on the specialist's book. During the remainder of trading the stock declined to 130 on approximately 62,500 shares of which the specialist purchased 12,700 and sold 1,200 shares; 2,800 shares were purchased at a price of 133½ and 1,800 shares were purchased at 132½. Most price changes were eighths and quarters; only one change exceeded ½ point.

November 26

Reported Volume	245,400
Open	140*
High	140
Low	138⅛
Close	138¾
Change	9¾ (7.5%)

* The stock was ex-dividend $1.

American Telephone & Telegraph opened at 12:59 P.M., at a price of 140 on 150,000 shares, of which the specialist supplied 11,000 shares. The stock traded for the remainder of the day at prices ranging from 138⅛ to 140 and closed at 138¾. Of 95,400 shares traded after the opening the specialist purchased 3,500 and sold 4,800 shares.

FLOOR TRADING: NOVEMBER 22

From the opening until 1:41 floor traders purchased 5,100 and sold 4,500 shares. From 1:41 until the close floor traders sold 1,000 shares (100 short) near the beginning of the decline at prices ranging from 137⅝ to 137⅛. During that period they purchased 800 shares at 135 and 134½ and 400 shares at prices from 131½ to 130⅛. The stock closed at 130.

NOTE: Reference was made, in the attached memorandum,[3] to the specialist's profit in American Telephone & Telegraph Co. This computation was made on a FIFO basis and only included the specialist's transactions between 1:41 P.M. on November 22 and the opening transaction on November 26.

The use by Saul of the FIFO (first in first out) method of accounting, and his decision to limit the accounting to the period after 1:41 P.M. warrant examination. Were it not for the FIFO method of accounting and the exclusion from accounting of purchases made before 1:41— and further, the exclusion of figures on segregated investment accounts—we would have had a different picture of what happens on the floor of the Exchange in the course of a crisis. For one thing, any investment account purchased six months or more earlier would not appear in the accounting.

In the memorandum attached to the *Profiles* report, Saul observed:

Specialists registered in certain of the most important stocks studied (from the standpoint of market leadership) appeared to meet their obligations. Thus, the specialist registered in the stock of American Telephone & Telegraph purchased, on balance, 11,200 shares of stock as the price declined from 138⅜ to 130.

Instead of this bit of graffiti, Saul should have supplied the prices at which George La Branche, the AT&T specialist, purchased stock. Since he appears to have sold at the top and bought at the bottom, this specialist's, and others', contributions to that day's activities should have been examined with a microscope. Such an examination would have discovered a number of noteworthy points, since:

1. Commissioner Cary had admonished that "the reconstruction of the market . . . was based entirely on reports filed by individual specialists." In other words, no meetings were held in which face-to-face questions and answers occurred between the SEC and the Exchange specialists. Each specialist prepared and filed his own report.

2. Commissioner Saul's report states that the specialist in AT&T "was long 1,800 shares" at the opening on November 22. Yet it seems probable that this specialist had segregated investment accounts and that the figures he supplied refer only to his trading account. Most likely, Commissioner Saul's statement should have said "1,800 shares long in his trading account." References to segregated investment accounts are rare finds in Exchange literature. However, both Telephone and RCA were racing toward their highs. The specialist in RCA—Bill Meehan—stated that he was long 136,900 shares. Since RCA opened at 90½, this amounted to a position of approximately $12.5 million. Specialists rarely, if ever, carry this kind of position in their trading account; it is logical to assume that most of this 136,900 shares represented Meehan's segregated investment account. Since both Telephone and RCA were close to their highs and actively traded and since the specialists in each are enormously wealthy, it is probable that they had investment accounts of comparable value.

3. Commissioner Saul's report states that this specialist was long but does not state whether he was or had been short stock in another account. This is important because, though the specialist cannot be long and short at

the same time in his trading account, his financing firm or another segregated account can, according to the rules, be short when the trading account is long; this information is included in a report by the Special Study group.

4. In Commissioner Saul's memorandum we are told the specialist "sold 4,800 shares" between the opening and 1:41 P.M. Examining the transactions in AT&T that follow below, we see that there are a number of big blocks for a thousand shares or more; we see that while there were no big blocks at that day's high of 138⅜, there were six big blocks at 138:

$$
\begin{array}{r}
1,300 \\
1,000 \\
1,000 \\
1,000 \\
1,000 \\
\underline{1,100} \\
\end{array}
$$

Totaling 6,400 shares at 138.

Commissioner Saul tells us that the specialist "sold 4,800 shares," but he does not say whether or not he sold most or all of those 4,800 shares short at the top.

AMERICAN TELEPHONE & TELEGRAPH
TRANSACTIONS NOVEMBER 22, 1963

10 A.M. to 1 P.M.

3000	137⅛	1500	137½	200	138⅛
100	137⅛	100	137½	100	138¼
400	137⅛	100	137⅜	100	138¼
700	137¼	100	137½	100	138¼
200	137¼	200	137⅝	100	138¼
100	137¼	100	137¾	100	137¾
200	137¼	200	137⅞	100	137⅞
200	137⅜	1300	138	100	138
700	137⅜	300	138	100	138
500	137½	200	138⅛	100	138

AMERICAN TELEPHONE & TELEGRAPH
TRANSACTIONS NOVEMBER 22, 1963 (*continued*)

10 A.M. to 1 P.M.

1000	138	200	137¾	200	137⅛
500	138	300	137⅞	600	137¼
100	138	100	137⅞	200	137⅛
100	138	100	137⅞	800	137
200	138	1500	137¾	400	137
200	138	100	137⅝	100	137
200	138	200	137⅝	400	137
100	138	100	137⅝	100	137¼
100	138	500	137½	600	137
100	137¾	100	137¾	100	137
400	138	200	137½	200	137¼
100	138	100	137½	100	137⅛
200	138	100	137⅝	200	137⅜
100	137⅞	100	137⅝	400	137¼
100	137⅞	100	137¾	300	137⅛
100	137¾	100	137¾	1000	137⅜
200	137⅝	100	137⅝	200	137⅛
400	137⅞	100	137⅝	200	137⅜
400	137⅞	900	137½	300	137⅛
100	137⅞	100	137⅜	300	137⅛
100	138	200	137⅜	1000	137
1000	137⅞	100	137¼	100	137
100	137⅞	200	137¼	300	136⅞
100	137¾	100	137½	100	136⅞
100	137⅞	100	137½	200	136⅞
100	137⅞	200	137½	500	136¾
600	137⅞	100	137⅜	500	137
200	138	100	137½	500	137
1000	138	200	137¼	1000	137
1000	138	100	137⅛	200	136¾
200	138	100	137¼	200	136¾
300	137⅞	200	137⅜	100	136⅞
300	138	400	137¼	100	136⅞
200	137⅞	200	137¼	100	136⅞
1100	137¾	100	137⅛	200	137

AMERICAN TELEPHONE & TELEGRAPH
TRANSACTIONS NOVEMBER 22, 1963 (*continued*)

10 A.M. to 1 P.M.

300	137⅛	100	137⅝	200	137⅝
100	137⅛	200	137½	100	137⅞
200	137⅛	200	137½	100	137¾
100	137⅛	100	137⅝	100	137¾
100	137⅛	100	137½	100	137⅞
100	137⅛	500	137½	100	137⅞
100	137⅛	200	137⅝	200	137¾
100	137⅛	100	137⅝	200	137¾
100	137¼	700	137⅜	100	137⅞
200	137¼	300	137⅜	600	138
100	137⅜	100	137½	800	138
100	137¼	300	137⅝	500	138
200	137⅜	300	137¾	500	138
100	137⅜	500	137¾	100	137⅞
500	137½	100	137¾	1000	138
500	137½	100	137¾	1100	138
100	137½	100	137¾	100	138
100	137⅝	300	137¾	100	138
100	137⅝	100	137⅞	200	138
200	137⅜	100	137⅞	100	138⅛
100	137⅝	100	137⅞	200	138⅛
100	137½	200	137¾	200	138
100	137½	100	137⅞	500	138¼
300	137⅜	100	137⅞	500	138¼
100	137½	300	138	100	138¼
100	137½	100	137⅞	500	138¼
200	137½	100	137⅞	100	138⅛
100	137⅜	100	137⅞	100	138¼
200	137⅜	500	137⅞	100	138¼
300	137⅜	100	138	200	138¼
100	137½	100	137⅞	100	138¼
100	137⅝	100	137⅞	200	138¼
100	137⅝	200	137¾	100	138¼
100	137½	100	137¾	100	138¼
100	137⅜	100	137¾	100	138¼

AMERICAN TELEPHONE & TELEGRAPH
TRANSACTIONS NOVEMBER 22, 1963 (*continued*)

10 A.M. to 1 P.M.

100	138¼	100	138½	100	138⅜
100	138¼	100	138⅜	100	138½
100	138½	100	138¼	300	138¼
100	138½	100	138⅜	100	138⅜
400	138½	100	138¼	100	138¼
600	138½	300	138⅜	100	138¼
200	138½	100	138⅜		

AMERICAN TELEPHONE & TELEGRAPH
TRANSACTIONS NOVEMBER 22, 1963

After 1 P.M.

100	138⅜	200	138¼	1000	137
100	138¼	100	138⅜	2000	137
100	138¼	100	138⅜	100	137⅛
100	138¼	100	138⅜	1000	136¾
100	138¼	100	138⅜	100	136½
100	138⅛	400	138⅜	100	136½
100	138¼	100	138⅜	100	136½
300	138¼	200	138⅜	100	136½
200	138⅛	200	138¼	500	136¼
100	138⅛	200	138¼	500	136¼
100	138¼	200	138¼	1000	136¼
100	138¼	500	138	1000	136¼
100	138¼	1000	137⅝	2100	136
100	138⅛	300	137½	200	136
100	138⅛	100	137½	500	136
100	138⅛	100	137¾	500	136
100	138¼	100	137½	400	136
100	138¼	200	137¼	100	136
100	138¼	300	137½	100	136
200	138¼	100	137⅛	10000	136
300	138⅛	100	137¼	500	136
100	138¼	500	137⅛	600	136

AMERICAN TELEPHONE & TELEGRAPH
TRANSACTIONS NOVEMBER 22, 1963 (*continued*)

After 1 P.M.

500	136
400	136
500	136
100	135½
100	135½
500	135½
1000	135½
5000	135
200	135
100	135
200	135
100	135
700	135¼
100	135⅛
1400	135
500	135¼
1000	135
300	135
400	135
100	135¼
100	135⅛
100	135⅛
200	135⅛
100	135
200	135
700	135
500	135
800	135
200	135
300	135
400	135
500	135
500	135
1000	135
400	135
500	135
3000	135
900	135
800	135
700	135
3000	135
900	134½
200	134½
400	134½
500	134½
300	134½
200	134½
300	134½
500	134½
200	134½
700	134½
800	134½
700	134½
800	134½
200	134½
100	134
600	134
500	134
400	134
700	134
800	134
1000	134
100	133¾
100	133½
800	134
100	133⅝
100	133½
300	133½
200	133½
300	133½
400	133½
100	133⅝
100	133½
200	133½
100	133½
100	133½
200	133½
100	133½
200	133½
1000	133½
400	133½
500	133½
100	133½
200	133½
300	133½
400	133½
500	133½
200	133½
300	133½
300	133½
200	133½
500	133½
100	133½
300	133½
100	133½
100	133⅝
100	133½
200	133½
100	133⅝
500	133½
100	133⅝
100	133½
100	133½
100	133½
100	133½

AMERICAN TELEPHONE & TELEGRAPH
TRANSACTIONS NOVEMBER 22, 1963 (*continued*)

After 1 P.M.

200	133⅝	200	131½	100	130½
100	133⅝	200	131½	100	130½
200	133⅝	300	131½	200	130½
200	133½	200	131½	300	130½
300	133½	600	131	100	130½
400	133½	500	131	200	130½
600	133½	400	131	100	130½
100	133½	200	131	200	130½
200	133½	1000	131	100	130½
300	133½	500	131	100	130¼
300	133½	100	131¾	200	130¼
200	133½	100	131¾	100	130¼
1600	133	100	131½	100	130½
300	133½	400	131½	500	130½
200	133½	500	131½	500	130½
100	133½	100	131¾	600	130½
300	133	100	131½	500	130¼
200	133	300	131¾	300	130½
800	133	100	131¾	100	130¼
100	132⅞	200	131¾	100	130¼
100	132⅞	200	132	200	130¼
100	132½	200	132	100	130¼
100	132½	100	132	500	130¼
100	132	100	131½	100	130¼
200	132	100	131¾	400	130¼
400	132	700	131½	500	130¼
800	132	100	131½	100	130¼
200	132	200	131	200	130¼
300	132	600	131	500	130¼
400	132	500	131	600	130¼
300	132	400	131	1000	130¼
200	132	400	131½	1000	130¼
700	132	400	131¼	500	130⅛
700	131½	700	131	500	130⅛
300	131½	200	130½	500	130⅛

AMERICAN TELEPHONE & TELEGRAPH
TRANSACTIONS NOVEMBER 22, 1963 (*continued*)

After 1 P.M.

600	130⅛	500	130	300	130
500	130⅛	500	130	400	130
400	130	500	130	100	130
1000	130	1000	130	500	130
200	130	400	130	400	130
200	130	200	130	200	130

Telephone opened on November 26, 1963, at 140.

Although specialists' trades are indistinguishable from public trades, at least until 1 P.M., it is my opinion that this specialist is *not* buying, but *selling* at the top—and doing a fairly creditable job of it.

Moreover, looking at the list and what happened after the 72,000 shares mentioned by Commissioner Saul had gone across the tape, we note big blocks for 10,000 shares, 5,000, 2,000, and so on. None of this activity was likely to be institutional. It would be almost impossible for pension fund or mutual fund portfolio managers to be in there selling on such short notice. Certainly, they would not be buying at top prices when they knew that specialists use every crisis to drop prices in order to clean out their books, engaging in a mad scramble to pick up stock bargains for themselves and their friends.[4] Professionals would, in consequence, be waiting for lower price levels.

If we venture to explain the performance of the specialists in AT&T and other stocks on the 22nd and 26th of November, we can say that during periods of crisis they are best able to sell out their accounts at the top and the public's at the bottom of the market. As for Commissioner Saul's statement that the specialist in AT&T purchased 13,700 shares after 1:41 P.M., if the transactions are counted beginning at 130¼ and continued to the close, a pattern seems to emerge suggesting that this specialist "acquired" the stock he needed at this price level to cover his short position and go long in preparation for the opening on the 26th. It is also my assumption that having completed this task, and not wishing to have to execute incoming buy orders, the specialist closed shop as soon as possible, without waiting for the Exchange to close—which it did seven minutes later.

Saul fails to say whether the specialists' sales or purchases were for a trading account, investment accounts or omnibus accounts. Since specialists' greatest profits may well be in their long-term investment accounts, it's logical to assume that the specialist unit in AT&T had one or more such accounts. If my assumptions are even partially correct this specialist's profit was far greater than the $80,000 quoted by Saul.

It is my opinion that Commissioner Saul provided a far from adequate picture of what happened in AT&T during this period of crisis. Taking a profit in such a situation is not illegal, but it certainly raises questions in view of the specialist's stated function as a broker and his mandate to maintain an orderly market.

With ease, Chairman Staggers stated:

In your special study report you set forth certain recommendations concerning the specialist, which you have indicated you intend to carry out through the rule-making power of the Commission, although it appears from testimony before our committee last week the exchanges are opposed to many of these particular recommendations. The special study group made an analysis of the work of the specialist on the May 28 selloff and had several comments to make concerning the effectiveness of certain specialists and the seeming inactivity of others. Among the specialist's activities the special study considered was that in the share of American Telephone & Telegraph.

I note that on Tuesday last American Telephone & Telegraph did not open until 12:30 and then up 10 points from Friday's close. It would seem interesting to me were the facts developed regarding specialist activity in this stock on the preceding Friday and on Tuesday the 26th, namely, what purchases they made on Friday; what sales they made on Tuesday; and what may have been their profit in this connection . . .[5]

Chairman Staggers' question about this specialist's profits in AT&T was in response not only to several telegrams from my office but to wires and letters from thousands of others, and his questions had given life to what was a generally sterile investigation.

And Ralph Saul wriggled out:

In answer to the specific question as to the profitability of the specialist's trading it would seem that on the liquidation of his position on November 26, there was a profit of approximately $80,000. This was on a capital commitment of $1,600,000 as of the close on November 22. *It should be pointed out that this profit figure has no bearing on the performance of the specialist in American Telephone and Telegraph stock.*[6]

On November 26, American Telephone opened at 140, 10 points higher, and "the specialist supplied 11,000 shares." In other words, he had sold 11,000 shares of the 12,000 he had in his long position, at a price increase of $10 a share, an increase of $110,000. Add to this what the omnibus accounts could have provided, and it is difficult to see how his profits could have been a mere $80,000!

Next, Commissioner Saul came up with an argument in support of Bill Meehan, the specialist in RCA:

RADIO CORPORATION OF AMERICA
TRANSACTIONS NOVEMBER 22, 1963 (*continued*)

10 A.M. to 1 P.M.

200	89¼	500	89½	600	89⅝
100	89¼	100	89½	100	89¾
200	89⅛	100	89½	100	89¾
100	89⅜	300	89½	100	89¾
200	89¼	100	89⅜	100	89¾
100	89¼	100	89½	100	89⅞
500	89¼	200	89⅝	100	89⅞
500	89⅛	100	89⅝	100	89⅞
100	89⅜	500	89⅝	100	89⅞
200	89¼	100	89½	100	89¾
100	89¼	200	89⅜	100	89¾
300	89¼	100	89⅜	300	89⅞
200	89¼	400	89½	200	89⅞
100	89⅜	100	89⅜	200	89⅞
100	89⅜	400	89½	100	89⅞
400	89½	100	89½	100	90
200	89⅜	100	89½	900	90
100	89½	200	89½	200	90
100	89⅜	100	89⅝	500	90
500	89¼	100	89⅝	1000	90
100	89¼	100	89⅝	200	90
100	89¼	100	89¾	500	90
200	89⅛	200	89⅝	100	90⅛
200	89⅛	200	89¾	100	90
200	89¼	200	89⅝	100	90⅛
200	89	100	89⅝	100	90⅛
100	89	100	89⅝	200	90⅛
600	89	100	89⅝	500	90¼
100	89	400	89¾	100	90¼
100	89⅛	600	89⅞	100	90¼
200	89⅛	100	89⅞	500	90⅜
100	89⅜	100	89⅞	400	90⅜
100	89⅜	100	89⅞	100	90⅜
100	89⅜	100	89⅞	100	90⅜
100	89⅜	100	89¾	300	90⅜
100	89⅜	200	89⅞	100	90¼

RADIO CORPORATION OF AMERICA
TRANSACTIONS NOVEMBER 22, 1963 (*continued*)

10 A.M. to 1 P.M.

100	90⅜	100	89¾	100	89⅜
300	90½	400	89⅝	100	89⅜
200	90⅝	200	89½	100	89⅜
500	90½	800	89¼	100	89⅜
100	90½	200	89¼	100	89⅜
100	90⅜	100	89¼	500	89½
500	90½	200	89⅛	100	89½
200	90½	100	89⅜	100	89½
100	90½	200	89¼	300	89½
100	90½	100	89¼	100	89⅜
100	90½	500	89¼	100	89½
100	90⅝	500	89⅛	200	89⅝
100	90⅝	100	89⅜	100	89⅝
100	90½	200	89¼	100	91⅞
200	90⅝	100	89¼	500	91⅞
300	90⅝	300	89¼	100	91¾
100	90⅝	200	89¼	500	91¾
400	90¾	100	89⅜	200	91¾
700	90½	100	89⅜	200	91¾
200	90½	400	89½	400	91¾
100	90⅜	200	89⅜	300	91¾
100	90⅝	100	89½	100	91⅞
100	90⅜	100	89⅜	100	91⅞
200	90¼	500	89¼	200	92
400	90¼	100	89¼	100	92
200	90¼	100	89¼	500	92
100	90½	200	89⅛	1000	91⅞
100	90¼	200	89⅛	100	92
100	90¼	200	89¼	200	91¾
700	90	200	89	100	92
200	90	100	89	200	92
1000	90	600	89	100	92
200	90	100	89	100	91⅞
500	90	100	89⅛	100	91⅞
100	89¾	200	89⅛	100	92

After examining the figures that show the trades in RCA between 1:00 P.M. and the close, it is my opinion that this specialist was in all probability "acquiring" stock at the close in 1,000-share and 500-share blocks—and if Meehan is going to cover shorts he's going to do it at the bottom and he's going to need a lot of stock. Here again we have an example of a specialist's accumulating stock at the bottom in preparation for the next day's trading.

RADIO CORPORATION OF AMERICA
TRANSACTIONS NOVEMBER 22, 1963

After 1 P.M.

200	91⅞	100	91⅜	200	90⅛
100	91¾	200	91½	100	90⅛
200	91¾	400	91⅝	200	90⅛
100	91¾	200	91¾	200	90⅛
100	91⅝	300	91¾	1000	90⅛
100	91⅝	100	91¾	1000	90⅛
100	91⅝	400	91¾	1000	90⅛
200	91⅝	100	91¾	1000	90
100	91½	100	91½	2100	90
100	91½	200	91½	1500	90
500	91½	100	91¾	1000	90
200	91⅜	100	91¼	1000	90
200	91¼	100	91¼	500	89¾
100	91⅛	400	91	100	89¾
200	91⅛	300	90¾	100	89¾
300	91⅛	200	91	1500	89½
100	91⅛	100	91	100	89½
500	91⅝	200	91	100	89½
300	91¼	400	90¾	1500	89¼
100	91¼	700	90½	200	89¼
100	91¼	400	90½	100	89¼
200	91¼	200	90⅜	1000	89
200	91¼	800	90¼	1000	88¾
300	91⅜	1000	90⅛	1500	88½

RADIO CORPORATION OF AMERICA
TRANSACTIONS NOVEMBER 22, 1963 (*continued*)

After 1 P.M.

100	88½	1000	87¾	500	86¾
100	88½	200	87¾	500	86½
100	88½	100	87¾	500	86¼
1000	88½	200	87¾	500	86¼
100	88½	1000	87½	1000	86
100	88½	500	87½	500	86
1000	88¼	500	87¼	1000	85
1000	88¼	500	87	100	85
1000	88	500	86¾	100	85
500	88	500	87		
1000	88	500	87		

RCA opened on November 26, 1963, at 89¾ on 31,000 shares.

Figures for some of the other big stocks follow:

GENERAL MOTORS TRANSACTIONS
NOVEMBER 22, 1963

10 A.M. to 1 P.M.

6300	77½	100	77½	100	77½
100	77½	100	77⅜	500	77½
200	77½	100	77⅜	100	77½
100	77½	100	77½	100	77½
100	77½	200	77⅜	100	77⅜
300	77½	300	77¼	100	77⅜
300	77½	100	77¼	100	77⅜
100	77⅝	100	77⅜	200	77⅜
300	77⅜	100	77⅜	500	77½
100	77⅜	100	77¼	200	77½
200	77½	200	77⅜	100	77⅜
				100	77⅜

GENERAL MOTORS TRANSACTIONS
NOVEMBER 22, 1963 (*continued*)

10 A.M. to 1 P.M.

200	77⅜
400	77½
100	77⅜
100	77½
200	77⅜
300	77⅜
200	77⅜
100	77½
500	77¼
100	77⅛
300	77
100	77⅛
100	77⅛
200	77⅛
100	77⅛
300	77
100	77
100	77
500	76¾
100	76¾
1000	76⅞
100	76⅞
100	77
100	77
300	76¾
700	76⅝
500	76½
700	76¼
100	76¼
100	76⅜
100	76⅝
100	76½
200	76⅝
200	76⅜
100	76⅜
100	76⅜
100	76½
100	76⅜
100	76⅝
100	76⅝
100	76⅝
200	76⅝
100	76⅝
100	76⅝
200	76¾
100	76⅝
400	76⅝
400	76⅝
400	76⅜
300	76⅜
200	76⅝
100	76⅞
100	76¾
100	76¾
100	76¾
200	76⅞
100	76⅞
100	76⅞
300	76⅝
100	76¾
100	76¾
100	76¾
100	77
100	77
500	77
100	77
100	77
100	76⅞
100	76⅞
100	77
100	77
100	77
200	77
100	77
100	77
300	77
100	77
100	77⅛
100	76⅞
100	76⅞
100	77
300	77
700	77¼
200	77
100	77¼
400	77⅜
200	77¼
300	77⅜
100	77⅜
100	77⅜
200	77⅜
400	77¼
100	77½
100	77⅜
100	77½
500	77½
100	77⅜
700	77⅜
100	77½
300	77⅜
100	77½
100	77½
100	77½
500	77½
700	77½

GENERAL MOTORS TRANSACTIONS
NOVEMBER 22, 1963 (*continued*)

10 A.M. to 1 P.M.

100	77½	200	77⅞	100	78¼
100	77⅝	100	78	100	78¼
100	77¾	100	77⅞	200	78
200	77¾	200	78	200	78¼
100	77¾	300	78	100	78⅛
100	77⅝	100	78¼	100	78
100	77¾	100	78¼	100	78
100	77¾	200	78		

After 1 P.M.

100	77⅞	400	77⅞	3000	76
100	77¾	500	77¾	700	75½
100	77¾	600	77½	2000	75⅛
300	77¾	1400	77⅜	500	75⅛
100	77⅝	100	77⅛	500	75⅛
100	77¾	100	77	400	75⅛
200	77¾	200	77	500	75⅛
100	78	100	77	200	75⅛
300	78	500	77¼	6000	75
200	77⅞	200	77	5000	75
100	78	400	77	1000	75
100	77⅞	100	77	1000	75
500	78	100	77	200	75
100	77⅞	400	76¾	1000	75
200	77⅞	100	76⅝	500	75
100	78	100	76½	500	75
900	78	100	76½	300	74⅞
300	77⅞	200	76½	100	74⅞
100	77⅞	100	76	200	74¾

General Motors opened on November 26, 1963, at 77¾ on 78,000 shares.

UNITED AIRLINES TRANSACTIONS
NOVEMBER 22, 1963

10 A.M. to 1 P.M.

600	39¾	100	39¾	100	39½
200	40	100	39¾	300	39⅝
100	37⅞	900	39⅝	100	39⅝
100	40	100	39¾	200	39¾
200	40	100	39¾	100	37⅞
200	40⅛	100	39⅝	1300	40
100	40⅛	100	39½	100	40
100	40	100	39½	100	40¼
200	39¾	100	39½	100	40¼
100	39⅝	500	39½	100	40
100	39¾	200	39⅝	100	40

After 1 P.M.

100	40⅛	100	37½	100	36¼
300	39¾	100	37⅛	100	36¼
500	39½	100	37⅛	200	36
100	39¼	100	37⅛	200	35½
300	39	400	37	100	35½
200	38¾	100	36⅝	100	35⅛
100	38⅜	200	36⅝	100	35⅛
100	38⅛	100	36½	300	35
100	38	100	36½	100	34¾
300	37¾	300	36½	100	34⅝

United Airlines opened on November 26, 1963, at 39½ on 10,500 shares.

EVERSHARP TRANSACTIONS
NOVEMBER 22, 1963

After 1 P.M.

100	31¼	100	31	100	30¼
100	31¼	100	30⅞	100	30⅛
200	31	400	31	200	30

EVERSHARP TRANSACTIONS
NOVEMBER 22, 1963 (*continued*)

After 1 P.M.

100	30	500	29	100	28⅜
200	30	500	28⅞	100	28⅜
200	29¾	200	28¾	300	28
300	29¾	200	28¾	100	27
500	29½	100	28¾	200	26½
1300	29⅜	100	28⅝	300	26⅜
100	29⅜	100	28⅝	100	26⅜
400	29¼	300	28⅝	300	26¼
200	29⅛	100	28⅝	500	25¼
100	29⅛	100	28⅝	100	25¼
200	29⅛	100	28⅝	1600	24
500	29	200	28½	500	24
				4000	23

Eversharp opened on November 26, 1963, at 31 on 90,000 shares.

BURROUGHS TRANSACTIONS
NOVEMBER 22, 1963

After 1 P.M.

100	24⅜	100	24¼	11000	22½
100	24⅜	300	24⅛	2000	22½
100	24⅜	100	24⅛	100	22¼
100	24⅜	1800	24⅛	100	22⅛
1000	24¼	100	24	100	22½
700	24¼	5500	24	100	22⅛

Burroughs opened on November 26, 1963, at 24½ on 12,800 shares.

POLAROID TRANSACTIONS
NOVEMBER 22, 1963

After 1 P.M.

200	170¼	100	169½	100	162
100	170¼	200	168¾	100	162
100	169½	200	168	300	161
100	169½	300	167¾	100	160
100	169	100	167	100	160
100	169	100	166⅝	100	160
100	169	500	166	100	160
100	169⅛	200	165¾	100	160
100	168¾	400	165	100	160
200	168⅜	100	164¾	100	159
100	168⅞	100	164⅝	300	159
100	169	300	164½	100	158
300	169	500	163	300	158
100	169	1200	163	300	157
100	169½	100	162¼	300	156
100	170	100	162¼	200	155¼
100	170½	100	162⅛	400	155¼
100	170	100	162	100	155¼
100	169¾	100	162	500	155

Polaroid opened on November 26, 1963, at 165 on 12,000 shares.

It must be remembered that RCA had been trading at its highs. When he does not wish to record a huge short position in his stock, a specialist will often set up an omnibus account with another firm or with a bank. This account is then able to sell short anonymously and thereby supply the auction market with whatever stock is needed to supply demand. This is less conspicuous than selling short from the specialist's trading account, and it avoids investigation. Furthermore, tax advantages often accrue when specialists also maintain stock in segregated investment accounts that must be held for delivery (after six months) for long-term capital gains purposes.

The tremendous run-up (in October and November) in the price of RCA, as well as the fact that its specialist had more than $12.5 million in what appears to be a segregated investment account, suggests that he had been utilizing short sales from one omnibus account or another to distribute stock to the public and that he intended to transfer stock from his segregated tax account to an omnibus account to cover his short sales. If this isn't what happened it would be of interest to learn what did. Of course it will be asserted that specialists can no longer "sell short against the box"[8] and then deliver over a segregated tax account to their trading account in order to establish long-term gains, but it's certain that sophisticated loopholes exist and are employed to turn short-term into long-term gains.

A profit-and-loss statement from the Internal Revenue Service for 1963 and 1964 would have been interesting evidence of specialist activity on the days in question. The question was never raised why the body in charge of the regulation of the Exchanges did not halt trading immediately when word of the assassination hit the floor. It is well known, after all, that specialists use such occasions to advantage. Great waves of "panic selling" are by and large a myth. After he has found and used the opportunity to unload his own and friends' investment accounts, a specialist then takes his stock down as fast as possible and then executes all other sell orders. To have halted trading immediately would have prevented all this. Saul states:

> In times of crisis . . . the excess of sell orders can then be absorbed only by two major sources of buying power. The first is the stored-up demand represented by limit orders on the specialist's "book." These are orders previously left with the specialist to purchase at specific prices below the market . . . The second major source of potential buying is the specialist.

We would be failing in the use of intelligence if we did not bear in mind the facts revealed (pp. 192–194) and the way in which General Motors was dropped on light volume until big blocks could be "acquired" at the lows. On pages 195–197 are examples of the manner in which so many other stocks were dropped full points on 100-share lots.[9] Commissioner Saul's statement that the results of his "study of floor trader activity shed little new light on this subject" is completely accurate.

NOTES, chapter 12

---

[1] From a conversation with the author.

[2] From a January 21, 1964, letter to Congressman Staggers from William L. Cary, Chairman of the SEC.

[3] *Memorandum Prepared by the Division of Trading and Markets in Reply to Chairman Staggers' Letter Dated December 2, 1963.*

[4] It was common knowledge that AT&T was moving toward its highs and that this was the beginning of the season for selling it—*not* buying it. The same set of circumstances surrounded the transactions in RCA.

[5] Letter of Congressman Harley O. Staggers to William L. Cary, Chairman of the SEC, dated December 2, 1963.

[6] Emphasis supplied. *Memorandum Prepared by the Division of Trading and Markets in Reply to Chairman Staggers' Letter Dated December 2, 1963.* The stock quotations are from the Francis Emory Fitch, Inc., *Stock Sales on the New York Stock Exchange.* The stock profiles are from the *Memorandum.*

[7] Institutions pay for their privileges with special, high commissions; again, "nonmembers" means individual investors. Note (on pp. 185–187) how Jacobson, the specialist in United Airlines, pulled his stock down 5½ points on approximately 5,000 shares,

and Goldberg, the Polaroid specialist, dropped his 8 points on 4,200 shares. Yet Keith Funston testified on February 4, 1964, before a House committee investigating that day's events (*Investor Protection,* p. 1104), ". . . it was the public that made the decline, I mean more people wanted to sell than wanted to buy, so it was a mass panic." Yet, judging from the big blocks we saw going across the tape on the announcement of President Kennedy's assassination, is it not feasible to assume this was NOT public selling—is it not more likely that, for reasons already elaborated, this was *member* selling? And, as it concerns the drop of 8 points in Polaroid on 4,200 shares, can we conceivably consider this as "panic selling" warranting such a drop?

[8] "A method of protecting a paper profit. Let's say you own 100 shares of XYZ which has advanced in price, and you think the price may decline. So you sell 100 shares short, borrowing 100 shares to make delivery. You retain in your security box the 100 shares which you own. If XYZ declines, the profit on your short sale is exactly offset by the profit in the market value of the stock you have retained. You can close out your short sale by buying 100 shares to return to the person from whom you borrowed, or you can send him the 100 shares which you own."—NYSE, *The Language of Investing: A Glossary,* April, 1960.

[9] The other stocks that dropped full points—and sometimes more —on 100-share lots that afternoon were: Beckmann Instruments, Celanese Corp., Cluett & Peabody, Consolidated Cigar, Dupont de Nemours (7 points on 1100 shares), Delta Airlines, Electronic Associates, Eversharp, Hayes Industries, Georgia Pacific, GE, Johnson & Johnson, International Paper, IBM, High-Voltage Engineering, Minnesota Honeywell, MCA, Pan American, George Roper, Smith Douglas, Timken Roller Bearing, Xerox, and Youngstown Sheet & Tube.

13

The Era of
American Political Impotence
or
Paradise Lost

The powers of the impotent are terrifying.

In 1964, it was necessary to offer the public further appeasement for the unregenerate manner in which specialists had conducted themselves subsequent to the assassination of President Kennedy. The blame for this had been deposited where it belonged—on the doorsteps of the politicians.

In his book *Congress: The Sapless Branch,* Joseph S. Clark, former Senator from Pennsylvania, gives us this picture of the legislatures:

> It is the third branch of government, the legislative, where things have gone awry. Whether we look at city councils, the state legislatures or the Congress of the United States, we react to what we see with scarcely concealed contempt . . . This is where the vested interest lobbies tend to run riot, where conflict of interest is concealed from the public . . . the legislatures of

America, local, state and national, are presently the greatest menace in our country to the successful operation of the democratic process.[1]

And in *The Rich and the Super-Rich,* Ferdinand Lundberg cites a series of articles that appeared between June 9 and June 15, 1965, in *The New York Herald Tribune*:

"Anyone who wants any legislation, buys it with cold, cold cash. I don't mean you go up to a Senator and ask him if he'd like to make $5,000 by voting for your bill. That's out today. So are broads and booze."

The words were those of a well-known veteran Washington lobbyist who was explaining his modus operandi.

"What you do is arrange to meet him alone somewhere—but not at his office. I almost never go up on the Hill, except maybe to show friends or relatives around," the lobbyist added.

"You don't tell him what you want. He knows. You tell him you understand he has a tough campaign coming up—or he had a tough campaign—and you'd like to help cover the costs. Then you leave an envelope with cash in it. The real reason you are giving the money is never mentioned.

"Of course, you can't do this with all Congressmen. But generally it takes only a couple of votes in subcommittee to swing a bill one way or another. After you've been here awhile you know who to deal with." [2]

The public, though it occasionally hears of a scandal involving outright bribery, refuses to believe that it is the subtler forms of bribery, hidden from sight and often within the law, that make the legislative wheels turn. But mere corruption is not the only problem; in fact it is not even the greatest one. The greatest problem—one about which the public knows even less than it knows about unethical lobbying—is the bureaucratic mind as it influences legislation.

Nowhere does the bureaucratic mind present a greater obstacle to sound and helpful legislation than in the area of relations between Congress and the Stock Exchanges and, by implication, the specialist system.

Just how inherently hostile the bureaucratic mind is to recognizing economic necessity and why legislation is often condemned by its origins can be seen in the dialogue between members of the Subcommittee on Commerce and Finance and members of the Stock Exchange hierarchy. Congressman Harley O. Staggers of West Virginia was the Chairman of the Subcommittee on Commerce and Finance.[3] There was nothing new about the underlying premises of this committee's investigation of the Stock Exchange.

A dim recognition of the problem had already been hinted at in two editorials, one in the *Washington Post* of January 2, 1964,[4] and the other in *The New York Times* of January 29, 1964. To demonstrate that he was in harmony with the spirit of the *Times,* Congressman Staggers introduced both editorials into the record and then, for practical purposes, proceeded to ignore them. The *Times* examined the activities of specialists subsequent to President Kennedy's assassination:

Specialists of the New York Stock Exchange, who are charged with maintaining orderly markets, turned in a mixed performance on November 22, 1963—the day that President Kennedy was assassinated.

An investigation of their activities by the Securities and Exchange Commission shows that some specialists contributed to the extremely disorderly conditions that took place in the 30 minutes that the Exchange remained open following the news of the shooting in Dallas. Its findings reveal that specialists dumped shares on the market ahead of the public, which led to a nosedive in prices and was hardly consistent with the claim by the New York Stock Exchange that specialists play a vital role in maintaining stability.

Keith Funston, the Exchange president, acknowledged that "not all specialists acted alike," observing that "some people do not perform as well as others in a crisis." But he neglected to mention that the ability of specialists to provide stability depends to a large extent on their financial resources, which in many cases are inadequate. In Mr. Funston's view, specialists did a good job simply because they ended up buying more shares than they had sold.

Specialist purchases do not constitute a true measure of their performance, for it is quite possible to play a destabilizing role and still increase commitments. Mr. Funston also clouds the issue by suggesting that the responsibility of specialists can be set aside in a crisis, which is precisely the time when their stabilizing function is most needed.

Even then there is no expectation that specialists can prevent panic or halt a decline. Specialists could be wiped out if they tried to stem a selling wave. But they are supposed to provide a temporary cushion when there is a large gap between supply and demand. And they have a responsibility to avoid adding to any selling or buying pressure.

This limited responsibility demands that specialists have adequate financial resources. It also requires the Exchange to strengthen its own supervision, with tougher disciplinary penalties against specialists who contribute to disorder. The problem cannot be explained away simply by saying that there will never be another crisis like November 22. There are bound to be new crises that will test the nerves and purses of the specialists.

Now we come to the testimony. The specifics of specialists' short selling and covering operations are ignored throughout, as are their profits and the manner in which many of them dropped the prices of bellwether stocks full points on 100 shares. Funston, in his testimony to the subcommittee [5], states:

A copy of our report, entitled "President Kennedy's Assassination and the Stock Market," has been filed with the committee and is attached to my statement. Some of the major findings of our analysis may be summarized here. We found:

1. Selling pressure after 1:40 P.M. November 22 was primarily the result of market orders by active individual customers (the so-called volume accounts).

2. Stop orders placed by the public before the assassination also contributed significantly to the selling wave after 1:40.

3. Odd-lot investors were also swept up in the selling panic, even though they were moderate buyers on balance. Virtually all their purchases after 1:40 were the result of limit orders entered on the books before President Kennedy was shot. Most market orders placed by odd-lotters after 1:40 P.M. were sell orders.

4. Buying support came mainly from specialists and floor traders and limit orders placed by individual investors before 1:40 P.M. Buy orders at the market by public customers were negligible after 1:40. Specialists increased their net holdings in the 25 stocks by 99,800 shares, representing an additional commitment of $5,161,700 in the final 27 minutes in these 25 stocks.

5. Institutional customers and off-floor members and allied members were buyers on balance. But they accounted for a relatively small share of the volume after 1:40.

6. The strong recovery of the market Tuesday, November 26, was a tribute to the orderly transfer of the reins of Government and public confidence in its fundamental stability. A contributing factor certainly was the plan for liquidation of Ira Haupt & Co. announced during the night before trading reopened.

As regards the performance of individual specialists under these unusual conditions, our study shows that in all but 4 of the 25 issues, the specialists closed the day on November 22 with more shares than they had had at 1:40 P.M. Using continuity as a yardstick, 86.5 percent of the transactions in these 25 issues after 1:40 P.M. were at the same price as the previous sales, or varied by not more than one-fourth of a point. This continuity ratio is as high as that achieved by all specialists for all of 1961 and 1962, and equals the standards achieved at the time of the market break of May 1962, and the ensuing recovery.

Funston's comments would have had more meaning for the Committee if they had examined a list of that day's sequential transactions in any one of several hundred stocks.

Funston's statement included this:

The specialist's stabilizing function can only be evaluated by a transaction-by-transaction study of the extent to which he buys on declining prices and sells on rising prices. Nearly all of 144,200 shares bought by specialists were in transactions which had the effect of cushioning the decline . . .[6]

In other words, specialists were covering their short positions or adding to their long accounts. Why didn't Staggers examine this?

Funston's testimony is at odds with Commissioner Saul's. A glance at the list of that day's transactions (see pp. 188–197) would have proven this to the Committee. According to Saul's statement, on November 22, Bill Meehan, the specialist in RCA, was long 139,600 shares at 1:41.[7] Yet Funston asserts: "At about 1:40 P.M. specialists in the 25 selected issues had an aggregate position of 129,500 shares long, and 4,100 shares short."[8]

The possibility exists that Saul had included Meehan's investment account as a part of his trading account.

Funston, on the other hand, would have seen to it that he did not include investment accounts and would have provided only the totals for specialists' trading accounts. This is a discrepancy it would have been interesting to have had Funston explain. Instead, Funston pretty much went along with the specialists' rationalizations for the November decline—which is not surprising, when one remembers that one of the historical and political functions of the President of the New York Stock Exchange is to defend the powers of the specialist. Funston does this by attributing the drop to the public.

Funston does not attend these meetings to answer for policy, but to make it. And listening to Representative Milton W. Glenn of New Jersey we can understand why:

MR. GLENN: Mr. Funston, it is a little difficult for we [sic] laymen to understand the position of specialists on the exchange. I first want to ask you, could the exchange operate without specialists?

MR. FUNSTON: No, sir.

MR. GLENN: We have read in your statement and in the report of the SEC that they occupy an inside position, they make certain brokerage fees, they have certain obligations to act as dealers in maintaining an orderly market even though it may cost them money, and that in essence they act against the market trend and buy when the market goes down and sell when the market goes up.

Now this is sort of an unusual position for anyone who is earning a livelihood and trying to make money. Do they keep the profits which they make on the market when it goes up and do they sustain the losses likewise when it goes down?

MR. FUNSTON: Yes, sir. The specialist income roughly depends on the specialist and it varies with different specialists but they get about half their income from commissions which they share in that are left with them to execute and about half of the profits overall are made as a dealer.

Now a dealer sometimes loses money, sometimes they make money. Of course, if they are going to stay in business over a period of time they have to make it more often than they lose it although sometimes a firm will lose money in a year on the dealer position and have enough on the commission position to offset their dealer losses.[9]

It might have helped to have had someone from Internal Revenue there to cite the short-term profits from omnibus and other accounts in which specialists have a "direct or indirect interest."

Congressman Staggers now sets it up for the reader to examine his and Mr. Frank's attitude toward "the book."

MR. STAGGERS: Mr. Funston, you were talking about working against the specialist book. Now when he acts as dealer or broker and if on his book he has a certain amount, would you explain to this committee the workings of the book? I do not think many of them know.

Also, how long is he required to keep that book under your rules and what are the regulations and requirements? Is that not really the fundamental duty of the specialist?

MR. FUNSTON: Yes, sir.

MR. STAGGERS: Would you explain?

MR. FUNSTON: May I start and ask my colleague, Mr. Frank, who is vice chairman of the board and who is a specialist, to correct me if I say anything wrong. I, being much more of a layman than he, maybe I can at least put it in more layman's language, at the start anyway.

The specialist has a so-called book. The book has buy orders on the one side and sell orders on the other side in which he records the transactions that are desired by another broker representing the public at different prices away from the last market price.

Just to give you an example: It may well be that in a particular stock there is a member of the public who through his broker is willing to buy a stock at $40 a share. There is someone who is willing to sell it at $45 a share. Say the last sale was about 42½ in between. Well, a member representing a customer comes in to that particular specialist and says, "I want to buy some stock, say, at the market." So the broker representing the public comes to the specialist and says, "How is the X-Y-Z stock?" The specialist seeing the 40 to 45 which is the public's spread there, that is much, much too wide, so he says, "42⅜ to 42⅝." The specialist does not know whether the person who is coming up to him is a buyer or a seller but he has to be willing to do the opposite of what that person wants to do.

So if the person wants to buy the stock, he would sell it to him at 42⅝; if he wants to sell it, he would buy it from him at 42⅜. In other words, the specialist has narrowed the market and as a dealer is quoting a quarter-point spread in this stock instead of the 5-point spread that would be there if the specialist was not on the floor and charged with the responsibility of making a close continuous and orderly market.

MR. STAGGERS: May I interrupt you there. I would like to ask Mr. Frank if that specialist has the authority to say that it is 42⅜ and 42⅝ or should he quote his book as given to him what the bid is and asked?

MR. FRANK: The specialist should quote the bid and the offer expressed by the public if he deems that it is a proper one and a wise one and one that would relate to the recent price activity and price history of the stock. If in his judgment he can better serve those who come to him by putting in his own bid as a dealer or his own offer to sell from his inventory and to improve that spread, then he must so do. He must combine both functions. He must combine his agency function and his dealer function in such a way as to give a continuity and a depth and a proper market in the relation that is called upon him by this price action of the stock.[10]

The harsh methods of the specialist in his use of the book have already been suggested. But how does one put congressional option and congressional debate in touch with realities?

MR. STAGGERS: You do not believe, then, they ought to be segregated?

MR. FUNSTON: I certainly do not.

MR. STAGGERS: This has been one of the big questions of the stock exchange rules in this committee starting way back in the manipulation in 1934 of the markets. You go ahead with your statement.

MR. FUNSTON: Sir, the reason why I—

MR. GLENN: Will the chairman yield?

MR. STAGGERS: Surely.

MR. GLENN: This is a terrific responsibility on the part of these specialists, is it not, Mr. Frank?

MR. FRANK: It is a responsibility placed on him by our rules, which he understands, and is supervised by the stock exchange.

MR. GLENN: He is in effect sitting under two hats and doing the work of two different entities; is that not so?

MR. FRANK: No, sir. We are agents when called upon so to act. When there is a lack of balance between public supply and demand, then we are dealers to fill in that void.

MR. GLENN: And only you make that decision?

MR. FRANK: In line with the rules and regulations of the stock exchange and the requirements placed on me.

MR. GLENN: Now there is no appeal from your decision when you make it, it is acted upon and that is the end of it; is that not so?

MR. FRANK: No; the auction market is open for all to enter. I make my market and if it can be improved upon by others who enter the market it is done.[11]

The answer to Congressman Glenn's question, obviously, is that there is no appeal from the specialist's decision. But let's read further:

MR. GLENN: When these dealers come to you do you have to buy if you do not feel like it?

MR. FRANK: I must buy to furnish the continuity and the depth which is expected of me when I am registered as a specialist.

MR. GLENN: But you decide that continuity and depth, do you not?

MR. FRANK: The decision on the continuity and the depth is always reviewed. It cannot be spelled out exactly and the decision is based on its price history and previous action and total market conditions.

MR. GLENN: But you do all that?

MR. FRANK: It is my responsibility to make sure that it is orderly.

MR. FUNSTON: Mr. Chairman, may I break in here to say that the thing that keeps happening, what you say this conflict of interest, is not only the caliber and quality of the men who are honest men who do this but also the very tight and stringent rules that are imposed by the stock exchange to watch this operation.

Now we mentioned continuity. You remember in my statement I reported that even in this chaotic break from 1:40 to 2:07, 86 percent of all the trades were at no more than one-quarter of a point away from the last trade. This is continuity.

If the specialist group do not have continuity in the checks that are made, surprise audits that are made of them, we would catch that and subject them to some disciplinary action. It is fair to say that the SEC in their most intense study of the market did not conclude as you have, Mr. Chairman, that this was a place where people were not representing the public's interest but they made no recommendation at all about segregating the broker-dealer function . . .[12]

Mr. Staggers continues:

. . . We are not talking about the ones who did keep faith, we are talking about the ones who did not keep faith. There were those that did not and we know they did not according to the records and that is what we are after as protectors of the public welfare.

So we are trying to close the loopholes and that is why you are here today.

MR. FUNSTON: Yes. I might say if anyone is not doing their job we are anxious to chastise them because our interests and yours are the same.

MR. STAGGERS: We do not want only to chastise them, we want to do something about it. . . . I do not believe we have it fully explained yet as to how it would protect the public; that he must give these orders as they come down the line from the brokers. The names he takes from the top and he may never get to the bottom or the rates there. When they buy and sell both and he comes here and as you say, he may step in on his own to say, "Well, I will make the market here."

MR. FUNSTON: Yes, sir.

MR. STAGGERS: But the public is here on the book.

MR. FUNSTON: Yes.

MR. STAGGERS: And this book represents the public: is that right?

MR. FUNSTON: Well, it represents the orders that the public have seen fit to place on the specialist book away from the marketplace because in this illustration that I gave you of 40 to 45, the book, the public if they would come in and say, "I want to buy at the market," they would buy as I said at about 42⅝, whereas if the specialist was not acting as a dealer they would come in and buy at 45.

MR. STAGGERS: I understand that. I wish you would go ahead with the responsibility of the specialist to this book, how he is bound by this book, the rules that make him adhere to the book itself, and its importance. I want you to explain that. I do not believe it is too well understood by the public.

Also, is it right that the specialist is the principal dealer in one stock but he may have fifteen?

MR. FUNSTON: That is right.

MR. STAGGERS: But in order to deal with this stock you are going to have to go to a specialist.

MR. FUNSTON: That is correct.

MR. STAGGERS: Then he controls to a great degree many of these things. Now you say that his job is to protect and keep the continuity of the market and we will agree to that. The theory is fine, but we are trying to get to the exceptions and why some of these events happened and why there is a responsibility to the book.

I wish you would go a little further into that.

MR. FUNSTON: You are asking me what is the responsibility of the specialist to the book?

MR. STAGGERS: I want you to explain just a little further the book itself and what part it plays in the activities of the stock market.

MR. FUNSTON: The book itself is in essence only the vehicle in which the public's orders, which are away from the market, are recorded. In other words, most people when they go in to buy stock say, "Well, I want to buy stock at the market." In this illustration that I gave you it would be 42⅝. However, many people say, "Well, I don't want to pay 42⅝, if it ever falls to 40 I will buy it."

People on the other side say, "Well, I don't want to sell it at 42⅝, but if it ever gets to 45 I will sell it."

So they go to their broker and they say, "Put in a limit order to sell at 45." They give that to their broker and the broker takes that offer to the specialist and gives it to him and says, "Look, here is an order to sell at 45."

Where the specialist comes in, the specialist can never compete with the public. In other words, if the specialist can't buy at 45, if on his book a public customer wants to buy at 45—and I misspoke a minute ago when I said they had to come to the specialist, they don't. They have to come to the post where the specialist stands, but a commission broker representing a customer and another commission broker representing another customer can stand there in front of the post and trade by themselves and often do.

MR. STAGGERS: I wanted to get this thing in the book that the specialist is not supposed to compete with the public.

MR. FUNSTON: Never.

MR. STAGGERS: That is what we are trying to get at the bottom of, and I think we will before we get through.

MR. FUNSTON: Yes.

MR. STAGGERS: Mr. Glenn.

MR. GLENN: Mr. Funston, how many specialists are there on the floor of the New York Stock Exchange?

MR. FUNSTON: Well, there are 350 individuals collected together in about 110 specialist units.

MR. GLENN: And you say they are appointed by the board of governors?

MR. FUNSTON: Yes, sir.

MR. GLENN: Are there any specific qualifications that they must meet?

MR. FUNSTON: Yes, sir. They have to be a member of the exchange and as a member of the exchange have to be persons of integrity and have gone through all kinds of investigations. They have to be of adequate financial capacity and then they have to show evidence that they know by experience on the floor how to run a book, how to be a specialist.

MR. GLENN: Now is this considered quite an honor or a profitable plum to be awarded the position of a specialist?

MR. FUNSTON: Not necessarily. It is a very demanding, risky business that requires a certain kind of person. The only way that you can ever learn it is by the experience of being one and working in it which is the big advantage that the New York Stock Exchange has over all the other stock exchanges of the world, who, if they would try to establish a full-blown specialist system cannot find the people to do it.

MR. GLENN: Is the risk greater than one would ordinarily encounter as traders on the floor?

MR. FUNSTON: May I defer that to Mr. Frank? I think it is but I would like to hear what he says.

MR. FRANK: To broadly describe risks would be delicate. The risks vary according to the particular experience that one has. I mean if we are called upon to make a bid of greater size than another, possibly a risk in one case would be more than another but they vary with each entrance into the market of a customer.

MR. GLENN: Let me put it another way, then. Are the opportunities to make profit greater as a specialist than an ordinary trader on the floor?

MR. FUNSTON: Are you using, sir, the word "trader" on the floor as a floor trader, a man who spends all his time on the floor buying and selling, or are you using "trading" in the sense of a commission broker representing the public?

MR. GLENN: Well, an ordinary broker-dealer.

MR. FUNSTON: I would say it would be hard to say. Undoubtedly there are, it varies. There are very successful specialists, there are those who are not successful. There are very successful floor brokers and those who are not so successful. So it is hard to say.[13]

As you will recall, Saul quoted the profits of the specialist in AT&T at $80,000 for November 22, 1963, and the next day of trading. We can also recall Saul's admonition: "It should be pointed out that this profit picture has no bearing on the performance of the specialist in AT&T stock." [14]

The burlesque continues:

MR. HARRIS [Oren Harris of Arkansas, Chairman of the full Committee]: . . . being a member of the exchange they ordinarily are a member or employee of a broker-dealer firm?

MR. FUNSTON: The specialists, yes, they are members and they associate themselves together in specialist firms because one man can't stand there from ten in the morning—

MR. HARRIS: I know but that does not answer my question.

MR. FUNSTON: I am sorry.

MR. HARRIS: What association or relationship do they have with a broker-dealer firm?

MR. FUNSTON: Well, they are a broker-dealer firm.

MR. HARRIS: That is what I asked.

MR. FUNSTON: Yes. They are formed in a broker-dealer firm.

MR. HARRIS: In other words, it is the broker-dealer that has its own employee who becomes a specialist?

MR. FUNSTON: No, sir: a man cannot be an employee and be a specialist, he has to be a partner of a firm and a member of the exchange.

MR. HARRIS: Well, all right, say he is partner then. That is where he gets his money, his income.

MR. FUNSTON: He gets it from specializing on the floor as a broker-dealer.

MR. HARRIS: Well, he is paid, though, through a broker-dealer firm as a partner of that firm?

MR. FUNSTON: Yes, sir.

MR. HARRIS: And his income and his financial interest comes through his being a partner and associate of the firm.

MR. FUNSTON: Yes, sir; that is right.

MR. HARRIS: Well, that clears it up.[15]

It is a source of great comfort to know that Congressman Harris has accepted no compromise with his critical vision.

Now we come to our favorite congressman, John D. Dingell of Michigan, and the most interesting statement in the course of the hearings:

MR. DINGELL: Would the gentleman yield for a brief question?

MR. GLENN: Yes.

MR. DINGELL: I don't understand the specialist functions.[16]

Now the congressmen address their attention to an issue that is equal in importance with anything the hearings may shed light on: the implications of the 1963 bankruptcy of the Ira Haupt brokerage firm usually known as the salad-oil scandal.

MR. STAGGERS: Mr. Funston, I want to compliment you on answering the questions we asked you to come here to answer and on giving us the benefit of your views. I think you have done an excellent job.

However, I am sure that the members of the subcommittee have a number of questions that they would like to ask, and I will also have a great number later.

We will start with Mr. Dingell.

Do you have any questions, Mr. Dingell?

MR. DINGELL: Yes, Mr. Chairman.

Mr. Funston, I would like to refer to a few editorials that our chairman put in the record of hearings. Now, you indicated in your statement at the bottom of page 5:

"It cannot be too strongly emphasized that the exchange had no obligation to act, and that customers of exchange member firms cannot regard the unusual action taken in this case as setting any kind of precedent for the exchange to assume liability for customers' losses stemming from financial problems encountered by member firms in any of their activities."

Is that the position of yourself and the position of the exchange?

MR. FUNSTON: Yes, sir.

MR. DINGELL: That means that what was done in the case of the failure of the Haupt Co. was simply an act of grace on behalf of the exchange toward the various customers and clients who might have been injured in that failure. Am I correct in that?

MR. FUNSTON: No, sir. I would not say it was an act of grace. I would say it was an act that the board made because of what we felt our responsibility was in the particular circumstances of this particular case.

MR. DINGELL: But essentially it was an act of grace because the exchange had no responsibility in this matter and expressly disclaims that it would take the same action in a future case.

MR. FUNSTON: No. I would not agree that it was an act of grace. As I say, I think there is a difference. I think that we reviewed this particular case with the facts surrounding it as a responsibility which we should assume, and should in the future any other case come up with specific circumstances that we would feel it was our responsibility to assume, we would do likewise.

MR. DINGELL: But there is actually no requirement in the constitution of the exchange or in the bylaws as they stand at this moment?

MR. FUNSTON: No, sir. That is correct.

MR. DINGELL: Which would so require?

MR. FUNSTON: No, sir.

MR. DINGELL: Were the exchange to so view the matter at some future time if there were similar failures, there would be nothing to compel the exchange to do other than to leave the various applicants of the customers, of the customer firms, very much at the mercy of the exchange?

MR. FUNSTON: There is nothing in the law or in the constitution. However, there is the authority vested in the board of governors for looking after interests of the security customers that we serve.

MR. DINGELL: But you expressly disclaim there is a responsibility on the part of the exchange to assume liability for customers' losses, and I am quoting now from your own statement here, "Stemming from financial problems encountered by member firms in any of their activities."

MR. FUNSTON: Yes; that is correct.

MR. DINGELL: Now, conceivably there could have been substantial losses to customers in the Haupt Co. under the set of circumstances—the exchange has come up with $7½ million, I think—referred to in this paper; is that correct?

MR. FUNSTON: That is correct.

MR. DINGELL: The Washington Post says that $6.7 million have been paid out to date.

Now, in the editorial in the Washington Post and in similar articles appearing in the press, the law, it goes on to specifically state, as follows: "The law makes no provision for protection of free balances in the event of bankruptcy," which means that a client of the member firm whose stocks were hypothecated or were sold indeed by a member firm would be treated just as a general creditor; am I correct?

MR. FUNSTON: No, sir.

MR. DINGELL: The firm in bankruptcy?

MR. FUNSTON: No.

MR. DINGELL: It would not be?

MR. FUNSTON: In general, the fully paid securities which have been segregated, the customer would get those back.

MR. DINGELL: He would?

MR. FUNSTON: Yes.

MR. DINGELL: Assuming they had been sold, how would he get them back?

MR. FUNSTON: Assuming they had been sold?

MR. DINGELL: Assuming they had been sold or assuming they had been pledged.

MR. FUNSTON: Those kinds of securities could not be pledged.

MR. DINGELL: They could not be?

MR. FUNSTON: No. Not fully paid securities. Those that were in margin accounts could be pledged.[17]

Contrary to Funston's assertion, the margin agreements signed by Ira Haupt's customers along with the margin agreements of almost all other brokerage firms stipulate:

All monies, securities, commodities, contracts, or other property (referred to herein as collateral) held or carried by you from time to time for me (either individually or jointly or in common with others) shall be security for and shall be subject to your lien for all my liabilities to you, including contingent and unmatured obligations; and any part or all of such collateral may from time to time and without notice to me be pledged or repledged by you, either separately or in common with the property of others, as collateral for your loans, without limitation as to amount (except as otherwise required by law or by any applicable exchange rules) and without your retaining possession or control of property of like kind and amount.

In other words, once a customer signs a margin agreement, whether or not he makes use of it, he consents to the use of his cash and to the use of his stock in any other cash accounts that he may leave with the broker in street name.

> MR. DINGELL: The point I am coming to, Mr. Funston, is that I am very much concerned about this and I think that the committee is going to have to be very careful in consideration and recommendations to the Securities and Exchange Commission and perhaps have to make some independent judgments on this point.
>
> I notice here in the communication received in response to a letter by myself to the SEC the following language, and I am quoting from the letter now: "At the same time broker-dealers holding free credit balances may use them to obtain positions in securities and otherwise in their general operations without notifying the customers or obtaining their specific consent."
>
> MR. FUNSTON: That is correct.
>
> MR. DINGELL: This is true?
>
> MR. FUNSTON: Yes, sir.
>
> MR. DINGELL: And conceivably this is something which in the event of a failure or major insolvency by a large firm could result in substantial injury to the investors.
>
> MR. FUNSTON: Yes, sir; but may I just say on that in twenty-five years and maybe even longer, I know it is for twenty-five years, there have been no losses of free credit balances by any member firm of the stock exchange. It is our aim, our concern—we are concerned too; your interests and ours are the same—we are concerned also and this Haupt case has opened our eyes to a new threat that we did not realize was there before.[18]

The "threat" that the specialist system "did not realize was there before" involves the entire credit structure of the specialist and Federal Reserve Systems. With each question, Dingell spins the gun chamber. Funston knows it, and so does the congressman.

The problem presented by the Haupt failure is raised the following day by Congressman John B. Bennett (Michigan) and we come one step closer to reality. However, the Exchange spokesmen are masters at this kind of parry and thrust:

MR. BENNETT: I have to leave, too. I am sorry I was not here to listen to your statement yesterday, Mr. Funston. I confess that even after having read the statement I am still very much confused about the bankruptcy of this broker-dealer.

The one thing that I have been interested in for many years is the ratio of dollars that a broker-dealer had to have for every dollar of customer-issued money for the securities that he held. For a long time the ratio has been 20 to 1; is that right?

MR. FUNSTON: Yes.

MR. BENNETT: Under Commission rule.

MR. FUNSTON: It was 20 to 1 under exchange rule and 15 to 1 under Commission rule—no, wait a minute, it is the other way around.

MR. BENNETT: The Commission had a 20 to 1 ratio.

MR. FUNSTON: That is right. They had a 20 to 1 ratio, we had a 15 to 1 ratio and then we changed and went to 20 to 1 ratio. That is right now.

MR. BENNETT: If the credit requirements of broker-dealers had been tighter or the ratio had been closer to the amount of capital that they hold as against the assets the customers hold, would this kind of situation, as in the Haupt case, have occurred?

MR. FUNSTON: Yes, it would have. The Haupt failure in terms of the—well, let's see. The Haupt failure probably, as best could be told, will be the cause of this inventory being—it will be three times the capital of the firm. So any reasonable relationship would have made no difference at all.

MR. DINGELL: Would you yield to me at that point?

The Haupt failure really occurred because of the failure to have capital requirements applied to other trading, in other words, commodity trading, as opposed to the stock trading, is that not a fact?

MR. FUNSTON: No, the Haupt failure really occurred because of fraud and $23 million worth of inventory that everybody thought was there that was not there.

MR. DINGELL: Yes, but also the fact that they did not have sufficient capital in the other areas, the commodities area, as opposed to trading within the framework of your exchange.

In other words, they did not have the capital with regard to the commodity engaged in.

MR. FUNSTON: Well, yes, that is right. In other words, they didn't have the $23 million capital that they should have had if they are going to have losses of $23 million in commodity trading.

MR. DINGELL: That is right, but they also did not have enough commodities, they did not have enough capital to meet reasonable costs with regard to their commodity trading.

MR. FUNSTON: Oh yes. They had plenty of capital to meet reasonable calls for their commodity trading.

MR. DINGELL: They did?

MR. FUNSTON: Oh, yes.

MR. BENNETT: A 10 percent margin requirement applies as I understand it. Does it have anything to do with this failure?

MR. FUNSTON: May I ask Mr. Coyle to answer that question? Did you hear the question, Mr. Coyle? Mr. Coyle is vice president in charge of the member firm division of the exchange.

MR. COYLE: I heard the question but I did not quite understand it, sir.[19]

The door is opened on cloud-cuckooland and as quickly closed again because no one "quite understands." But ask yourself, why did the Exchange pay off the Haupt customers?

The answer is simple. Had Haupt's customers lost their stocks held in street name, it might have involved the specialist system in legislation preventing the use of customer credit balances and stock as a part of their net capital (at a 20 to 1 ratio) on behalf of their own speculations. If the use by brokers of more than $3 billion in free credit balances plus the stock from almost 900,000 margin accounts [20] were ever called into question, and new legislation made it illegal to borrow these items, it would mean a whole new ball game.

As for the Exchange's responsibility to discipline the specialist, Funston's protestations notwithstanding ("Disciplinary actions undoubtedly will be taken. Some action is going to be taken tomorrow on instituting disciplinary action in a very few cases" [21]), no disciplinary measures were taken against any specialist. Like the emperor, he can walk naked. He is dressed in the latest law.

NOTES, chapter 13

---

[1] New York: Harper, 1964, p. 22.

[2] On p. 505.

[3] Representing the New York Stock Exchange were Keith Funston, President; Walter N. Frank, Vice Chairman of the Board of Governors; E. C. Gray, Executive Vice-President of the Exchange; S. L. Rosenberry, Exchange counsel of the firm of Milbank, Tweed, Hadley & McCloy; William O'Reilly, Director of the Floor Procedure Department; Frank Coyle, Vice-President in charge of the Member Firm Department; and A. B. Chapman, Vice-President.

[4] Quoted in Chapter 9.

[5] *Investor Protection, Hearings before a Subcommittee of the Committee on Interstate and Foreign Commerce, House of Representatives, First and Second Sessions, on H.R. 6789, H.R. 6793, S. 1642, December, 1963, through February, 1964.*

[6] *Investor Protection*, p. 1084.

[7] Commissioner Saul reported this in his *Profiles of Specialist and Floor Trader Activity in Twenty-five Selected Stocks on November 22 and November 26, 1963*. The profile on RCA can be found on p. 959 of *Investor Protection*.

[8] *Investor Protection*, p. 1084.

[9] P. 1094.

[10] P. 1095.

[11] P. 1097.

[12] P. 1097.

[13] Pp. 1098–1100.

[14] This assertion also appears in *Investor Protection* on p. 948.

[15] P. 1101.

[16] P. 1102.

[17] P. 1088.

[18] P. 1092.

[19] P. 1133.

[20] The figures are from the June 20, 1969, *Monthly Review* put out by the New York Stock Exchange.

[21] *Investor Protection*, p. 1107.

14

Under the Spreading Apathy
or
La Dolce Vita in the SEC

**Judas was born 2,000 years ago.
The American bureaucrat was created later.**

In the early 1930s, there was a movement afoot to reform the Stock Exchanges. This movement culminated in the Securities Exchange Act, which in turn gave birth to the Securities and Exchange Commission. It had originally been intended that the Federal Trade Commission administer the act, but Richard Whitney, the President of the New York Stock Exchange and spokesman for the specialists, opposed the FTC.

Writing for *The New Republic* of May 16, 1934, John T. Flynn[1] said:

> The Federal Trade Commission will probably be ditched and a separate commission agreed on. This, then, puts the whole subject up to the President [of the U.S.]. Whether we have real stock-market regulation or not will depend on the kind of men appointed to the Commission. And that is up to the President . . . It will not do to name just one or two good strong men

and then put in three others who are friendly to the Exchange or just respectable nonentities.

The friends of the Exchange are busy behind the scenes now on this vital point. They have powerful friends in Washington, friends close to the throne. But the President will make the greatest blunder of his administration if he attempts to placate these anti-social men.

The entire financial community opposed the Securities Act and continued to attack it even after it went on the statute books, until well into 1934. The principal outcry against the Act came from the specialists, who were in control of the Exchange and who regarded it as their private property. It became clear that the new Commission chosen to replace the FTC was to have no jurisdiction over the most important factor in the speculative markets—credit. That had been left to the hopelessly partisan Federal Reserve Board.

Then came the final blow. The public had assumed that the SEC, once its members were designated, would at least act to prevent the speculative manipulations that Congress had identified as the real evil in the market, the cause of the 1929 crash and subsequent depression. But a rumor soon spread that Roosevelt, at the request of the Exchange's high priests, was about to appoint to the SEC chairmanship one of the country's shrewdest and most persistent speculators—Joseph P. Kennedy.

On June 30, 1934, in a meeting at the White House attended by Raymond Moley, Bernard Baruch, and Kennedy, Roosevelt appointed Kennedy to the SEC as Chairman for a full five-year term. John T. Flynn, like many others at the time, was completely stunned by the appointment. He could not have been more amazed had Roosevelt appointed a card-carrying Communist. He expressed his amazement in *The New Republic* of July 18, 1934:

This is indeed an impossible world. Last summer Ferdinand Pecora was busy probing the sins of Wall Street. At the same time Joseph P. Kennedy was busy with a group of his pals—Mason Day, Harry Sinclair, Elisha Walker, of Kuhn, Loeb and Company, and two or three others—putting over a pool in Libbey-Owens-Ford Glass Company stock. The pool was inspired by Walker of Kuhn, Loeb in whose office at the time Pecora was drilling for facts. It was managed by Mason Day of Redmond and Company, stock brokers, where Joseph P. Kennedy had his office. This was one of the pools that produced the squalid little boom of 1933 and when these poolsters withdrew and the boom collapsed the administration denounced the men who had operated them. Pecora was directed to investigate them. And when he did, the trail brought him at once to the office of Redmond and Company, from which Mason Day and Kennedy were operating. There Pecora dragged into the light the activities of this pool in which, without supplying five cents of capital or intelligence, Kennedy made $60,000. Day described Kennedy to Pecora as a capitalist and he defined, at Pecora's request, a capitalist as one who makes money but does not have to work. Kennedy fitted the definition perfectly.

This pool, mind you, was formed in the moments when the New Deal was mounting to frenzied heights of piety, in the midst of the Wall Street investigation, when Mr. Pecora's agents were swarming over the Street.

Only four months ago Pecora submitted his findings about these pools to the Senate. Immediately thereafter he was directed to prepare the Stock Exchange Control Bill. He did so. And in time the bill, with its most effective sections cut out, was passed . . . I did not in my wildest dreams imagine [Roosevelt] would appoint a speculator as chairman of that body . . . I say it isn't true. It is impossible. It could not happen.

Robert E. Healy was appointed to the Commission for one year and Ferdinand Pecora for two. Pecora was thus to serve under the man he had been investigating only four months earlier.

Kennedy's appointment more or less set the pattern the SEC was to follow from then on—that is, one of working hand-in-glove with the Exchanges. It also sealed the fate of the Securities and Exchange Act as a regulatory instrument. Flynn said that the Act was so imperfect that even a good commission could not do much. He felt that headed by a man like Kennedy, it could be counted a complete loss.[2]

As Kennedy's successor Roosevelt appointed James M. Landis. Prior to his appointment, Landis had distinguished himself as an apologist for the Exchanges and as an arch-opponent of meaningful reform. In 1932, for example, when Fiorello LaGuardia proposed a plan to regulate the Exchange, the Exchange hired Landis, then a law professor at Harvard, to write a legal brief showing that any attempt to regulate or limit Exchange speculations was unconstitutional. Landis did his job well, and LaGuardia's proposal was defeated. Later, as SEC Chairman, Landis was to prove equally effective thwarting reform. When two economists of the SEC, Kemper Simpson and Willis Ballinger, were given authority to make a study of the economic implications of specialist activity and the system's use of credit, they were given only $300 for expenses. Despite this, they finally produced a good report—and it was buried.[3] The study was then given to a group of Wall Street and SEC stooges, who produced a report in praise of specialists. The two SEC economists, Simpson and Ballinger, were fired on Landis' orders.

Since the days of Kennedy and Landis, the SEC has changed very little. It still presents a public face of integrity and impartiality, while working hand-in-glove with the Exchanges and the specialist system behind the scenes. In 1962, for example, the Commission's Special Study group was occupied with an investigation of the securities markets. Using a specialized jargon, the SEC persuaded investors that it was in pursuit of their vital interest that it had launched the investigation. In fact, it undertook the investigation only because Congress insisted it do so. Indeed, in view of its history, it is obvious the leadership of the SEC would never, on its own initiative, have instituted an investigation of the specialist system. The thrust of its efforts is in another direction— not to the attack, but to the defense, of the system's point of view. How then did Congress come to issue the orders demanding an investigation of the Exchange?

When speaking of the 1962–63 investigation of the securities markets, even former members of the Special Study group completely leave out of account the explosive circumstances surrounding the specialist system— and these were the circumstances that actually precipitated the investigation. Sidney Robbins, Professor of Finance at Columbia's Graduate School of Business, was retained by the SEC to act as chief economist for the Special Study group. In his book, *The Securities Markets: Operations and Issues,* he says:

> Various circumstances combined to induce Congress to authorize the study: the record number of companies that were going public; the "hot issue" phenomenon marked by the appearance of a number of newly formed, inadequately capitalized dealer-firms that marketed the issues of little known companies whose stocks had a rapid initial rise and subsequent collapse; the elevated price-earnings ratios of many companies; the high trading volume and high "fails" to deliver or receive stock certificates, and the spreading of interest in securities manifest by the rapid growth of the investment companies.[4]

Yet there is not the slightest doubt that it was the series of revelations provided by the case against Alexander Guterma—not the events described by Robbins—that led

to Congress' decision to call for an investigation of th
securities markets. Guterma was convicted on a numbe
of rules-violation counts in 1960 and was sentenced t
four years and eleven months in prison and fined $140
000. Without the Guterma case, and the congression
pressure it generated, it is extremely unlikely that th
SEC would have set up the Special Study group.

On November 28, 1969, in an article illustrating th
formula of militant partiality demonstrated by U.S. regu
latory agencies, columnist Jack Anderson had this t
say: "All too often . . . these agencies protect th
public the way a fox guards a chicken coop . . . th
Securities and Exchange Commission does nothing t
stop stock manipulators from using boiler room tactics t
run up the price of next-to-worthless stock offerings . . .
Indeed, the partnership between the SEC and the Ex
change provides a training ground for future executive
in industry and the Stock Exchanges. Working on th
Commission staff, a man soon perceives that he just ma
be able to follow in the footsteps of Ralph Saul, goin
from a $19,000-a-year securities analyst for the SEC t
a Commissioner of the SEC, and then to President of th
American Stock Exchange itself. Ralph Saul is a case i
point. After he was appointed President of the Exchang
he was described by *Business Week* as follows:

> . . . he happens to believe that the SEC and the Ex-
> change are partners in the regulation of trading, and
> therefore there is "no moral issue involved in serving
> with one partner after serving with the other . . ." [5]

I am not accusing Saul of tempering his actions as Com
missioner in order to ensure his acceptance by th
Exchanges; I do accuse him of having been a lax Com
missioner. And I believe the order of things invites lax
ness on the part of any Commissioner. Though Saul ma
not have succumbed to temptation, it is not necessary t
elaborate on the idea that a man in a relatively low

paying government position, enticed by a future high-paying position on the Exchange, could be tempted to do a less than rigorous job as a government-paid regulator.

In nominating Saul as President of the American Stock Exchange, specialists maintained that:

> he had earned a reputation for open-mindedness among those exchange officials who bargained with him over implementation of the proposals in the 1963 study. "He was one of the few people at the SEC who was reasonable," says one . . .[6]

Saul was ordained for higher things than the SEC:

> I felt that I liked public service, its problems and pressures . . . the job looked terribly interesting but I went down with the intention of staying only a couple of years and then returning to legal work.[7]

The *Wall Street Journal* of November 7, 1966, quotes from the gospel according to St. Ralph:

> Under the scheme of regulation as contemplated by law, the stock exchanges have the primary responsibility for regulating the marketplace, while the Government has a supervisory role in relation to the exchanges. This will work only if there is full disclosure and understanding between the partners; otherwise the relationship will get out of kilter. That may have been the problem in the pre-1961 days, partly because the Government wasn't adequately supervising the exchanges. This isn't the case now . . . The relation is in focus: the SEC believes in the process of self-regulation and at all times it must say to itself: "The exchanges aren't doing the job precisely the way we'd do it, but nevertheless they're doing it effectively and in the public interest.
>
> "Therefore we must forbear." The SEC realizes that the exchanges have the flexibility that Government lacks, by its very nature . . .

In an age in which the computerized man has solved regulatory problems a moon's distance from earth, Saul maintains that the Exchanges

> have an on-the-spot understanding of regulatory problems that a Government 250 miles away can't possibly have. Exchanges can act more promptly here, without having to go through detailed administrative procedures.[8]

Saul is quite obviously a trailblazer of the coming order. "I think I'm going to be pretty busy," he said, "but I wouldn't have taken the job unless I felt the Exchange had a great future." Had anyone cautioned him to beware of a great future in an enterprise with a dark past?

In 1912, in its investigation of the financial establishment, the House Banking and Currency Committee viewed the New York Stock Exchange as a "private club." It recognized that society had been unable to mobilize its powers in order to enforce laws that would prevent fraud by Stock Exchange members. The committee therefore recommended a solution that is as relevant today as it was then—that the Stock Exchange become incorporated.[9] "Regulation" by the SEC has failed, since 1934, to force the public disclosures of Stock Exchange operations that would be our only guarantee of justice; and the Stock Exchange is still, as it was, a "private club."

Another case in point. At the very moment when the auction-market investor was most vulnerable, we find the Chairman of the SEC, Manuel Cohen, pushing "confidence" and "the securities markets."

> Investor confidence . . . is reaching new highs . . . the securities markets have done an outstanding job in performing their economic function during this period of heightened business activity.[10]

Unfortunately, as investors soon learned, the price level of stocks was high, and shortly the stocks went down. Now, sounding like the President of the New York Stock Exchange, Cohen raises his voice to push "self-regulation" and, of all things, *exemption from the anti-trust laws:*

> The stock exchanges must be free to exercise their self-regulatory responsibilities in the interest of protecting the public. To that extent, if necessary and required by the Federal securities laws, they must be free to take part in concerted action which might otherwise constitute per se violations of the antitrust laws . . . there is evidence that concern over possible anti-trust consequences may be dampening the vigor of self-regulation.

But he does not tell us how such exemptions from the anti-trust laws would:

1. Cause specialists and other members to abandon their short-selling activities;
2. Prevent the cataclysms caused by the Exchange's pursuit of special fees from big-block distributions or prevent the violence to which these distributions subject the market;
3. Prevent the bull raids that are conducted by the financial establishment subsequent to its pooling operations at the bottom of each and every crash;
4. Prevent brokers from acting as investors' agents and functioning, at the same time, as principals for their own accounts;
5. Prevent specialists from using exemptions from margin regulations to buy stock for their own accounts;
6. Limit Exchange members' use of credit when trading for their own accounts;
7. Prohibit members from using their customers' cash and stock as a part of their own capital;

8. Prevent specialist transactions in omnibus accounts;

9. Prevent the specialist from exploiting, for his own or a "friend's" advantage, the monopoly of information he has gathered from his book or the privilege it gives him to clean out this book so that he can fill his own and his big-block customers' orders at low price levels;

10. Prevent the establishment from so controlling the fluctuations in the stock market's 1,400-odd stocks that an advance is nothing more or less than a function of decline;

11. Alter the conditions that cause hundreds of stocks to decline to the accompaniment of good earnings and advance to the accompaniment of bad earnings;

12. Change the fact that today, because their customers have left their stock with them in street name, the New York Stock Exchange controls the proxies and, therefore, the board directors of every major corporation in the country;

13. Prevent the partners of member firms or financing banks from sitting on the boards of directors of these corporations, thereby causing a major division of interests between the corporation's board of directors and the stockholders of that corporation;

14. Prevent specialists and other members from employing sophisticated techniques to turn their short-term into long-term capital gains;

15. Resolve the inequities that exist in the margin regulations, which allow the nonmember investor 20 per cent margin and members 2,000 per cent;

16. Prevent the Exchange's monopolistic agreement to restrain trade one day a week by closing down so that specialists may continue to do manually work that could be computerized.[11]

According to economist Milton Friedman,

> Private monopolies seldom last long unless they can get governmental assistance in preserving their monopolistic position. In the stock market, the SEC both provides that assistance and shelters the industry from antitrust action . . . Remove this assistance and, while private monopoly will not disappear, it will be greatly reduced in scope and importance.[12]

It is the social relationship existing between the SEC Commissioners and the Exchange hierarchy that provides the Exchange with this "assistance and shelter." If one is open-minded enough to admit this, it is not difficult to see how the Exchange has employed this more or less social relationship as a technique of maintaining power. In conjunction with its other persuaders it has been a simple matter for the Exchange to fragment the regulators' sense of values. Nor is it difficult to understand how the regulator happens to develop class interests that cause him to seek positions on the Stock Exchanges. Anticipating a job with a "great future" on the Exchange, he gives little thought to the duties of his job as a regulator. He assists the Exchange in its efforts to defeat and dominate the competing power system he is supposed to represent. The community has failed to properly gauge the power and ruthlessness of the Exchange in pursuit of its goals.

William Cary, Cohen's immediate predecessor as Chairman, had this to say in his letter of transmittal on the report of the Special Study of the Securities Markets:

> While the report focuses upon shortcomings in the industry and in the self-regulatory authorities, in certain respects it is an express or implied criticism of the Commission as an institution. The Commission has not fully exercised its powers nor coped effectively with all the problems confronting it . . .

Soon afterward William Cary resigned as Chairman of the SEC.

The regime of Manuel Cohen as Chairman, then, further illustrated the SEC response to the demands of the specialist subculture. At the same time he demonstrated for the benefit of the Appropriations Committee the extraordinary range and diversity of investigations that could be conducted by his department.

The present Chairman of the SEC, Hamer Budge, is another political animal. It is noteworthy that he was appointed to the Commission by President Johnson at the insistence of the late Senator Everett Dirksen in return for Dirksen's support of the 1964 Civil Rights Act. Richard Nixon then appointed him Chairman in early 1969. In July, 1969, a Senate Securities Subcommittee began hearings into the possibility of a conflict of interest when it was revealed that, at the same time mutual fund legislation was pending. Budge had been negotiating terms for a position with the management team of a mutual fund complex.

In the course of these hearings it was also revealed that Richard Nixon had served as a director of four of these funds from late 1964 until 1968.

According to the *Wall Street Journal* (July 24, 1969):

> The SEC chairman asserted that neither the Federal statutes nor the rules of conduct prevent members and employees of the commission from becoming employed in the securities or mutual-fund industries "and this frequently occurs."

On August 5, it added to this statement: "Mr. Budge said any IDS sensitivity in this area 'must be very recent,' noting that the management company had, in the past, hired such SEC men as Ralph Saul, then director of the SEC's Trading and Markets division and now president of the American Stock Exchange."

NOTES, chapter 14

---

1 John Flynn was born in Bladensburg, Maryland, in 1882. Over the years he became recognized as one of the country's foremost writers on economics, finance, and political science. He served as editor of the *New York Globe* and left that post in order to devote all his time to writing and lecturing. He contributed regular articles to *Collier's* and the *Reader's Digest* and was most celebrated for his column in *The New Republic*. In addition to writing a number of books on politics, finance, and history, he found time to serve in Washington as adviser to a number of Senate committees. He was particularly helpful to those committees concerned with banking and currency legislation, and in his assistance in the investigations of the New York Stock Exchange.

2 John Flynn was, I believe, right.

3 That is, it was buried until John Flynn got hold of it.

4 New York: Free Press, 1966.

5 October 29, 1966.

6 *Business Week,* October 29, 1966.

7 *Business Week,* October 29, 1966.

8 *Wall Street Journal,* November 7, 1966.

9 *Report of the Committee Appointed Pursuant to House Resolutions 429 and 504 to Investigate the Concentration of Control of Money and Credit,* February 28, 1913. On pp. 116 and 117, the committee said: "Your committee, however, is of opinion that to a great extent the objectionable features of operations on stock exchanges would be eliminated if the following conditions were met:

"*(a) Incorporation.*—If such exchanges were to become bodies corporate of the States or Territories in which they are respectively located.

"Whilst, of course, they can not now do anything contrary to law, nevertheless the State can not exercise in their case that comprehensive control and close and summary supervision which it may exact of corporate bodies as a condition of permitting them to exist at all. If such exchanges were required to incorporate, the State could write into their charters provisions calculated to restrict them to legitimate purposes and suppress the abuses described; and by a system of examinations and penalties could enforce such provisions.

"The principal objection urged by the exchange against incorporation is that it will interfere with its power of discipline over its members and thus lower the standard that has been reached and that can only be maintained by an unquestioned final authority. Not wishing to criticize harshly, we are yet bound to say that we do not consider the standard attained by the exchange under freedom from governmental supervision to be of such character as to constitute a valid reason against such supervision.

"But aside from that, no reason is perceived why any such result as suggested should follow from giving to an accused member whose reputation and entire business career and means of livelihood depend on the action of his comembers and competitors the manifest measure of justice of a review by an impartial authority. There is no danger that the courts will deal less severely or less effectually than has the exchange with the frauds practiced upon the public which it is the purpose of incorporation and regulation to prevent and punish. That would be difficult. Nor are they likely to regard manipulation with any less disfavor."

Implementing this recommendation now would go a long way toward reforming the financial attitudes of the Stock Exchanges' unconverted multitudes.

[10] Address by Manuel Cohen, Chairman of the Securities and Exchange Commission, before the Investment Bankers Association of America, Hollywood, Florida, November 30, 1965, as quoted and abridged in the *Wall Street Journal,* December 1, 1965.

[11] This is one of the major reasons the Exchanges were shut down one day a week. Otherwise, firms like Merrill Lynch, whose back offices are up-to-date, would never have tolerated keeping their doors closed in order to make it possible for less efficient firms to catch up on their paperwork. In the thinking of the Exchange hierarchy, it is better to lose one day's business than to have to program computers according to the laws of a viable auction market.

[12] *Newsweek,* August 26, 1968.

15

The Merits of Speculation

> Most traders don't make money because
> they worry too much,
> and they worry too much
> because they're traders.

On September 5, 1961, because of the practices un-
earthed by Robert Kennedy's investigation of the activities of Alexander Guterma, Congress enacted Public Law
87–196 and directed the Securities and Exchange Commission

> to make a study and investigation of the adequacy, for
> the protection of investors, of the rules of national
> securities exchanges and national securities associations,
> including rules for the expulsion, suspension, or dis-
> ciplining of a member for conduct inconsistent with just
> and equitable principles of trade . . .

The Commission was called upon to report to Congress
"the results of its study and investigation, together with
its recommendations, including such recommendations
for legislation as it deems advisable."

For practical purposes the investigation accomplished
nothing insofar as the specialist system was concerned.

241

In fact, the only recommendations accepted by the Exchanges were those that further implemented the specialist system. Rather than new laws, what is wanted is theory that will enable Congress to grasp the problems presented by speculation. Some of the questions that should shape such a theory are:

1. Should speculation on our Stock Exchanges continue to shape the future of life in the United States?

2. How does Congress stand in relation to speculation?

3. Does such speculation provide a mature response to the needs of investors and the economy?

Congress must decide if the Exchanges are to be run like a vast roulette wheel and if speculation on the Exchanges best expresses the needs of investors. In that event, it would be accepted by everyone that economic roulette is a good thing for investors and the country, that it is "part of our way of life." If Congress should decide that investor gambling is of value, then the function of the laws and regulations would be to see that the wheel is not rigged in favor of the house and that the whole operation of the Securities Exchanges is looked on as being no more than fun and games on a national scale. Government, as in Monte Carlo, could sit as a sort of referee to see to it that the tourists have a good time and are not cheated.

On the other hand, it is possible that Congress might decide to accept the theory of a true auction market, in which securities are bought and sold for legitimate investment purposes by men willing to accept the obligations as well as the rights of ownership in our industrial economy. By this theory, the gambling approach to the securities markets would be seen not only as without purpose but as inimical to our economic way of life. It would be recognized that the purpose of the rules and regulations governing the Exchanges is not to provide codes of ethical practices for gamblers but to provide laws to protect investors and an economy of 200 million people from the consequences of speculation.

The Securities Acts of 1933 and 1934 were rooted in the idea of government control of all the sources of money from banks all the way down the ladder to money-lenders. This involved the rigid regulation of corporation executives, the issuers of corporate securities and their commission, and banking-house underwriters. Congress acknowledged that the activities, purposes, and preoccupations of this group determined the character of the securities markets.

The acts provided that there should be a government agency that supervised the markets and that the terms of trading and the media supplying information to the public from the Exchanges should no longer be controlled and dictated by brokers and floor traders. It was intended by the acts that the control of the Exchanges should be exercised in equal proportions: by the brokers, by the listed corporations, by the bankers who finance the system, and by government-appointed representatives of the public.

The 1933 Securities Bill was enacted to make it incumbent upon every New York bank to operate in either the banking business or the securities business, but not in both. It was easy, therefore, to line the bankers up against the Securities Bill. However, the heaviest of the attacks launched against the Stock Exchange Bill of 1934 in its journey through Congress came from corporation executives across the country. The ammunition for all this was provided by the Exchange itself. The reader has earlier been made aware of the Exchange's controls over the boards of directors of most of the corporations listed with it.[1]

A note from Richard Whitney, then the President of the New York Stock Exchange, to corporation executives, asking for their help against the Securities Bill, brought an immediate response.

Even then, Congress had recognized the fact that the American corporation will never serve its stockholders properly until broker control has ended and until the brokers are evicted from the corporations and the corporation executives are evicted from Wall Street. The authors of the 1934 law knew that high-powered bankers like Winthrop Aldrich, the head of the Chase National Bank, along with other leading New York bankers, went to Washington as the personal guests of President Roosevelt and that their objective was to emasculate those provisions of the Act that would have served to curtail the activities of their banks on the Exchanges. Aldrich also had a conference with Senator Fletcher, who, along with Senator Rayburn, had been responsible for the Fletcher-Rayburn Bill to regulate the Exchanges. Immediately following these conferences, the bill to separate the banks from their Wall Street affiliates was left toothless. John T. Flynn, writing for *The New Republic* on May 9, 1934, wondered:

Will Wall Street and the racketeering banks all over the country, which have robbed countless thousands of trusting depositors and investors through these predatory and unconscionable affiliates, succeed in getting away with this? I predict they will . . . They have succeeded in taking out of the Stock Exchange Bill almost every important tooth designed to bite into Wall Street and in transferring the power to a still unnamed commission.[2] Whether that bill amounts to a hill of beans depends on this same appointive power that put . . . powerful subordinates who were the worst enemies of the Stock Exchange bill into the Federal Reserve Board and the Treasury . . . the most powerful enemies of the Exchange Bill were to be found in the President's own official family . . . the most successful raids on the bill were engineered by men in the Federal Reserve

Board, the Treasury, and the Department of Commerce . . .

The Stock Exchanges, under Whitney's guidance, went one step further. Harris Upham & Co. sent their customers a letter quoting a telegram sent to them by Richard Whitney. It concluded: "In my opinion, the practical consequences of the Stock Exchange Bill will be the disruption of our securities markets, deflation of security prices and postponement of economic recovery."

The effect on those who had bought stock on margin was, of course, immediate. They sold and in fury took up arms against the bill. They succeeded in perpetuating de facto self-regulation, which operates on the principle that, if you remove law and authority on the one hand and grant special privileges and monopoly powers on the other, the good hearts of members will be free to automatically inspire them to good deeds.

Two major forms of speculation legally coexist in the United States today: the speculations of entrepreneurs in industry, and the speculations of gamblers in securities. In the former, capital is committed into one or another kind of business for the production of goods and services in anticipation of a profit from the success of the enterprise. Profit, in this sense, stimulates initiative. It encourages willingness to accept economic uncertainty. Those who accept such risks are entitled to a return on their investments commensurate with the nature of their risks and the value and creativity of their insights. The importance of this kind of speculation is not questioned here. It merits maximum freedom from regulation, compatible with the well-being of the economy and people.

Our concern is with the financial establishment's privileged hierarchy—those who speculate in securities in order to profit from their price fluctuations.

It is probable that most of the Exchange's activities are devoted to purposes that have nothing to do with the needs of industry or investors. The Exchange, refusing to recognize that regulation of whatever kind would be preferable to the present anarchy, may point out that you cannot stop the inherent instinct of men to gamble, and it may say that it is useless to pass laws that forbid speculation. The experience of England, France, Holland, and Germany is cited by the Exchange in this regard.

The failure of regulation in Holland extends back three hundred years; according to the records, the major decline in Dutch stock prices was caused by short selling. In an effort to eliminate this practice, the government first banned short selling and when this wasn't successful (the law was ignored), it levied a tax on all short sales. This, too, was ignored. Inevitably, the government repealed the laws. It is important to point out, however, that there was no attempt made by the Dutch government to eliminate overall speculation per se. The only speculative "talents" they wished to circumscribe were those of the speculators who forced prices down.

In fact, the history of speculation shows that the major reason for controlling speculation should be not to keep prices from declining once they have risen but to eliminate the pooling operations and other practices of insiders that push prices up to abnormal peaks. The Exchange's talented swindlers have always made their major killings by driving prices up, not down. Depressions and investor losses are caused by bull raids.

Ferdinand Pecora's Securities Exchange Bill was drawn up along the lines laid down by the Dutch experiment: emphasis was placed on the causes of price declines instead of on the reasons for abnormal price advances. The English and French had experienced much the same regulatory problems. Their emphasis was also on short selling; in the end, the effort merely to restrict short selling served to minimize the impact of other evils attendant on speculation. The point is often made that the failure of the German experiment of 1896 is proof that it is impossible to eliminate speculation. But those who make this point neglect to mention that the German experiment failed because, like the Dutch experiment, it also placed its emphasis on the elimination of short selling.

Begun in 1896, the German experiment was shelved in 1908. It did not take into account the differences between the speculations on a security market and those on a commodity exchange. For example, a share that was sold on the German Bourse on the third day of the month didn't have to be delivered until the thirtieth, settlements of trades being made once a month. Transactions on the Berlin Bourse were, therefore, transactions in futures. This presents quite a different problem, particularly in terms of credit, from a market in which delivery of stock must be made almost immediately—hence, the regulatory problems were quite different from the problems faced by our regulators. Brokers and bankers found it a simple matter to evade the new law. The technique employed to evade regulations was to borrow stock and then purchase it—cover—at a later date, in order to eliminate the loan obligation—the same activity we call, on the New York Stock Exchange, short selling.

In 1908, the German government introduced a new law recognizing the need of government supervision and regulation of the exchanges. The government appointed its own man to the principal post on each of the exchanges. While each exchange could elect its own board for self-rule purposes, each board had to be approved by the government's appointee.

On the Berlin Bourse, half of the exchange's governors were elected from the membership of the exchange, while the other half were chosen from the representatives of banks and industrial and agrarian interests. Under this law, brokers were forbidden to trade for their own accounts except when necessary to fulfill the orders of their principals. With the passage of time, this section of the law came to be enforced less and less, and brokers, inevitably, went back to their own accounts. However, a customer could bring a complaint in which judgment would be leveled against the broker if the customer could show that he suffered an injury brought about by his broker's trading.

In this system, the government also appointed the specialists, called the "agents of quotation." Such an agent was forbidden to trade for his own account except when it was absolutely necessary to take a portion of a trade in order to complete a transaction. Even then, he was in each instance obligated to obtain the permission of the exchange, and his trading was subject to strict surveillance. It is the one successful aspect of the German law that most terrifies those on our Stock Exchanges who are aware of the impact that such a law would have on specialist speculations and the speculations of their friends.

The Securities Exchange Act of 1934 left it to the Commission to apply whatever regulations it believed expedient. Congress and the SEC had before them the experience of the German government. The SEC should have prohibited traders and specialists from trading for their own accounts. Trading on the Exchange floor should have been limited to commission brokers acting as agents for investors. The major loophole in the Act prohibited brokers and floor traders from placing orders for their own personal accounts while on the floor of the Exchange, but all they had to do was telephone their brokerage firms off the floor and have them place their orders.

The original wording of the Act recognized the need for complete segregation of the functions of the specialist as a dealer for his own account and as a broker acting as an agent for others. However, the Exchange managed to have a clause inserted into the Act whereby the Commission was told to "make a study of the feasibility and advisability of the complete segregation of the functions of dealer and broker, and to report the results of its study and its recommendations to the Congress on or before January 3, 1936." In 1936, the matter was again pigeonholed by the Commission "pending further study." For every congressman and senator the truth was there to observe and act upon. The 1934 Act failed because it was meant to fail.

But laws regulating the activities of specialists, even if effective ones could be passed, would not go to the heart of the problem. For the truth is that there is no need for the specialist. He does not perform one useful function that could not be carried out by another broker operating, as in Germany, as a "quotations clerk." As for the service he provides that allows brokers to leave limit orders on his books, the use he makes of his book proves that this service costs the investor far more than it is worth. If the book is to be used this way, we should expand on the German law, and specify that such limit orders be placed on the book of a "quotations clerk" who would not be allowed to buy or sell for his account or anyone else's—under *any* circumstances.

The original proposal included in the first Stock Exchange control bill sought to limit the specialist's functions. The most important part of this proposal was that he was allowed to act only as a broker and was forbidden to trade for his own account; this, of course, was eliminated from the Act. The other important part was that he was not allowed, under any circumstances, to disclose the contents of his book to any other person. This rule was adopted but is being evaded. Another provision was that the function of a specialist, at the order of the Commission, could be taken over by the Exchange. The Exchange saw to it that this was eliminated from the Act. As things stood, the Commission was empowered to segregate the broker and dealer functions of the specialist if it deemed it wise. However, Joseph Kennedy, when he was Chairman of the SEC in 1934, decided that the broker and dealer functions of specialists should not be segregated.

In the original proposal for the Securities Exchange Act a broker was forbidden "to engage himself or be a member of any firm engaged in the issuance, underwriting, or primary or secondary merchandising of securities of any sort." The Exchange also had this prohibition eliminated from the original bill.

Concerning big-block offerings such as secondaries, specialist offerings, or other such underwriting, the Commission was granted the power in a blanket clause (Section 10B), which forbids "any person to use any manipulative or deceptive device or contrivance which the Commission may make rules against."

When one of the leading congressmen was asked what he thought of the law after its enactment, he answered: "I cannot tell. I do not know how much law we have and cannot know until I see the Commission."

Short selling by corporate insiders was forbidden in the Act. Short selling by specialists and others was left to the discretion of the Commission (Section 10A). What attitude the Commission would take was a foregone conclusion. Its decisions served only to make it possible for the specialist, when he had decided to distribute stock, to do it via the short sale or to so utilize investor demand that it could be turned against the investor.

According to the Act, the rules central to margin were removed from the jurisdiction of the SEC and were handed over to the Federal Reserve Board. This, in the opinion of the Exchange's intellectuals, was too important a matter to be left to the nonbanking fraternity, who could quite conceivably upset the whole apple cart one day by eliminating margin. Without question the Exchange edifice is founded on how it employs the public use of margin on the one hand and, on the other, the use it has been privileged to make of credit on its own behalf. Margin is one of the Exchange's major instruments for sabotage, second only to short selling and the almighty big-block fee. The overly ambitious investor, too involved in his workaday world to do any hard thinking about the matter and offered no coherent objection to its premises, is only too happy to buy on margin.

According to the April, 1966, issue of *Fortune*:

> At some firms, the most important source of profit—or loss—is the trading the house does for its own account; indeed, there are some that earned more on their own portfolios last year than on all their "operations" combined. Just about every firm that does an appreciable over-the-counter business takes positions in a number of issues so that it will have an "inventory" to offer prospective buyers. Finally, there are some firms that invest actively most of the time, taking both short- and long-term positions, and seeking profits from the investment itself. Whatever the reason for its holding, it is clear that a brokerage firm with a big portfolio has a big stake in the trend of the market. At the same time, the firm that trades for itself has a problem about offering impartial recommendations to its own customers.

The apostles for this commercial substitute for crapshooting have managed to contrive a system in which your borrowing makes it possible for them to win with your money year after year. The mistake Marx, Engels, and others made was to confuse this with capitalism. Margin speculation is anything but capitalism. It is a system of finance that facilitates member speculations and slowly and inevitably consumes the corpus of the capitalist economy like a cancer. When the full history of speculation is revealed in official documents and sworn testimony, it will be unbelievable.

NOTES, chapter 15

---

[1] In a 1965 census of share owners, conducted by the New York Stock Exchange, the value of shares in publicly owned corporations held by nominees in street name was said to be $141 billion out of a total of $648 billion. The control this gives the NYSE over these corporations and the nation's industrial complex staggers the imagination. As indicated in Chapter 7, the percentage of stock being purchased in street name is estimated to be 75 per cent.

[2] The unnamed Commission later became the SEC.

16

The Challenge

Are there enough customers to feed all mouths?

Critics of American politics have long pointed out that, with too few exceptions, it is the pastime of second-rate men. They have not been without facts to support their view. I became aware of how this prejudice could take root and grow when, in June, 1963, I appeared before the Senate Subcommittee on Banking and Currency. First of all, I was asked when I arrived to submit my testimony for the record, not to read it. I protested that I was traveling 6,000 miles to read it—not just to hand it over for the record. Chairman Willis Robertson then said: "We understand that you have come 6,000 miles, and we want to be as generous as we can, but *please* make it brief."[1] Robertson belonged to the team of men opposed to everything I wished to discuss. According to Drew Pearson and Jack Anderson, Robertson

pushed through a bill in 1965, legalizing six bank mergers that had been blocked by the Justice Department as blatant violations of the antitrust laws. Robertson's legislation nullified Supreme Court rulings against two of the mergers and prevented prosecution of the other four . . . at eighty-one, he is employed by the bankers as a consultant.[2]

253

Now let me show, by way of illustration, the manner in which the Chairman of the Subcommittee, Senator Harrison Williams, addressed Keith Funston the following day:

> Mr. G. Keith Funston, president of the New York Stock Exchange, is our first witness. Mr. Funston has been a highly respected figure in the securities industry for many years, and he has been of significant help to this committee on many occasions.
>
> Mr. Funston, we welcome you. You may proceed in any way you want.[3]

When the President of the New York Stock Exchange opened his mouth Senator Jacob Javits opened his:

> I attended this morning especially to welcome Mr. Funston, who is president of the New York Stock Exchange, and Mr. Etherington, president of the American Stock Exchange, as important witnesses before this committee . . . Mr. Chairman, I have no idea how long the witness will take, and if I have to leave before he is through, I would like the privilege of welcoming him here as another distinguished citizen of New York and an important leader in its affairs and the affairs of the Nation . . .[4]

Javits' additional remarks are understandable when it is realized that Funston was the spokesman for the wealthiest members of the financial establishment—some of whom are clients of the law firm of Javits, Trubin, Sillcocks, Edelman, and Purcell.[5]

The failure of my trip can be gauged by the *Wall Street Journal*'s gratuitous comment (June 21, 1963) subsequent to my appearance: "It is doubtful that Mr. Ney will change the course of securities legislation." Then on April 4, 1966, *Newsweek* stated: ". . . a Securities and Exchange Commission official, while calling some of Ney's comments 'helpful,' says, 'I don't think he knows anything we don't.' "

If they know, why don't they act?

More than thirty-five years ago, John Flynn's pent-up hunger for action called out from the pages of *The New Republic* (March 28, 1934):

> When the moment for writing the history of this period arrives, let it be remembered that in the battle behind the scenes over the Stock Exchange Bill, the most powerful friends of the New York Stock Exchange were to be found in high posts of the Roosevelt Administration.
>
> It is a simple trick to deceive the people of the United States with strong words. It is easy, for instance, to announce that "Congress must pass a strong bill" against Wall Street and at the same time turn all the energies of the Administration to weakening the bill. The strident announcements please the people. The tooth-drawing behind the scenes pleases Wall Street. In the end, the performance leaves one who sees the bill from behind the wings a little sick at the stomach.

This sort of thing is still going on. It comes about because no method has been devised to insulate our lawmakers from the systematic corruption of the Exchange and its lobbies.

Two forces have come to dominate the economy—money spent on war-making and money spent on space. Both are immensely profitable to Wall Street, and both have been taken under Wall Street's control. In his book *The Weapons Culture*, Ralph Lapp declares:

> It is no exaggeration to say that the United States has spawned a weapons culture which has fastened an insidious grip upon the entire nation . . . pressures exerted by powerful corporations are felt in the Pentagon, in the White House, and are reflected in the Congress.[6]

The overt manner in which the broker mentality has encouraged this weapons culture is typified in the advertisement quoted by Lapp (on his p. 29) that appeared in *The New York Times*:

NIKE-X
$30 Billion for Whom?

If the U.S. deploys its Nike-X defense, $30 billion could flow into certain electronics, missile, and computer companies. The impact would be enormous.

About $2.4 billion has already been spent on Nike-X development. Some companies are benefiting from this spending now, are likely to continue benefiting even if the program remains in the R & D stage, and could profit handsomely if a full-scale program is approved.

The ad was paid for, Lapp wrote, by the brokerage firm of Arthur Wiesenberger & Co.

Just how far our leaders have moved from integrity and how willingly they have attached themselves to the Exchange can be imagined when, forced out of Washington by the advent of a new administration, the politician joins—of all things—an Exchange brokerage firm. When we learn that former Secretary of the Treasury Henry Fowler was admitted as a general partner of the Goldman Sachs brokerage firm on December 30, 1968, and that on January 8, 1969, Lawrence F. O'Brien—another former member of the Cabinet—was named President of McDonnell & Co., another brokerage firm,[7] we can better understand why it is that so much of what happens in Washington has, as its ideal extension, a job in the financial establishment.

President Nixon has followed the same dreary tradition, filling his Cabinet with "tricky Dick" lawyers and bankers. Choosing his former law partner as Attorney General, he made it plain that, in his opinion, the great legal issues confronting the Justice Department are best decided by a lawyer—John Newton Mitchell—whose main qualification is a career as a municipal bond expert.[8]

"You don't set a fox to watching the chickens just because he has a lot of experience in the henhouse," Truman once said.[9]

Effective, meaningful government regulation of the securities industry is imperative.

Section 2, Paragraphs 1–4, of the Securities Exchange Act outlines the government's jurisdiction in this matter. It assumes that the problem is one for which public remedies are to be found by controlling the manipulation of security speculation that might cause excessive expansion or contraction of the credit available for industry involved in interstate commerce. The Act also asserts that such fluctuations in the value of credit seriously affect the valuation of bank loan collateral, which in turn affects the operation of the Federal Reserve System and the national banking system.

Because of our ignorance they have littered our statute books with laws that are of value only to the securities industry. The thought processes of a congressman like Dingell (Chapter 13) and the naïveté expressed in his question "What is a specialist?" after days of questioning suggest that if ignorance paid dividends then our congressmen have made most of their fortunes from what they don't know about the securities markets. Yet, these are men we've allowed to shape and mold the capitalist system's financial institutions.

Drew Pearson and Jack Anderson pointed out that "the back door to many a congressman's office can be reached through his law practice. Of the 535 members of Congress, more than 300 are attorneys. Few have bothered to take down their shingles." [10] We can make an uncomfortable comparison between the men who wrote the Constitution and the primitive patterns of the Dirksens, Dodds, McIntyres, Bibles, Allotts, and a host of other senators—all of whom can be expected to pursue whatever course of action is consistent with their law firms' financial interests. The public would get a better idea of the genuflections of politicians like Senator Jacob Javits if a law existed that compelled congressmen to reveal the names of the Stock Exchange members and bankers who retain the services of their New York law firms.

Until higher standards and tests of qualification are introduced—other than those of seniority or influence—to qualify a legislator to sit on a committee involving banking or securities legislation, then politicians will only add to the evils that have metastasized.

The Specialist

Neither the New York Stock Exchange nor its specialist system is equal to the difficult task of performing its obligations within a framework of "self-regulation." There is only one yardstick by which we need test the specialist system. That yardstick is whether its continued existence is good for the nation. Specialists provide one useful function (which they have proceeded to abuse): they make it possible for brokers to leave orders with them at prices above or below the existing market price of a stock, which, of course, are subsequently executed when and if the stock touches these price levels. A computer could now more effectively perform this function.

It was recognized in the original Act that the specialist should only act as a broker and be prohibited from trading for his own account. The Exchange was, of course, powerful enough to eliminate this provision. It is interesting to recall, however, that the original Act included a provision that the SEC could, if it wished, insist that the specialists' functions be assumed by the Exchange itself!

The specialist is the greatest single enemy of the capitalistic-democratic tradition. The most important responsibility of government is to prevent the further waste of resources caused by his existence. And the inadequacy of economic preparedness cannot be allowed to serve as a pretext for delaying this legislation. According to IBM technicians, it would be a simple matter to replace specialists with a System 360, Model 85 computer, served by "agents of quotation."[11] But in the event our elected legislatures continue to abdicate their responsibilities in this matter, let them remember that the victims of their delaying tactics are tomorrow's children.

The Payment of Commissions by Brokers

Everyone participating in the investment experience must be treated equally. Members should be accorded no privileges, in terms of commissions or otherwise, that are not available to the public. Big blocks should not be granted lower commissions, thereby making it more attractive to swing in and out of the market. The Exchange is aware that by paying lower commissions for big-block accumulations and distribution it makes its big-block customers more willing to pay the Exchange its special big-block fees. The Exchange is operating a facility that is in the nature of a public utility. It should be regulated as such. The Exchanges are as much a public necessity within the framework of our economic and political structure as are gas, water, and electricity.

Broker Trading

It must be stipulated by Congress that the function of the Stock Exchanges shall be to offer their services and facilities to the public. All members of the Exchanges must therefore be prohibited from trading or investing for themselves if they wish to act as brokers for others. Section 10 of the Securities Exchange Act, before Roosevelt's appointees emasculated it, included this provision. That this prohibition be extended to include allied members and others associated with members is critical to the whole issue of reform.

Day Trading

Wherever those in any way associated with members participate as investors in the market or are powerful enough to control the fluctuations in the price of stocks, they must not be allowed to day-trade in the market in competition with the public. If members sell stock for this group, it must be at the stock's low price for that day or at the following day's low price—whichever is lower. They cannot be allowed to "get out" before the public. No announcement of any kind that might affect the price of an individual stock or the price of stocks as a whole can be used as a cause of entering or leaving the market before the public. The wisdom of such a rule would minimize the impact of any announcement. At present, the art of investing consists in the art of knowing how to distinguish between rumor and fact.

Specific Disclosure of Member Holdings and Profits

There is an enormous margin of privilege accorded members not granted other corporation executives. We take it for granted that corporation executives must disclose the nature and extent of their stock holdings; they are also obliged to submit financial statements to government agencies. In this crucial area it is imperative that the responsibility and mission of those associated in any way with the Exchanges be clarified. Not only must there be a prohibition against any member effecting transactions (as an "agent of quotation") in any stock in which he is registered, but full disclosure must be made of any holdings he or any of his associates may have in any other stock. The logical difficulties inherent in implementing this rule can be considerably eliminated in a market in which all investors are treated alike and the income tax reports of all those doing business as members or those associated with members are, by law, made a matter of public record.

Directorships and Proxies

Congress must recognize the conflicts of interest inherent in brokers acting as directors. The Stock Exchange must be taken out of the corporations, and the corporations must be taken out of the Stock Exchange. Members of the Stock Exchange must also be prohibited from voting or otherwise controlling the proxies of stock left with them by customers in street name. Proxies should be sent to customers, using the same methods employed in sending dividends. The prerogative to vote must be reserved exclusively for the shareholder. No recommendation should be given or solicitation allowed by the brokerage firm.

Broker Credit

Brokers must not be allowed to use credit or to extend it to customers. Bankers are not allowed, by law, to lend money that will be used in violation of Section T (that is, for the purchase of stock). This is a law that should be, but is not, enforced. Obviously, brokers should not be granted the privilege by the Federal Reserve Board to do what banks are not allowed to do—but the intent of this law is constantly evaded.

According to law, brokers should not be in the banking business. If loans are to be extended to investors, they should be granted by banking institutions that are equal to the difficult and onerous responsibility of determining who should be extended credit and for what purpose the loan is to be used. Moreover, it would ensure better control of the expansion and contraction of credit if this function was placed under the jurisdiction of a central bank, similar in its real objectives to the stated objectives of the present Federal Reserve Bank.

In this connection, listed corporations should not be allowed to extend call loans to Stock Exchange members. It should be against the law for any corporation to lend its money to any individual or corporation for speculation in shares.

Member Credit Exemptions

The special credits exemptions granted members and specialists must be eliminated, along with the privilege to use investor capital and stock as part of their net capital. Margin loans to customers should also be prohibited.

Omnibus Accounts and Options

Further precautions must be taken concerning pooling operations by specialists and other members in order to accumulate stock for themselves, their friends, and their big-block customers. A member must not be allowed to segregate stock for himself, his partners, associates, or others. Omnibus accounts must also be outlawed. Brokers must be prohibited from trading against options that are held either by the broker or by someone else. Option trading was, of course, outlawed in the original Act, but the provision was amended so as to leave the matter up to the SEC. As might be expected, the SEC went along with the Exchange on this, and so one of the greatest sources of overstimulation, manipulation, and gambling still exists and exercises an appalling influence over the market. Members employing options (and thereby making it even easier to use their incredible sources of credit) can manipulate stock prices up and then, having exercised their options, unload their stock into the portfolios of unsuspecting investors. On all counts, therefore, the use of options should be outlawed.

Short Selling

Many of the market's evils stem from the members' ability to borrow stock in order to sell short.

The elimination of short selling can do away with one of the market's worst evils: the manner in which big blocks are suddenly dumped into the market. Eliminate short selling and you eliminate the specialists' and other members' ability to quietly and inconspicuously lay the groundwork for chaos by establishing omnibus or other accounts from which they then sell short. Eliminate short selling and you also eliminate one of the principal tools used by brokers to help them "stabilize" prices when they are intent on dumping big blocks into the auction market. As a major instrument of manipulation, it has no place in an investment-oriented environment.

Brokerage Trading Accounts

At present, a brokerage firm's trading accounts are often its greatest source of profit. Nevertheless, brokerage firms should be prohibited from trading as principals for their own accounts in the stocks in which they are supposed to be "making a market."

Broker Market Letters and Related Matters

The broker's function should be limited to that of acting exclusively and solely as a broker. Brokerage firms should not be allowed to operate investment advisory services, since many brokers tend to stimulate speculation in order to stimulate commissions. Inevitably, they tend to become tipping services.

Every effort must be employed to use the ticker tape and the broad tape to provide investors with the latest information concerning stocks that are being actively traded. These tapes should be used to announce proposals for the inception or cancellation of mergers, take-overs, spin-offs, proxy fights, splits, and special situations. They should be employed as media for transmitting investment information rather than trading information; they should be confined to the statement of facts. They should not be employed in a manner that stimulates gambling. Their proprietors should be held accountable for the dissemination of any statement that can be directly linked to investor losses. Increasing proprietary responsibility will bring the shell game that now exists in the place of honest information under control.

Disclosure of Information

A facility must be provided that records up-to-the-minute information for investors on the volume of all big-block transactions in a stock—whether they are on the Exchange or in the third market and whether they are purchases or sales. Furthermore, if corporate insiders are buying or selling stock, then their stockholders have the right to know immediately how their management teams are exercising the power vested in them by their stockholders.

Concerning Conflicts of Interest Between Management and Stockholders

As stockholders, investors should be able to believe without reservation in the integrity of their management teams. In practice, however, they have learned that their officers and directors are indifferent to their well-being and are interested solely in their own ability to profit from the fluctuations in company stock. This circumstance has inevitable consequences in terms of management's relationship with its stockholders; it creates, for one thing, a rivalry between a company's management and its stockholders. Management now seeks to exploit its employers—the stockholders—by collaborating with members of the Exchange in order to buy and sell their shares at the most favorable prices, thereby placing their stockholders at a disadvantage. Equally important, the noncash methods of most takeovers and mergers involve management's willingness to accept high prices for their stocks and stock options, offered in order to gain their acquiescence in the merger or takeover. In the event a tender offer (a takeover) is anticipated, the company against which the raid is to be made must be so advised. If they do not wish to be taken over, they should not be, provided they have observed their obligations to their stockholders. There is no reason why a man who has built up a corporation should have to give up his life's work merely because a company like Gulf and Western Industries decides it wants the company. The laws governing the protection of property rights should be extended to cover this area. As for stock options exercised by management, these should be prohibited. On all counts they are inimical to the interests of stockholders. There is no legitimate argument that can be made for the existence of options; they are legal larcenies exercised against a corporation's owners—its stockholders.

Big-Block Transactions

The insights of Robert Healy into the larcenies surrounding big-block distributions (quoted in Chapter 10) show that it is imperative that these distributions be prohibited along with price pegging, short selling, "special brokerage incentives," and other discriminating activities ancillary to these transactions. Furthermore, no member should be allowed to provide one investor with a service for a fee that makes it possible for him to take advantage of another investor who has not paid or is not able to pay such a fee. The payment and receipt of such fees should be prohibited.

Overhauling the Federal Reserve System

Legislative interpretation of the Federal Reserve System's prevailing credit practices, its collusive restraints, and, in general, its anti-public practices must be re-evaluated and considered with impartiality by persons who are familiar with the nature of credit and related monetary and business problems—but who are not themselves businessmen.

As an economic engine the potentials of the Federal Reserve System are formidable. However, not even the United States can survive the enormous waste and continuing crisis occasioned by its prejudices. At present its loyalties are invested in a militant minority instead of the country's plurality, though it was for this latter group its creation was sanctioned.

Interlocking Directorates of Banks

The banking fraternity's link with the Stock Exchanges makes it imperative that bank directors be prohibited from serving on the boards of other corporations and exercising control over a corporation because the bank controls a large percentage of the corporation's assets. No more than a broker, and for the same reasons, should bankers be privy to the inside information of corporations they may serve.

Regulating Regulators

Much might be said about the relations between government-agency regulators and those they are supposed to regulate. Obviously, regulators must see a great deal of the men they are supposed to regulate, and the bureaucrat ultimately finds himself compelled to choose between his interests and his integrity. When the regulators find their next employment with the regulated, the choice they had made is obvious.

In the *New York Review of Books* (November 21, 1968, p. 27), Ralph Nader points out that

> political patronage has undermined local and state consumer protection agencies; it has, for example, helped to make the Federal Trade Commission as ineffectual as it is . . . business lobbying—including campaign contributions, powerful law firms, trade associations, and public relations—works against vigorous enforcement. Finally, so many regulatory officials resign to go into high-paying jobs in the industry they were once supposed to regulate that these government posts are viewed as on-the-job training by cynical appointees. The Federal Aviation Agency, Interstate Commerce Commission, and Federal Communications Commis-

sion all carry on a tradition that inhibits officials from action and attracts appointees who are temperamentally reluctant to act.

A footnote to his article informs us that "The last two chairmen of the Interstate Commerce Commission are now President of the National Association of Motor Business Carriers and Vice-President of Penn Central. Both industries are supposedly regulated by the ICC." The issues confronting us are urgent, indeed inescapable. We are not dealing here with a mere scandal, but with the future of the nation and perhaps the world.

NOTES, chapter 16

Emphasis added. *Hearings before a Subcommittee of the Committee on Banking and Currency*, U.S. Senate, June 18, 19, 20, 21, 24 and 25, 1963, p. 129.

Drew Pearson and Jack Anderson, *The Case Against Congress* (New York: Simon and Schuster, 1968), p. 193.

Hearings, p. 137.

Hearings, pp. 141–42.

Chuck Stone, in his *Black Political Power in America* (New York: Bobbs-Merrill, 1968), p. 102, points out that the problem exists in the highest court in the land: "Americans love to indulge themselves with the political opiate that the U.S. Supreme Court is above politics. It is not, and is, in fact, one of the most political institutions in the country. Judicial objectivity only exists when it depends on who is calling the political shots . . ." Gus Levy, former Chairman of the NYSE and senior partner of Goldman Sachs, and John Loeb of Loeb Rhoades continued to contribute to Justice Fortas' income while he was on the Supreme Court bench, as we noted earlier. The value of such a relationship when a host of law suits are pending against one's company is left to the reader's imagination.

New York: Norton, 1968, p. 29.

[7] According to *The New York Times* of August 12, 1968, Lawrence O'Brien, on resigning from McDonnell the previous day, had this to say: "I find that McDonnell & Company does not afford me the opportunity that I had envisioned it would."

[8] A story in *I. F. Stone's Weekly* (June 30, 1969) indicates that Mitchell was already showing where his sympathies lie: "Far from overstepping its authority, as some have alleged, the Supreme Court refused to be stultified and gulled when it took jurisdiction in the El Paso Gas case and remanded to the District Court for the full divestiture it originally decreed to block the El Paso–Natural Gas merger and to restore competition in natural gas in California. The Nixon Administration is far from abiding by the Caesar's wife rule. Nixon and Attorney General Mitchell were senior partners in the law firm through which El Paso has been fighting this case since 1961, and the firm's fees were three-quarters of a million dollars in 1961–67. Four days after Mitchell took office, the Justice Department ordered the anti-trust case against El Paso dropped. The Court declined to be fooled by shifts in California's representation and has ordered a 'cash sale' and the 'severance of all managerial and financial connections' to stop the merger and enforce its original order."

[9] Harry Truman on Vice-President Nixon's candidacy for the Presidency, October 30, 1960. It was Robert Taft, however, who pinpointed the problem when, after his defeat at the 1952 Republican convention, he said, "Every Republican candidate for President since 1936 has been nominated by the Chase Bank."

[10] *The Case Against Congress,* p. 101.

[11] *The New York Times* announced on October 2, 1969, that "An automated system of making markets in over-the-counter securities was introduced yesterday by Paine, Webber, Jackson & Curtis . . . It enables registered representatives in any of Paine, Webber's 63 offices around the nation to execute market orders instantaneously—within certain significant limitations—without dealing with any of the firm's market-makers. Inasmuch as an over-the-counter trader performs a function with unlisted stocks comparable to that of a specialist in listed shares on the floor of the New York Stock Exchange, the Computrade system indicates for the first time that some of the functions of the specialist can be eliminated by automation. The new system therefore has highly important implications for Wall Street, because the specialist and the function he performs provide the basis for the exchange market."

Survival in the Jungle

It's All in the Charts

**The door out of the ghetto
is hidden by a blueprint for larceny.**

It's curious how often even the most intelligent investor makes an investment decision based on fundamentals such as earnings ratios and the announcement of a merger, a new product, or split. He asks, "What makes investors pay $50 a share for stock at one time and $100 at another?" And an invisible world of myths supplies him with an answer: "A stock is worth what the public is willing to pay for it." On the strength of this, he commits himself to situations that may well bankrupt him.

Unless the investor understands that it is the specialist who determines the price of his stock, that a stock is only worth what its specialist is willing to pay for it, he doesn't understand the difference between fact and fiction in the stock market.

Specialists weave a web of relationships within their stock's price structure as they buy and sell. There is a pattern to the web that, seen through the medium of chart analysis, tells the investor what is going on in that stock. Major accumulations or distributions that are in

271

progress can show up or even be anticipated. Like the electrocardiogram, chart patterns can be interpreted and their future fluctuations predicted.

Brokerage firms are aware of the manner in which technical data supplied by charts can serve their fee-paying big-block customers. "Fundamentals" are a carrot that is placed just far enough in front of the investor's nose so that he will follow it to slaughter. These brokerage firms, in their ad copy, are careful to genuflect before the altar of fundamentals. In the *Wall Street Journal* of April 8, 1968, Merrill Lynch had this to say:

> Institutional investors know about our work in fundamental analysis. What they don't know is how big a job we do in technical analysis.

Aware that such an ad threatens the Exchange's traditional brainwashing techniques, Merrill Lynch is quick to add:

> We think the big size of our sample of public volume allows us to take some unique approaches to analyzing the market. That's one reason we spend nearly $230,-000 a year on technical work.
>
> But it is technical work, and its primary value is to institutions and the few really knowledgeable individuals who understand the limitations as well as the applications of technical work. To institutions and sophisticated individuals it can be very useful indeed and I'd like more of them to know about it.

So would I.

Correctly interpreted, charts can provide investors with a program and an insight into the changing intentions of specialists. There is, however, one major drawback to charting: there are too many chartists. Thus a situation exists that is used to advantage by specialists. A specialist knows that chartists can be counted on to buy and sell as a group whenever the fluctuations in his stock's price describe what chartists refer to as a "buy" or "sell" signal—therefore, chartists are playing with their cards face up. It is possible, too, that a specialist could manipulate his stock to provide false buy or sell signals; it's easy to guess who would lose money in that situation.

Many chartists have developed techniques that make it difficult for the specialist to trap them. With this thought in mind and as a part of this book's task, I would like to summarize my charting techniques.

To comprehend my charting techniques and their implications, the reader must know something about chart analysis.[1] Price changes tend to establish a trend and can often be depended on to continue that trend for weeks, months, even years; they establish this trend within the confines of parallels that form a channel.

Whereas today's chartists maintain that upward price movements must establish a trend before predictions can be made concerning future upward price movements, my techniques prove that once a major bottom has been reached in a stock it is often possible, analyzing the previous long-term decline, to come up with the exact angles that will be followed as the specialist begins his bull raid. The angles at which a stock advances are a function of the angles at which they declined. More than that: these advancing angles determine the future decline.

The fact that prices follow so consistent a trend cannot be attributed to traders' selling at the top of it and again buying at the bottom like automata—but to specialists. They have the position and the power to sell at the top and buy at the bottom. Recognizing the implications of my charts, one comes to understand the coercive control exercised by specialists over their stocks.

My charting techniques require four things: charts,[2] a protractor, a pair of parallel rulers, and the ability to recognize a pattern. It is suggested that the reader obtain instruction in the use of the protractor and rulers if he does not know how to use them. Expertise in the use of both can be acquired in a few minutes.

It will be more difficult to become adept at pattern recognition, to recognize patterns when they appear in any one of several different but closely related forms, to understand that all these patterns are located in the network of fluctuations that form a stock's long-term decline. In the 1953–1965 chart of Kerr-McGee Oil the lowest low has been marked *A*; the low preceding *A* has been marked *B*; the high between them has been marked *C*; the high prior to points *A*, *C*, and *B* has been marked *D*. Then the angles between these four points were measured. There is a major angle of 61 degrees (*CAB*), a minor angle of 41 degrees (*DAB*), and another minor angle of 20 degrees (*CAD*). A deeper understanding of the meaning and importance of these angles is formed once we begin to understand how they can be employed: each of these angles is a measure of the stock's forthcoming angles of advance (the 20-degree angle [*CAD*] is also capable of describing one of the angles of decline that will occur in Kerr-McGee in later years).[3]

Using the protractor I now construct the three angles on the lower right of the 1955–1966 Kerr-McGee chart. The next step involves the use of the parallel rulers. Placing them on the 41-degree line we have already con-

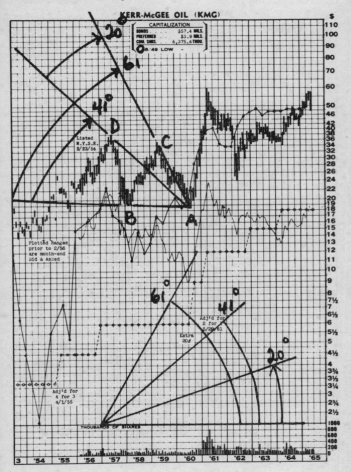

KERR-McGEE OIL (KMG)

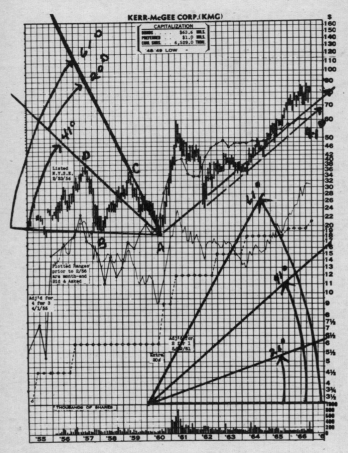

KERR-McGEE CORP.(KMG)

structed on the chart (lower right) we lift the angle with the parallel rulers until the ruler intersects the low at point *A*. Drawing a line from point *A* we now extend it out (to the right) to the end of the chart. We note that without any regard to the forces of supply or demand, earnings announcements, or a 2-for-1 split, the stock can be seen to have actually advanced along our 41-degree line!

However well defined my criteria, they cannot guarantee an appropriate evaluative response—even from market professionals. In the hopes of overcoming any bias, I have chosen Kerr-McGee Oil as a case in point—for it was Jiler who chose KMG to illustrate a "blow-off," [4] which provided me with this starting point. Happily this case provides an excellent setting in which to further test the efficacy of my principles and procedures.

Examining Jiler's chart of KMG (p. 278 here), we observe the standard approach of analysts toward a typical blow-off. Observe his description of the run up in price that culminated in the April, 1961, high in KMG.

PLATE 1   KERR-McGEE—*Uptrend Line and Channel*

The chart [p. 278 here] shows how Kerr-McGee Oil tripled in value in less than seven months. For the first six months, prices adhered remarkably close to an imaginary uptrend line (heavy line) and within the confines of a relatively narrow channel outlined by the dotted line drawn parallel to trendline. Further examination will reveal that the trendline was well established within the first month of the advance. In April, 1961, prices broke through the upside of the channel and accelerated into a blow-off or climax phase of development. This type of action often marks a temporary or major top. The vertical part of the rise was attributed to anticipation of a 2 for 1 stock split, which became effective May 31. By early 1962, prices were still well below the highs recorded on this chart.

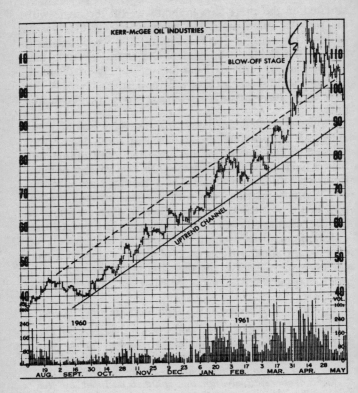

KERR-McGEE OIL INDUSTRIES

BLOW-OFF STAGE

UPTREND CHANNEL

1960   1961

INTERNAL TRENDLINE

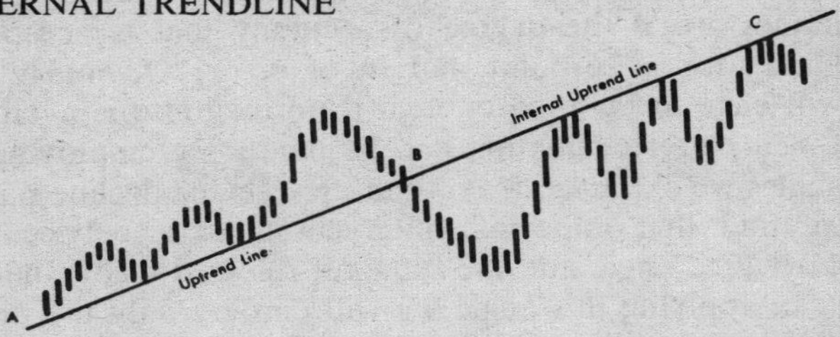

Internal Uptrend Line

Uptrend Line

Is it not fair to ask how good standard evaluative techniques are if the degree of accuracy that is acceptable allows for a 25-point margin of error? Obviously they will have to be good enough if nothing else is available. But a better evaluation can be made. By employing the angles we extracted from the Kerr-McGee decline pattern we find that important interactions exist between our 41-degree angle and the blow-off referred to by Jiler.

In applying this angle we will employ only the principles basic to Jiler's evaluative techniques. Hence, it will be seen that my procedures differ from his in only one respect (albeit an all-important respect), and that is in my premise that a stock's long-term decline pattern has built into it the angles that will determine its forthcoming angles of advance (and decline). In all other respects my charting techniques apply standard procedures. Thus, about the illustration reproduced here on p. 279, Jiler states:

> [This figure] shows how an internal treadline forms. The section from A to B is a normal uptrend line, while B to C, forming *beneath* the trendline, makes it an internal line.

Again on page 48, he states:

> Like trendlines, support and resistance can be found at almost any time and on any chart. In fact, they are the basic components that make up all the more sophisticated patterns that chartists look for in trying to predict price movements . . . trendlines help confirm support and resistance levels, while support and resistance levels help confirm and anticipate new trendlines.

If we are to logically pinpoint the 1961 "blow-off," we must select the critical points existing before 1961 that conform to Jiler's specifications concerning trendlines and measurement sophistication. At X we note such a

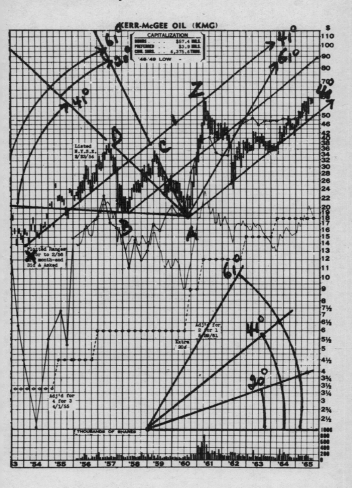

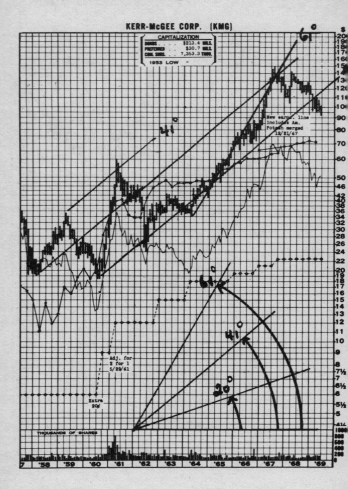

KERR-McGEE CORP. (KMG)

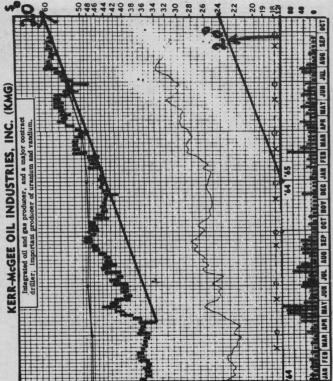

KERR-McGEE OIL INDUSTRIES, INC. (KMG)

Integrated oil and gas producer, and a major contract
driller; important producer of uranium and vandium.

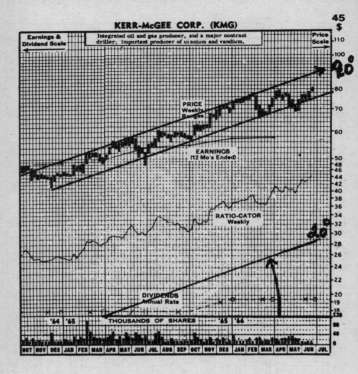

KERR-McGEE CORP. (KMG)

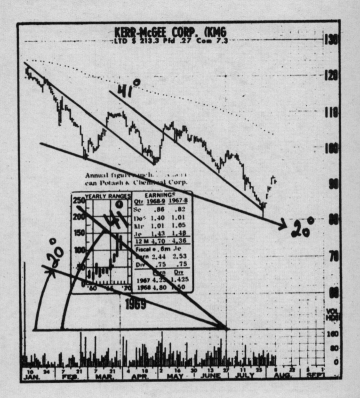

KERR-McGEE CORP. (KMG
LTD $ 213.3 Pfd .27 Com 7.3

41°

20°

20°

1969

Annual figures include . . . . .
ean Potash & Chemical Corp.

YEARLY RANGES	EARNINGS	
	Qtr.	1968-9	1967-8
	Se	.86	.82
	Do	1.40	1.01
	Mr	1.01	1.05
	Je	1.43	1.48
	12 M	4.70	4.36
	Fiscal ● .6m Je		
	Earn	2.44	2.53
	Div	.75	.75
		Earn	Div
	1967	4.25	1.425
	1968	4.80	1.50

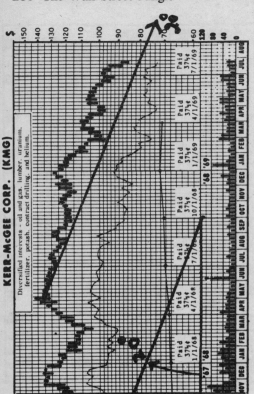

point. It is the beginning of the three-year uptrend in Kerr-McGee that began in 1954. In other words we have a situation in which, from 1954 to 1957, a "normal trendline" existed. From 1957 through 1961 an "internal line" formed "beneath the trendline." This internal line acted as a line of resistance; the price of KMG rose to meet it in 1961.

In the Kerr-McGee 1953–1966 chart, we see that the projection of the 61-degree angle from point *A* is useless —but note how it applies on the 1957–1969 chart to the specialist's bull raid from the 1964 low to the 1967 high!

A random sampling of the monthly charts in KMG shows the importance of another of our basic angles.

Possibly the most important application of our basic angles is in the prediction of long-term declines, as can be seen on the January-September and November-August KMG charts. Note the manner in which the 41-degree angle operated within the longer-term movement of the 20-degree angle.

We are now in quite a different position from the one we were in at the beginning of the chapter, when we first looked at the chart of KMG. Then we could assume that its pattern was determined by what investors are willing to pay for stock; now we know that this is not so. Yet the knowledge we now possess should have come as no surprise. The nature of the setting in which the public must buy and sell their shares was established in earlier sections of this book. We learned how the specialist exploits his book's privileges, how he uses public demand to send prices down instead of up, why and how he uses the short sale and short covering, and how he uses his trading and investment accounts.

It is valid to ask if it is possible to recognize a repetitive pattern from one chart to the next or if the chart of KMG was unique. The answer is that KMG is typical and that the pattern principles we evolved for KMG can be employed with other charts. To illustrate this I will provide the charts of several other companies. While there are variations in the manner in which the basic angles are extracted, the validity of the principle can be demonstrated by applying the technique to additional charts. By applying the same standards of measurement we rule out the possibility of coincidence. The importance of this approach toward understanding the real nature of the stock market cannot be overemphasized.

The series of four Boeing charts shows that the principle operating in the case of Kerr-McGee also operates in the case of Boeing.

In the 1965 chart of Boeing we employed the 18-degree angle (long-term) and in the 1968 chart the subsequent bull raid in Boeing by members exhibits the applicability of the 54-degree angle.

Since the accompanying weekly and monthly charts are now more or less self-explanatory, I can confine my comments to the following points. It's fair to assume that someone in the system makes a prior decision about the nature and variety of the basic angles to be locked into the initial decline pattern. The size of these angles will determine the stock's variations as it advances and declines.

A long-term channel trend can exist over a period of years, and the angles seem to remain fairly constant. Thus, it is not at all surprising to see our basic angles (included in the decline pattern) being subtly repeated within a stock's chart as the stock's price structure moves through time.

In the 1954–1966, 1956–1968, and March, 1967–March, 1968, charts of Rheem, the same basic angle formula can be seen at the higher low of 1966 (point *B* on the 1968 chart) as at the low of 1962 (point *A* on the 1966 chart). The repetition of these angles is important, since their reappearance signaled that Rheem was going

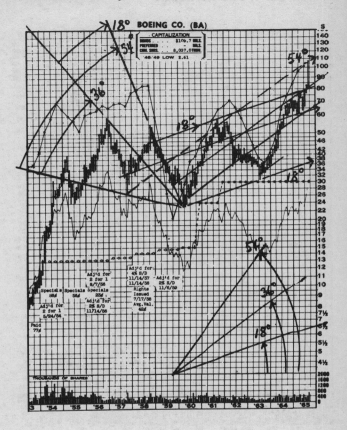

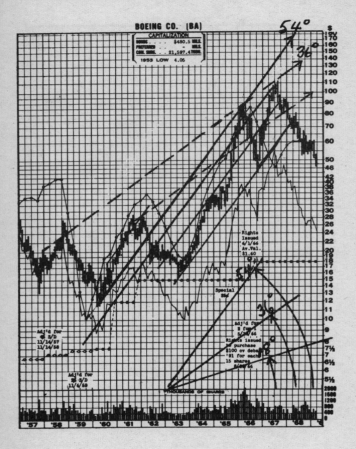

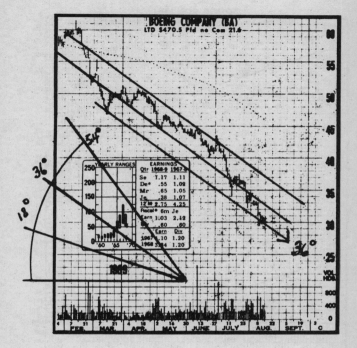

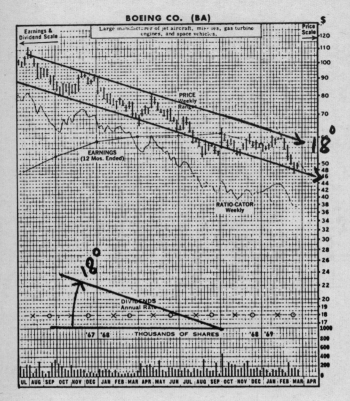

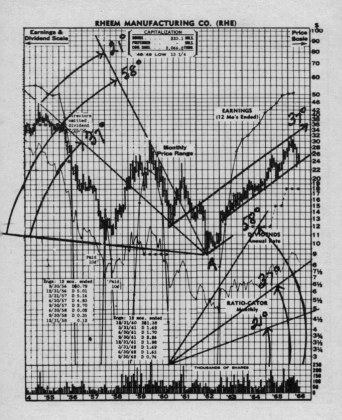

RHEEM MANUFACTURING CO. (RHE)

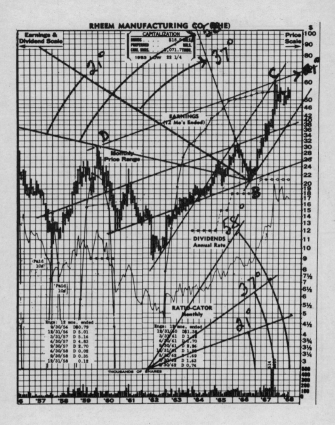

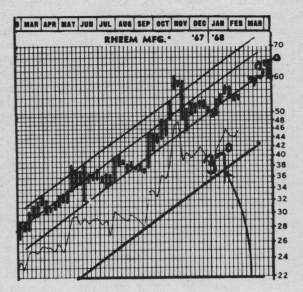

higher despite the fact that earnings had begun to flatten out—in fact one might say *because* earnings had begun to flatten out—thereby making it possible for members to accumulate all the stock they wished, the change in earnings rendering the stock unattractive to the public

It is my experience that few statements made by specialists can be taken at face value. For instance, Bill Meehan, the specialist in Ford, commenting on the May, 1962, break in the market had this to say about charts:

> Not that I am any student of charts, but I took a look at the Ford chart and it looked very dangerous to me . . . I liquidated our whole position and went short and we have maintained a short position, actually in only three of our stocks, all the way through, practically, during this whole period. During the day, we have become long, but almost every night, we were short stock.[5]

Implicit in the statement that "almost every night we were short stock" is the acknowledgment by Meehan that there was enough public demand for his stock to make it possible for him not only to sell the stock he had gone long on during the day but to further add to this selling by also selling short. As head of the Special Study group, Ralph Saul had failed to note that, from its May high to its June low, the price of Ford stock had dropped more than 30 per cent or that if this specialist was short stock, such short selling could have served to: (1) further depress the price of Ford stock, (2) make it profitable for Meehan to open Ford on the downside, (3) create a condition in which, by opening the stock lower in order to cover a short position, he could then claim to have stabilized as he cleaned out his book of any limit orders added to his long position and then, as prices advanced and public demand for Ford entered the market, controlled the advance by again selling short.

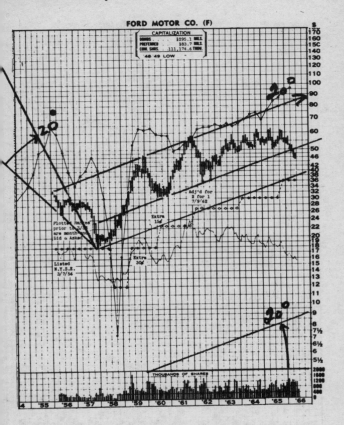

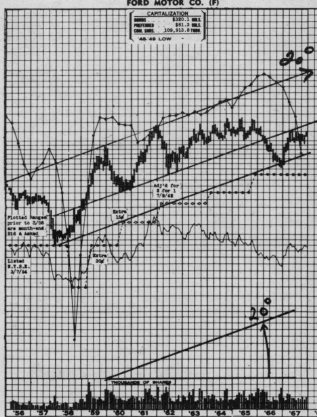

FORD MOTOR CO. (F)

Equally interesting is this specialist's assertion that he is not a "student of charts." He was nevertheless willing to make a multimillion-dollar decision to sell on the basis of a chart he didn't understand!

With unusual insight Ferdinand Lundberg asserted:

> It is true that all the persons to whom I refer [the public—R.N.] have their compensation determined by a market. The elite, however, do not have their revenues impersonally determined by a market, to the dictates of which they submit. They make market rules pretty much to suit their inclinations.[6]

And whether we see it as comedy, tragedy, or farce, that's the way it is. One way of establishing an index by which to evaluate the market rules is to examine the validity of the essential angle we extracted from the decline pattern in Ford stock at its 1957–1958 low.

NOTES

[1] William L. Jiler's *How Charts Can Help You in the Stock Market* (New York: Trendline, Standard & Poor) is easy to understand and deals effectively with the basic principles and problems of chart analysis. His theories differ from my own in that I do not believe charting can be adequately considered without reference to the larger context of specialist controls. Consideration is being given to this evaluative concept in a book on charting techniques I am now preparing. The tentative title for this book is *Charting Techniques for the Appraisal of Specialist Behavior*. For the purposes of the present book, a presentation of the elementary evaluative procedures and principles will serve.

[2] Securities Research Company quarterly edition charts are recommended for angle determination.

[3] The charts in this chapter and the next are reproduced by courtesy of Securities Research Co., 208 Newbury Street, Boston Mass. 02116, and Trendline, Inc., 345 Hudson Street, New York N.Y. 10014.

[4] A blow-off is the climax stage of a stock's development. It occurs long after the floor's virtuosities of deception have enabled members to complete their accumulations. In the course of a blow-off, prices break above existing resistance levels, signaling that the bull raid on the stock's price structure has entered its final phase and that as far as that stock is concerned, the floor like a circus, is about to pack up and move away.

[5] SSR, Part 2, p. 113.

[6] *The Rich and the Super Rich*, p. 278.

New Concepts for
Portfolio Evaluation

**It's impossible to tell where what is legal ends
and where justice begins.**

Preceding chapters have attempted to answer the question: "Why do most investors lose money in the stock market?" The answer pointed to the specialist system and a regulatory bureaucracy that knows what it ought to do but doesn't want to do it. We must now approach the question, "What must investors do to survive in the market?"

A substantial body of literature exists that attempts to answer this question. The fundamental limitation of most of it is that its thinking is sterile. It has been castrated by the Stock Exchanges. Its authors believed themselves to be pragmatists, yet their beliefs have done nothing to change the course of events.

Then there are investors, I'm told, who always buy at the bottom and sell at the top. They can be proud of their acumen—not so much because they know when to buy as because their ability to consistently sell at the top implies an ability to observe and pass judgment on the Exchange's carefully disguised objectives. The ability to

301

make such valid judgments, to employ procedures and criteria that not only define the timing and duration of distribution but identify its content, is rare indeed. If such investors exist, I've never met them.

In order to understand why I say this, all one need do is remember a little of what has been said in earlier chapters. Because the market's processes have been obscured, it is impossible for an investor to make consistently valid investment decisions or to employ the procedures that might identify the market's critical areas for him.

It is much easier for him to snap at the lures the Exchanges place before him.

He wants to *think* in a new way but he *feels* in the old way; thus, while he knows that earnings announcements and rumors are part of the ritual the Exchange uses to exploit him, all he need hear is that the XYZ company, whose stock has suffered a severe decline while its earnings rose, has just announced a 50 per cent decline in earnings. This is enough to depress him. Despite his intention to think in the new way, he identifies with the earnings announcement; it arouses old feelings, excites old thoughts. He forgets his intention to think in the new way, and he sells his stock. Almost immediately its price rises. He thought in the old way because the Exchange had conditioned him to do so.

The individual's early experiences as an investor and the responses he's been encouraged to make tend to determine his future development as an investor. For this reason he needs help. Ideally, he should be able to get it from his financial adviser, but it is more likely than not his financial adviser's thinking is notably inferior to that of the men with whom he is in competition—the Stock Exchange members who determine the direction of the market. His thinking is worse because he identifies with the Exchange hierarchy—right down to the lowly broker. He's concerned about their opinions and their attitudes toward him. He's anxious to advance in the investment industry, and so he has no higher loyalty than to its leaders. Thus the investor has conditioned himself to say and do nothing that might be construed as "biting the hand that feeds him."

What is required of the investor is a personal effort beyond the ordinary—beyond what others are doing to achieve their investment goals. Most investors are unsuccessful because they refuse to do anything unpleasant. They set themselves tasks and then attempt to solve them in the easiest possible way. Afraid to do anything on their own, they follow the crowd. Thus, they are unable to go beyond the ordinary aims, efforts, and goals laid down for them by others—most of whom have had their goals laid down for them by the Stock Exchanges. Like love at first sight, the Exchange is one of the greatest labor-saving machines ever invented.

But if investment is to be coherent and confident there must be an understanding of what properly constitutes a framework of principles that can motivate and safely guide the investor through the market's crises—so that, in the words of Confucius, one can follow what the heart desires without transgressing what is right.

To a considerable extent, the function of the following principles, and indeed of all security analysis, is to assist the investor in recognizing undervalued stocks and to provide the intellectual instruments that will tell him when these stocks should be sold.

Fashions in stocks and bonds and the percentages of each that one is advised to include in a portfolio are continuously changing. While it might be supposed that there was a point at which agreement could be reached, experience shows there is not. Nor is there likely to be, when opinions are dictated for the most part by brokers who have large inventories of shares on their shelves that they must get rid of in one way or another.

For example, Merrill Lynch is, in almost every way but one, a typical brokerage firm. Because of its size, however, the rumor of its power and, therefore, its wisdom, has become legendary. There is the instinct to capitalize on this. Thus, through 1969 Merrill Lynch has been waging a highly successful campaign to interest its one-and-a-half million customers and all others on the lookout for a new broker in the merits of convertibles. Many who read their full-page ads are either ill-informed, feeble, or too trusting. Without an adequate comprehension of the limitations inherent in these issues they will be persuaded that such knowledge is esoteric and reserved for the wise few—among whom they count Merrill Lynch. The re-education of the public from common stock to convertibles is a simple matter. True, Merrill Lynch was honest enough to state that "if the price of the common rises, the value of your conversion rights go up. So your convertible security is likely to go up too. And vice versa." What Merrill Lynch neglected to say anywhere in the ad was that, although the convertible is likely to go up with the common, in a down market it can most assuredly drop in percentage more than twice as much as the common.

Since convertibles are finding their way into the public's portfolios in increasing numbers it is worth spending a few moments on them. They are what might be called special debt contracts of a company. For the most part they are generated by public sale through a brokerage house, which can then arrange for competitive bids for the bonds from a number of brokerage houses—the bonds being awarded to the highest bidder. Sometimes what is known as a direct placement is negotiated with an insurance company or a large brokerage house. The broker then touts the convertible as a highly safe "senior security" and says that in the event of a liquidation the holder of the convertible would be paid off first. It's pointed out that convertibles are negotiable bearer instruments that are usually sold in units of $1,000 and that they give the investor a long-term call on the common shares of the company, since they can be converted into a specified number of shares of the common before the date specified on the bond. Emphasis is also placed on the low margin requirements of convertibles, but the interest one must pay on them at the bank is carefully passed over. Yet, compare this interest to the interest you can obtain at the bank on your savings; consider at the same time the amount that should be made on the convertible to make the assumption of its risk worthwhile. At today's interest rates, the investor has to make a minimum of 25 per cent on his convertibles to make them a worthwhile investment. All of which brings us to a rule concerning such issues that is sanctioned by time and experience: if the common stock is attractive there is no need to purchase anything else. It may be to a company's advantage to issue convertibles instead of common. They will then gild the convertible to make it seem as attractive as possible in order to attract the unsuspecting public. On the other hand, it may be that the common is held in disfavor by the public. In that case more common can't be sold and so the company sweetens the poison by offering the common disguised as a convertible —and possessing far greater risks on the downside than the common. Thus we have two points of view toward these issues, both of which, unreservedly, dispose of their value. Certainly, nonprofessionals should not assume the risks inherent in such issues.

Instead, the nonprofessional should follow the lead of big money as it pursues a steady dime in preference to the seldom dollar. Another advantage of the common is that it is listed. Although the Exchange has seen to it that many of its big-block transactions are not printed on the tape, and therefore not recorded in the daily volume figures, the figures for common stocks are better than for other issues—and they can be charted. However, it is extraordinarily difficult to arrive at reliable knowledge about when stocks can be bought, with a minimum of risk, with standard charting techniques. This is not surprising, for there are hundreds of thousands of chartists, and as was noted above, their responses to buy and sell signals are predictable—and profitable, but the profits are not the chartists'. Techniques are therefore required that supplement the more conventional methods of charting and that make it possible to elude the widespread kind of application. This is obtained by employing the system organized on the premises outlined in the previous chapter. The specialist's insights are subtle and, what is even more important, they are outside the scope of the ordinary chartist's awareness and therefore engage the attention of relatively few persons. For this reason it is now suggested that the system I have described be considered as a new tool for encouraging the preservation and growth of capital in the stock market.

Assuming the specialist knows we are aware of his operation and purpose, what are his alternatives? Let us begin with a consideration of the Ford chart that engaged our attention in the previous chapter. Projecting our uptrend angle lines of 20 degrees on a July, 1969, Securities Research Company chart (and adding one bar to show the decline to the 42 level in July), and three downtrend angle lines of 20 degrees from the highs of 1960, 1962, and 1965, we have a chart of Ford (p. 307) that tells us a number of things.

1. Three major declines occurred in Ford—in 1960, 1962, and 1966. From the stock's high the approximate percentages of these declines were 36, 38, and 38 respectively. An equivalent decline of 36 per cent from Ford's 1968 high would carry the price down to approximately 38, a 38 per cent decline to approximately 37. The pos-

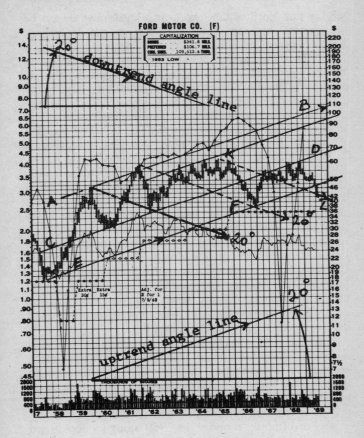

sibility that Ford could drop to this level must always be recognized. Investors tend to place on the specialist's book a great many stop orders just under 40.

2. These limit orders could quite possibly be employed by this specialist (by "cleaning up his book") to cover the shares he may have had to sell short to supply the demand for his stock in July and August.[1]

3. What had taken place in this stock in the past made it seem that a downside penetration in 1969 of the line *EF* on the long-term yearly chart was almost inevitable.

It's significant that after the 1962 bottom made it possible to draw the typical uptrend line (*CD*) many chartists were unreserved in the opinion that *CD* would act as a major support level for the price structure and, indeed, that purchases should be made once prices touched this line. Thus, when the stock's price structure went down to this level, chartists took the bait only to then see the line *CD* penetrated on the downside (in early 1966). Chartists found themselves in similar straits with line *EF* in 1969—the price structure penetrated *EF* when, having tested this line successfully twice in the past, chartists felt secure in the knowledge that it would perform on its third test—only to see the third attempt fail.

Chartists who came to the jarring realization that their techniques have little or no authority in the market often reacted by dismissing all charting. However there is no question but that the principles outlined in the last chapter are behind and underneath the market's machinery and in touch with the major forces at work.

4. Ford found "support" in 1969 along its downtrend line as it had in 1962 and 1966. The fact that these downtrend lines derive from the basic angles extracted from the Ford decline pattern (see the previous chapter) is witness to the fact that there has been no attempt to impose our casual prejudices on the reader. Rather it insists that our principle is in complete harmony with

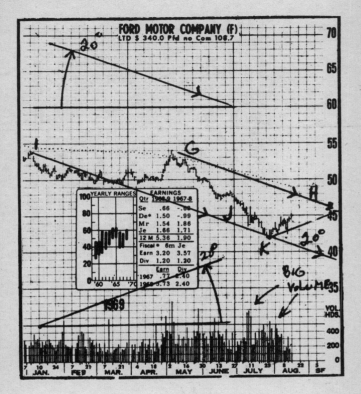

FORD MOTOR COMPANY (F)
LTD $ 340.0 Pfd no Com 108.7

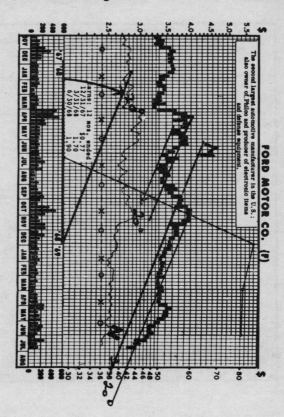

the specialist's rituals and can be employed to provide advance warning of them. Take, for example, the weekly and monthly charts of Ford.

5. A close relationship can be seen to exist between the three downtrend lines on our long-term chart of Ford and the downtrend lines on our weekly and monthly charts. The specialist's allegiance to this 20-degree angle seems to dominate no matter what agitations, economic or otherwise, one has been led to believe should influence the conduct of his affairs. It becomes clear, therefore, that we can make viable investment decisions by using their buy signals as our point of departure. For example, a buy signal showed up on the long-term chart when the Ford price structure dropped to this downtrend line in July, 1969, at 42. The 20-degree downtrend line (*II*) on the trendline weekly chart from the January high also signaled a buy in Ford when the price level touched this line during the last month in July. There is, therefore, between the long-term and the weekly chart, what might be described as a pathological coherence.

6. The specialist system and its processes must never be taken for granted. One must always anticipate the possibility of a specialist trap—a retracement of the price structure once it touches the line *GH,* another specialist "control" line. The possibility that such a retracement might occur is also suggested by the monthly Ford chart. Note that the downtrend line has not yet touched our line *MN.* Until it does, the possibility looms large that such a retracement will take place. The decision to buy Ford will depend on the basis of the signal provided first by the long-term chart and then by the weekly (and the long-term) chart. However, since their buy signals are not confirmed by the monthly chart this decision must be made with the possibility in mind of selling out if the price of Ford does not penetrate the line *GH* (on the monthly chart) on the upside to the accompaniment of

important volume or if at any time after this upside penetration, the price structure penetrates our uptrend line of 20 degrees advance by moving to the right of this line. No matter how unlikely it may seem, one must not forget the benefits to the specialist of a move under 40. Knowing his plans for the stock and that such a downside penetration of 40 could be as much as two or more months distant, the specialist is able to be patient. The investor can do no less, therefore, than anticipate this possibility. Should it occur he is ready for it. If it doesn't, he is protected by his purchase of Ford at the 42 level. (It attacked and failed to penetrate the line *GH* the last week of August.) Looked at in the light of subsequent events, the principles elaborated cannot be overrated. The investment decision was made under the focus supplied by our 20-degree angle's microscope—the weekly Trendline chart.

Taking two steps backward from these charts and glancing at them impartially we see that our angles, uptrend and downtrend lines, affect every investor. Practically speaking, they are the prime mover of the specialist system. The following rules, which supplement them, reflect the distrust and dread in which we hold the specialist. They can serve as guides to help investors through the specialists' jungle, culture, and climate:

1. Buy only the common stock of companies that are second or third in their respective fields. Their further growth will provide specialists with a built-in alibi for the bull raids they will conduct in the shares of these companies. Most of these bull raids will occur before the company's potential is publicized in terms of earnings or sales announcements. For this reason they are important candidates for the specialists' segregated tax accounts. Look for signs of big-block accumulations, therefore, in such stocks. There are several ways to pinpoint the best time to purchase these shares.

a. In conjunction with our other measuring instruments, look for them among companies that have had a spate of bad earnings—earnings that have been employed by specialists to rationalize a major drop in the stock's price. Concentrate on these "bargains" as they go through a period of unpopularity and indifference. They are patently worth considerably more than they are selling for.

b. A declining DJIA has a special charm for specialists. It allows them to take down the prices of stocks. In the course of an overall market decline, therefore, look for the shares of good secondary companies that have also been taken down, and as specialists acquire them for their segregated accounts, acquire them for yours. The advice that a sound portfolio should have only "quality stocks" is a valueless bromide.

2. Nothing puzzles me more than an investor's willingness to pay more than fifty dollars a share for stocks. Buy low-priced stocks. It's percentages you're after and you'll get them in these stocks in a bull market.

3. Unless you are highly skilled in the use of the analysts' evaluative tools, invest only in stocks listed on the New York Stock Exchange. The absence of significant institutional participation on the Amex makes it possible for specialists to conduct bull raids that can peak out in an hour's time. On the other hand, because of a stock's larger capitalization (number of shares outstanding) and the larger quantity of institutional sales taking place on the NYSE, these stocks tend to give the investor advance warning of distribution as institutions begin their selling near and at a stock's high. For the rest, the NYSE and the Amex are two specialist systems separated only by different opportunities.

4. Hold your broker responsible for telling you when big-block secondary offerings are about to take place in your stocks and then, as soon as possible, sell. You are better off in stocks for which the public still has some

appetite. Once demand for a stock peters out, it's ready to go down. For this reason secondaries and stock splits tend to occur most frequently at or near a stock's high. Most brokers will try to sell you into a secondary for the sake of the bonus. Most brokers have their hand in your pocket and their faith placed firmly in your ignorance.

5. Restrict purchases to stocks that have declined at least 35 to 50 per cent from their highs. In other words do *not* wait to buy until stocks are making new highs and attracting public attention. As a general rule, these highs tend to make their appearance after the halfway mark in a bull market—just when you should begin thinking of initiating your sales. On the other hand, buying a good secondary stock that has declined 50 per cent or more from its highs can cover a multitude of blunders.

6. The rule, "Cut your losses and let your profits ride," was invented by a broker. Follow it, and if you solve one problem you'll create ten more. You may have to sell sooner, but a good rule is to set an objective of 50 per cent on your investment. After that point has been reached you may have very little more to gain and much to lose. Too, much of the value you insisted on initially has evaporated. Find another situation that meets your initial requirements for purchase. For some strange reason investors want to see the stock they sell decline immediately thereafter. In any other field of endeavor when someone buys something from you you hope he'll be happy with his purchase. The test of an investor's breeding is the amount of return he demands on an investment. It is a species of unconscious autobiography.

7. The average investor is below the 30 per cent tax bracket. It is therefore absurd for him to feel he should wait for six months and a day before selling his stock. As for the investor who is in a top bracket and who listens to his accountant telling him not to take short-term gains—no matter the bracket—a short-term gain is better than a long-term loss.

8. Own your stock. Worry is the extra interest you pay when you buy stock on margin.

9. Do not sell short.

10. Do not allow your stock to be borrowed.

11. Credit balances should be immediately transferred to your bank.

12. Do not leave your stock with your broker in street name. It is in his power to vote this stock as the owner of record that gives the NYSE its power over the nation's political-industrial-military complex.

13. Invest only in growth-oriented rather than income stocks. If income is your objective, you belong in a bank; in a bank you can receive higher yields with no risk.

14. Four to five stocks are enough for a portfolio. If you know what you're doing you need no more. If you don't know you shouldn't be in the stock market.

15. Make arrangements with your bank to accept delivery of your stock from your broker against payment. Bank fees for this are nominal, and you will obtain faster delivery of your shares.

16. If there has been a major advance from June-July lows, look for nonmember sales for long-term capital gains purposes in December and the first weeks in January. Institutional sales will anticipate this and selling will begin in November and early December. In consequence, this, as a rule, is the best time to liquidate portfolios, since prices tend to be supported during this period. Prices aren't supported when nonmembers begin their selling, which is always postponed to the last minute in the hope of higher prices.

17. Heed the appearance of big blocks on the ticker tape after an important run up in prices. The specialist's trading account can sell stock short for a week, and subsequently his trading account can then purchase one of his segregated accounts. It is these shares that you may be seeing tumbling across the ticker tape in big blocks as

the specialist delivers them to his trading account. If so they signal an imminent decline in that stock. It is not unusual for the specialist to have two or more such segregated accounts maturing at different periods; this is one of the reasons behind a double or triple top in a stock. Often such tops will reflect double or triple bottoms. In this connection, there is nothing so well adapted to the specialist's purposes as to have the financial press publish the statement, "Brokers say it appears the market will test its bottom." The inevitable drop then takes place —and specialists acquire their second batch of stocks for their segregated accounts—with the approval of the entire investment community.

18. Look for bull raids in May. Specialists often want to unload stock during this month that they acquired from investors who had to sell at April lows for tax purposes.

19. A wise investor has this in common with a beautiful woman: neither ever surrenders by appointment. Therefore, do not enter stop or limit orders on the specialist's book.

20. When considering a stock for purchase, learn the name of the specialist listed in it (consult the appendix here) to determine the names of his other specialty stocks. If any of these are on the most active list as the stocks are making new lows, then it is possible that he will soon be committing his capital to one of these stocks. Unless a stock appears to have this kind of personal sponsorship (for his own account), it does not belong in your portfolio. Then too, it may be about to acquire this sponsorship. Look carefully then to see if any of his other stocks are being distributed or have just been distributed. If so, he may soon be transferring his credit resources from one group of stocks to another. Look for activity at such times in his inactive stocks. When his segregated accounts have been filled, shorts will be

"squeezed" and prices will leap forward. Advancing prices will add to further panic short covering and a further advance in prices. Prices often tend to retrace about 50 per cent after such nonmember short covering, since specialists tend to supply this stock by selling short. Prices then decline so that specialists can cover their short sales profitably. Specialists share Willie Sutton's sentiments: "It's a rather pleasant experience to be alone in a bank at night." [2]

21. Try to buy the stocks with the largest major and minor angles in their long-term decline patterns. These tend to offer the best prospects for specialist bull raids. Follow the specialist's footprints. Follow them far enough and they will always lead to conclusions that are contrary to reason but highly profitable.

The premise that portfolio evaluations *must* be conducted along the lines elaborated in this chapter is a major departure from the norms established by the Stock Exchanges. It is a premise that will be difficult for the average investor to accept. But then, the uninformed are always the most faithful.

A revolution in economics and in portfolio evaluation now turns upon the fact that the specialist system's hidden control of the stockmarket is no longer possible. Reason has entered the field. Now we possess the one thing that can protect us as we skate over the market's thin ice—an understanding of its cold realities. Now we can approach it without fear. We can even exploit it before it exploits us.

NOTES

---

[1] The Special Study Report (Part 2, pp. 144–45) cites a similar incident: "One incident from the floor department files shows that a specialist opened a stock 9 percent below the previous close so that he could eliminate a possible difficult situation. Before the opening of Erie Railroad on March 9, 1960, the specialist had public market orders to buy totaling 1,100 shares and public market orders to sell also totaling 1,100 shares; the stock had closed the night before at 9⅝. Although this exact 'pair-off' indicated that the public demand and supply were in balance, the specialist opened the stock at 8¾, down ⅞.[325] On the specialist's book was a stop order to sell at 8¾ for 1,200 shares, which was executed when the stock opened at that price and was purchased by the specialist. The specialist subsequently stated that there was also a limit order to sell, which had already been reduced in price and which he was afraid would be further reduced, placing him in a difficult situation. In light of this limit order on his book, the specialist deliberately opened the stock down 9 percent to enable him to 'clear up the stop order.' Had the limit order been reduced and the stop order not been 'cleared up,' the specialist might have had to purchase the stock represented by the stop order and the limit order at the same time, thus committing more of his capital than he wished—he already had an inventory of 2,000 shares. Before the specialist opened the stock, he obtained approval from a governor. The governor later stated that he misunderstood the facts. Be that as it may, the customer whose stop order was entrusted to the specialist would have been surprised to learn that the order he entered as his protection against a price decline had itself caused a price decline, and was executed only because the specialist was protecting himself.[326]

"As a result of a member firm complaint, the floor department made an inquiry into the situation. The vice chairman informed the specialist that he had used extremely 'poor judgment' and that he should have opened the stock at a price higher than 8¾. Vanderbeck testified as follows about this case:

Q. Is this an approved practice of the Exchange to open a stock down seven-eighths where this is an exact pair off?
A. [The specialist] was wrong in his judgment and he was so informed.
Q. Was any disciplinary action taken against [him]?
A. He was spoken to about this.

Q. Is this considered a disciplinary action?

A. No.

Q. Was he told to make an adjustment in price?

A. No, because it was a matter of judgment on his part with respect to the price.

"Other situations become quite complex and involve conflicts not only between the specialist and his customers but also possibly among customers.

"[325] After the opening, which was the low for the day, the price rose and by the end of the day was above the previous day's close.

"[326] Another example from Exchange files discloses that a specialist dropped the price of a stock 2½ points to pick up a 300-share stop order."

[2] In Quentin Reynolds, *I, Willie Sutton: The Personal Story of the Most Daring Bank Robber and Jail Breaker of Our Time*, New York: Farrar, 1953.

Stock Symbols and Specialists

There are a number of publications, including the *World Almanac,* that list stock symbols and what they stand for. I believe it is of interest to see which specialist units handle the different stocks.

Symbol	Post	
—A—		
A	4	BLAIR S. WILLIAMS & CO.
AA	3	ASIEL & CO., GENGLER BROS.
AAC	21	SPRAGUE & NAMMACK
AAD	8	C. V. GIANNI & CO., GILLEN & CO.
AAE	5	WEIL & DUFFY
AAE PR	5	WEIL & DUFFY
AAF	19	BENTON & CO.
AAS	1	COROON & CO., SIMON B. BLUMENTHAL, SHASKAN & CO., INC.
AB	22	SILVER, BARRY & VAN RAALTE

This list is from the New York Stock Exchange publication, *Stocks and Specialists,* August 15, 1969.

Symbol	Post	
ABA	14	CREEM & CREEM
ABC	17	WILLIAMS, EISELE & CO.
ABG	12	ARDEN & GITTERMAN, F. L. SALOMON & CO.
ABJ	5	WEIL & DUFFY
ABN	4	BLAIR S. WILLIAMS & CO.
ABT	3	H. L. GOLDBERG & CO.
ABW	18	J. W. TOOMEY & CO., VAUGHAN & CO., WRAGE & CO.
AC	6	LIEF, FOSTER, WERLE & CO.
AC PR	6	LIEF, FOSTER, WERLE & CO.
ACD	7	PICOLI & CO.
ACF	22	KINGSLEY, BOYE & SOUTHWOOD
ACI	22	KINGSLEY, BOYE & SOUTHWOOD
ACK	4	THOMAS F. FAGAN & CO.
*ACK PR	30	R. S. DODGE & CO., KERN SECURITIES CORP.
ACN	6	LIEF, FOSTER, WERLE & CO.
ACR	2	P. V. HALL & CO.
ACS	11	MARCUS & CO., TRAVERS & HUME, JEWETT, NEWMAN & CO.
*ACS PR	30	R. S. DODGE & CO., KERN SECURITIES CORP.
ACV	1	BENJAMIN JACOBSON & SONS
ACY	11	MARCUS & CO.
AD	12	M. J. MEEHAN & CO.
ADC	8	SPEAR, LEEDS & KELLOGG
ADL	4	BLAIR S. WILLIAMS & CO.
ADM	4	GAINES, REIS & CO.
ADP	2	J. J. CONKLIN & CO.
ADP PR	2	J. J. CONKLIN & CO.
ADS	8	SPEAR, LEEDS & KELLOGG
ADV	8	SPEAR, LEEDS & KELLOGG

* Ten Share Unit Stocks

Symbol	Post	
ADV PR	8	SPEAR, LEEDS & KELLOGG
ADX	9	ERNST & CO., WARE & KEELIPS, HOMANS & CO.
AEP	11	MARCUS & CO., TRAVERS & HUME
AET	3	ASIEL & CO., GENGLER BROS.
AET PR WI	3	ASIEL & CO., GENGLER BROS.
AEX	18	MURRAY & CO.
*AEX PR	30	R. S. DODGE & CO., KERN SECURITIES CORP.
AFI	15	LA BRANCHE & CO.
AFI PR A	15	LA BRANCHE & CO.
*AFI PR B	30	R. S. DODGE & CO., KERN SECURITIES CORP.
AFI PR C	15	LA BRANCHE & CO.
AG	4	GAINES, REIS & CO.
AG PR	4	GAINES, REIS & CO.
AGA	6	LIEF, FOSTER, WERLE & CO.
AGC	5	JEFFERSON MARCUS & CO., IRWIN SCHLOSS & CO.
AGC PR	5	JEFFERSON MARCUS & CO., IRWIN SCHLOSS & CO.
AGG	15	LA BRANCHE & CO.
AGM	8	SPEAR, LEEDS & KELLOGG
AH	2	CUNNIFF, ROMAINE, LAMM & STOUTENBURGH
AHO	1	MURPHY & CO.
AHP	14	STERN & KENNEDY
AHP PR	14	STERN & KENNEDY
AHS	8	C. V. GIANNI & CO., GILLEN & CO.
AIC	3	H. L. GOLDBERG & CO.
AII	17	FREIDAY & CO.
AIN	7	MALTZ, GREENWALD & CO.
AJ	5	JEFFERSON H. MARCUS & CO., INC., IRWIN SCHLOSS & CO., INC.

---

* Ten Share Unit Stocks

Symbol	Post	
AL	20	MURPHEY, MARSEILLES & SMITH
ALL	14	FAGENSON & FRANKEL CO., INC., J. STREICHER & CO.
ALM	10	HAUPT, MEFFERT, ANDREWS & HUG
ALS	20	MURPHEY, MARSEILLES & SMITH
*ALS PR	30	R. S. DODGE & CO., KERN SECURITIES CORP.
AM PR	13	ADLER, COLEMAN & CO.
AMA	8	SPEAR, LEEDS & KELLOGG
AME	7	E. H. STERN & CO.
AMF	22	KINGSLEY, BOYE & SOUTHWOOD
AMK	18	MURRAY & CO.
AMK PR A	18	MURRAY & CO.
AMO	10	BEAUCHAMP & CO.
AMP	22	KINGSLEY, BOYE & SOUTHWOOD
AMR	8	SPEAR, LEEDS & KELLOGG
AMT	15	JOHN E. BARRETT & CO., INC.
AMX	17	WILLIAMS, EISELE & CO.
AMX PR CL	17	WILLIAMS, EISELE & CO.
AMZ	12	ARDEN & GITTERMAN, F. L. SALOMON & CO.
AN	22	ALBERT FRIED & CO.
ANC	10	CYRIL DE CORDOVA & BRO.
ANG	6	STOKES, HOYT & CO.
ANK	12	ARDEN & GITTERMAN, F. L. SALOMON & CO.
AOG	22	STERN BROS.
AOL	21	SPRAGUE & NAMMACK
APA	21	J. F. NICK & CO.
APC	9	S. M. PECK & CO., CARL H. PFORZHEIMER & CO.

* Ten Share Unit Stocks

Symbol	Post	
APD	9	S. M. PECK & CO., CARL H. PFORZHEIMER & CO.
APD PR	9	S. M. PECK & CO., CARL H. PFORZHEIMER & CO.
APX	8	SPEAR, LEEDS & KELLOGG
APY	8	SPEAR, LEEDS & KELLOGG
AQM	13	ROBB, PECK, McCOOEY & CO.
AR	20	MURPHEY, MARSEILLES & SMITH
ARA	16	PHELAN & CO.
ARC	12	M. J. MEEHAN & CO.
ARD	12	ARDEN & GITTERMAN, F. L. SALOMON & CO.
ARH	8	SPEAR, LEEDS & KELLOGG
ARM	5	WEIL & DUFFY
ARO	18	J. W. TOOMEY & CO., VAUGHAN & CO., WRAGE & CO.
ARV	14	CREEM & CREEM
AS	17	COWEN & CO., F. H. SACKEN & CO.
ASA	20	HIRSHON, ROTH & CO.
ASC	15	LA BRANCHE & CO.
ASH	22	ALBERT FRIED & CO.
ASH PR	22	ALBERT FRIED & CO.
ASN	8	SPEAR, LEEDS & KELLOGG
ASR	11	LAURO & CO.
ASR PR	11	LAURO & CO.
ASR PR A	11	LAURO & CO.
AST	11	MARCUS & CO., TRAVERS & HUME
AST PR A	11	MARCUS & CO., TRAVERS & HUME
ASU	17	M. E. GOLDSTEIN & CO., WISNER & DE CLAIRVILLE
ASZ	6	H. L. KIMBALL & CO.
AT	13	ADLER, COLEMAN & CO.

Symbol	Post	
ATE	5	JOHNSTON & LUNGER
*ATE PR	30	R. S. DODGE & CO., KERN SECURITIES CORP.
ATE PR B	5	JOHNSTON & LUNGER
ATI	10	BEAUCHAMP & CO.
ATO	9	S. M. PECK & CO., CARL H. PFORZHEIMER & CO.
ATP	1	MURPHY & CO.
ATS	15	BENTON, CORCORAN, LEIB & CO.
AUR	1	SOMERS, SCHAFER & COLLINS
AV	9	S. M. PECK & CO., CARL H. PFORZHEIMER & CO.
AV PR	9	S. M. PECK & CO., CARL H. PFORZHEIMER & CO.
AVP	13	ADLER, COLEMAN & CO.
AVT	21	SPRAGUE & NAMMACK
AVT PR	21	SPRAGUE & NAMMACK
AVT PR C	21	SPRAGUE & NAMMACK
AVY	9	ERNST & CO., WARE & KEELIPS, HOMANS & CO.
AWK	1	MACKEY, SHEA & WINTER
*AWK PR A	30	R. S. DODGE & CO., KERN SECURITIES CORP.
*AWK PR B	30	R. S. DODGE & CO., KERN SECURITIES CORP.
*AWK PR C	30	R. S. DODGE & CO., KERN SECURITIES CORP.
AYL	10	HAUPT, MEFFERT, ANDREWS & HUG
AYP	1	MACKEY, SHEA & WINTER
AZ	4	THOMAS F. FAGAN & CO.
*AZ PR	30	R. S. DODGE & CO., KERN SECURITIES CORP.
AZP	14	CREEM & CREEM

---

* Ten Share Unit Stocks

Symbol	Post	
—B—		
BA	8	SPEAR, LEEDS & KELLOGG
BAI	12	ARDEN & GITTERMAN, F. L. SALOMON & CO.
*BAI PR	12	ARDEN & GITTERMAN, F. L. SALOMON & CO.
BAT	4	GAINES, REIS & CO.
BAW	16	PHELAN & CO.
BAX	2	P. V. HALL & CO.
BBK	18	HENDERSON BROTHERS, INC.
BBL	3	ASIEL & CO., GENGLER BROS.
BBL PR	3	ASIEL & CO., GENGLER BROS.
BBO	1	SOMERS, SCHAFER & COLLINS
BC	13	ADLER, COLEMAN & CO.
BCC	13	ADLER, COLEMAN & CO.
*BCH	30	R. S. DODGE & CO., KERN SECURITIES CORP.
BCR	1	MURPHY & CO.
BCX	10	LAURO & CO., C. B. RICHARD, ELLIS & CO.
BDC	4	THOMAS F. FAGAN & CO.
BDK	8	SPEAR, LEEDS & KELLOGG
BDX	20	HIRSHON, ROTH & CO.
BE	18	HENDERSON BROTHERS, INC.
BEC	20	BREGMAN & CO.
BER	3	H. L. GOLDBERG & CO.
BF	9	S. M. PECK & CO. CARL H. PFORZHEIMER & CO.
*BF PR	30	R. S. DODGE & CO., KERN SECURITIES CORP.
BFC	8	SPEAR, LEEDS & KELLOGG
BGE	17	COWEN & CO., F. H. SACKEN & CO.
*BGE PR B	30	R. S. DODGE & CO., KERN SECURITIES CORP.

* Ten Share Unit Stocks

Symbol	Post	
*BGE PR C	30	R. S. DODGE & CO., KERN SECURITIES CORP.
BGG	9	S. M. PECK & CO., CARL H. PFORZHEIMER & CO.
BGH	5	JEFFERSON H. MARCUS & CO., INC., IRWIN SCHLOSS & CO., INC.
BGT	20	BREGMAN & CO.
BHM	6	H. L. KIMBALL & CO.
BHW	20	BREGMAN & CO.
BHY	13	ROBB, PECK, McCOOEY & CO.
BI	10	HAUPT, MEFFERT, ANDREWS & HUG
BIG	10	HAUPT, MEFFERT, ANDREWS & HUG
BIW	15	BENTON, CORCORAN, LEIB & CO.
BIW PR A	15	BENTON, CORCORAN, LEIB & CO.
BJ	10	LENART, McHUGH & CO.
BKO	9	ERNST & CO., WARE & KEELIPS, HOMANS & CO.
BKY	19	FARRELL & CO., ALBERT ROTHENBERG, ROTHSCHILD & CO.
BLI	7	E. H. STERN & CO.
BLL	12	M. J. MEEHAN & CO.
BMA	22	KINGSLEY, BOYE & SOUTHWOOD
BMS	3	SHAW & ADRIAN
BMY	11	MARCUS & CO., TRAVERS & HUME, JEWETT, NEWMAN & CO.
BMY PR	11	MARCUS & CO., TRAVERS & HUME, JEWETT, NEWMAN & CO.

---

* Ten Share Unit Stocks

Symbol	Post	
BN	1	MACKEY, SHEA & WINTER
BND	11	LAURO & CO.
BNF	20	BREGMAN & CO.
BNK	4	EINHORN & CO.
BNK PR	4	EINHORN & CO.
BNK PR C	4	EINHORN & CO.
BNL	21	FOWLER & ROSENAU
*BNL PR A	30	R. S. DODGE & CO., KERN SECURITIES CORP.
BNL PR B	21	FOWLER & ROSENAU
BNL PR C	21	FOWLER & ROSENAU
*BNL PR V	30	R. S. DODGE & CO., KERN SECURITIES CORP.
BNS	1	BENJAMIN JACOBSON & SONS
BOK	20	MURPHEY, MARSEILLES & SMITH
BOL	18	J. W. TOOMEY & CO., VAUGHAN & CO., WRAGE & CO.
BOR	20	HIRSHON, ROTH & CO.
BOU	2	CUNNIFF, ROMAINE, LAMM & STOUTENBURGH
BPC	8	C. V. GIANNI & CO., GILLEN & CO.
BR	21	FOWLER & ROSENAU
BR PR	21	FOWLER & ROSENAU
BRD	5	WEIL & DUFFY
BRD PR A	5	WEIL & DUFFY
BRF	12	ARDEN & GITTERMAN, F. L. SALOMON & CO.
BRY	14	CREEM & CREEM
BRY PR A	14	CREEM & CREEM
BRY PR B	14	CREEM & CREEM
BS	11	MARCUS & CO., TRAVERS & HUME
BSC	6	H. L. KIMBALL & CO.
BSE	6	STOKES, HOYT & CO.

* Ten Share Unit Stocks

Symbol	Post	
BSH	19	WILCOX & CO.
BT	18	HENDERSON BROTHERS, INC.
BU	5	CHAUNCEY & CO.
BUG PR	30	R. S. DODGE & CO., KERN SECURITIES CORP.
BUR	7	PICOLI & CO.
BVA	12	ARDEN & GITTERMAN, F. L. SALOMON & CO.
BWN	4	GAINES, REIS & CO.
BWN PR	4	GAINES, REIS & CO.
BWS	19	FARRELL & CO., ALBERT ROTHENBERG, ROTHSCHILD & CO.
BX	18	HENDERSON BROTHERS, INC.
BX PR	18	HENDERSON BROTHERS, INC.
BY	15	JOHN E. BARRETT & CO., INC.
BYK	7	PICOLI & CO.

—C—

Symbol	Post	
C	2	ZUCKERMAN, SMITH & CO.
CAF	16	WAGNER, STOTT & CO.
CAF PR A	16	WAGNER, STOTT & CO.
CAL	4	GAINES, REIS & CO.
CAR	2	ZUCKERMAN, SMITH & CO.
CAX	12	ARDEN & GITTERMAN, F. L. SALOMON & CO.
CBE	7	E. H. STERN & CO.
CBE PR A	7	E. H. STERN & CO.
CBM	2	ZUCKERMAN, SMITH & CO.
CBO	13	ROBB, PECK, McCOOEY & CO.
CBS	17	FREIDAY & CO.
CBS PR	17	FREIDAY & CO.
CBT	4	GAINES, REIS & CO.
CCB	1	MACKEY, SHEA & WINTER
CCC	12	ARDEN & GITTERMAN, F. L. SALOMON & CO.

Symbol	Post	
CCC PR	30	R. S. DODGE & CO., KERN SECURITIES CORP.
CCF	22	KINGSLEY, BOYE & SOUTHWOOD
CCI	1	BENJAMIN JACOBSON & SON
CCI PR A	1	BENJAMIN JACOBSON & SON
CCK	11	MARCUS & CO.
CCK PR	11	MARCUS & CO.
CCL	16	WAGNER, STOTT & CO.
CCN	11	MARCUS & CO., TRAVERS & HUME, JEWETT, NEWMAN & CO.
CCN PR A	11	MARCUS & CO., TRAVERS & HUME, JEWETT, NEWMAN & CO.
CCN PR B	11	MARCUS & CO., TRAVERS & HUME, JEWETT, NEWMAN & CO.
CCP	8	COHEN, SIMONSON & REA, INC., ANDREWS, POSNER & ROTHSCHILD
CCX	17	M. E. GOLDSTEIN & CO., INC., WISNER & DE CLAIRVILLE
CCX PR	30	R. S. DODGE & CO., KERN SECURITIES CORP.
CDA	22	SILVER, BARRY & VAN RAALTE
CDA PR	30	R. S. DODGE & CO., KERN SECURITIES CORP.
CDD	16	ADOLPH SCHENKER & CO., KAUFMANN & CO.
CDP	2	CUNNIFF, ROMAINE, LAMM & STOUTENBURGH
CEA	14	FAGENSON & FRANKEL CO., INC., J. STREICHER & CO.
CEL	22	STERN BROS.
CER	15	BENTON, CORCORAN, LEIB & CO.

Symbol	Post	
*CER PR	30	R. S. DODGE & CO., KERN SECURITIES CORP.
CF	1	COROON & CO., SIMON B. BLUMENTHAL, SHASKAN & CO., INC.
CFD	14	SESKIS & WOHLSTETTER
CFD PR A	14	SESKIS & WOHLSTETTER
CFG	3	H. L. GOLDBERG & CO.
CFI	18	HENDERSON BROTHERS, INC.
CG	2	CUNNIFF, ROMAINE, LAMM & STOUTENBURGH
CGC	8	C. V. GIANNI & CO., GILLEN & CO.
CGE	5	JOHNSTON & LUNGER
CGG	10	HAUPT, MEFFERT, ANDREWS & HUG
CGI	13	ADLER, COLEMAN & CO.
CGP	17	M. E. GOLDSTEIN & CO., INC., WISNER & DE CLAIRVILLE
CGP PR A	17	M. E. GOLDSTEIN & CO., INC., WISNER & DE CLAIRVILLE
CGR	2	CUNNIFF, ROMAINE, LAMM & STOUTENBURGH
CH	3	H. L. GOLDBERG & CO.
CHC	10	CYRIL DE CORDOVA & BRO.
CHF	2	J. J. CONKLIN & CO.
CHI	1	COROON & CO., SHASKAN & CO., INC., SIMON B. BLUMENTHAL
CHL	19	BENTON & CO.
CHM	22	KINGSLEY, BOYE & SOUTHWOOD
CIC	5	WEIL & DUFFY
CIC PR A	5	WEIL & DUFFY
CIC PR B	5	WEIL & DUFFY
CID	2	J. J. CONKLIN & CO.
CIN	4	THOMAS F. FAGAN & CO.

* Ten Share Unit Stocks

Symbol	Post	
*CIN PR A	30	R. S. DODGE & CO., KERN SECURITIES CORP.
*CIN PR B	30	R. S. DODGE & CO., KERN SECURITIES CORP.
CIP	2	ZUCKERMAN, SMITH & CO.
CIT	14	CREEM & CREEM
CIT PR B	14	CREEM & CREEM
CJ	4	BLAIR S. WILLIAMS & CO.
CK	16	PHELAN & CO.
CKE	4	THOMAS F. FAGAN & CO.
CKL	7	E. H. STERN & CO.
CKO	7	E. H. STERN & CO.
CL	22	STERN BROS.
*CL PR	30	R. S. DODGE & CO., KERN SECURITIES CORP.
CLF	4	GAINES, REIS & CO.
CLL	20	MURPHEY, MARSEILLES & SMITH
CLL PR	20	MURPHEY, MARSEILLES & SMITH
CLU	2	CUNNIFF, ROMAINE, LAMM & STOUTENBURGH
CLU PR A	2	CUNNIFF, ROMAINE, LAMM & STOUTENBURGH
CLX	2	ZUCKERMAN, SMITH & CO.
CMB	16	WAGNER, STOTT & CO.
CMI	1	SOMERS, SCHAFER & COLLINS
CMN	18	J. W. TOOMEY & CO., VAUGHAN & CO., WRAGE & CO.
CMO	18	J. W. TOOMEY & CO., VAUGHAN & CO., WRAGE & CO.
CMR	17	DANIEL REEVES & CO.
CMS	16	PHELAN & CO.
*CMS PR A	30	R. S. DODGE & CO., KERN SECURITIES CORP.

* Ten Share Unit Stocks

Symbol	Post	
*CMS PR B	30	R. S. DODGE & CO., KERN SECURITIES CORP.
*CMS PR C	30	R. S. DODGE & CO., KERN SECURITIES CORP.
CMY	4	THOMAS F. FAGAN & CO.
CMZ	3	ASIEL & CO., GENGLER BROS.
CN	6	H. L. KIMBALL & CO.
CNB	13	ROBB, PECK, McCOOEY & CO.
CNC	19	BENTON & CO.
CNF	20	MURPHEY, MARSEILLES & SMITH
CNG	9	ERNST & CO., WARE & KEELIPS, HOMANS & CO.
CNH	17	WILLIAMS, EISELE & CO.
CNK	15	JOHN E. BARRETT & CO., INC.
*CNS	30	R. S. DODGE & CO., KERN SECURITIES CORP.
CNV	7	E. H. STERN & CO.
CNV PR A	7	E. H. STERN & CO.
CNV PR B	7	E. H. STERN & CO.
CO	20	MURPHEY, MARSEILLES & SMITH
COC	15	LA BRANCHE & CO.
COE	13	ADLER, COLEMAN & CO.
COS	19	FARRELL & CO., ALBERT ROTHENBERG, ROTHSCHILD & CO.
COT	20	HIRSHON, ROTH & CO.
COT PR A	20	HIRSHON, ROTH & CO.
COT PR D	20	HIRSHON, ROTH & CO.
COX	14	SESKIS & WOHLSTETTER
CP	10	LAURO & CO., C. B. RICHARD, ELLIS & CO.
CPB	6	LIEF, FOSTER, WERLE & CO.
CPL	16	WAGNER, STOTT & CO.
CPS	17	M. E. GOLDSTEIN & CO.; INC., WISNER & DE CLAIRVILLE

* Ten Share Unit Stocks

Symbol	Post	
CPX	5	WEIL & DUFFY
CQ	7	PICOLI & CO.
CR	18	J. W. TOOMEY & CO., VAUGHAN & CO., WRAGE & CO.
CRB	21	J. F. NICK & CO.
CRF	22	KINGSLEY, BOYE & SOUTHWOOD
CRH	15	LA BRANCHE & CO.
CRI	14	SESKIS & WOHLSTETTER
CRK	17	JOHN P. DUFFY
CRO	11	LAURO & CO.
CRO PR	11	LAURO & CO.
CRR	15	BENTON, CORCORAN, LEIB & CO.
*CRR PR	30	R. S. DODGE & CO., KERN SECURITIES CORP.
CRS	18	MURRAY & CO.
CRT	22	SILVER, BARRY & VAN RAALTE
CRT PR	22	SILVER, BARRY & VAN RAALTE
CRW	6	LIEF, FOSTER, WERLE & CO.
CRW PR	6	LIEF, FOSTER, WERLE & CO.
CS	9	LENART, McHUGH & CO.
CS PR	9	LENART, McHUGH & CO.
CS PR A	9	LENART, McHUGH & CO.
CSC	21	FOWLER & ROSENAU
CSK	11	MARCUS & CO., TRAVERS & HUME, JEWETT, NEWMAN & CO.
CSL	22	SILVER, BARRY & VAN RAALTE
CSN	8	C. V. GIANNI & CO., GILLEN & CO.
CSP	16	WAGNER, STOTT & CO.
CSP PR	16	WAGNER, STOTT & CO.
CSR	13	ROBB, PECK, McCOOEY & CO.

* Ten Share Unit Stocks

Symbol	Post	
CSS	5	JEFFERSON H. MARCUS & CO., INC., IRWIN SCHLOSS & CO., INC.
CSY	19	BENTON & CO.
CTB	6	LIEF, FOSTER, WERLE & CO.
CTB PR	30	R. S. DODGE & CO., KERN SECURITIES CORP.
CTC	10	BEAUCHAMP & CO.
CTL	8	SPEAR, LEEDS & KELLOGG
CTN	8	SPEAR, LEEDS & KELLOGG
CTP	17	FREIDAY & CO.
CTR	4	BLAIR S. WILLIAMS & CO.
CTS	8	COHEN, SIMONSON & REA, INC., ANDREWS, POSNER & ROTHSCHILD
CTU	6	LIEF, FOSTER, WERLE & CO.
CTX	17	CAHILL, SMITH & GALLATIN
CUD	22	STERN BROS.
CUD PR A	22	STERN BROS.
CUL	1	MURPHY & CO.
CUM	11	MARCUS & CO.
CV	12	M. J. MEEHAN & CO.
CV PR	12	M. J. MEEHAN & CO.
CVX	6	LIEF, FOSTER, WERLE & CO.
CW	13	ADLER, COLEMAN & CO.
CW A	13	ADLER, COLEMAN & CO.
CWD	13	ADLER, COLEMAN & CO.
CWE	15	BENTON, CORCORAN, LEIB & CO.
CWE PR	15	BENTON, CORCORAN, LEIB & CO.
CWL	6	LIEF, FOSTER, WERLE & CO.
CWO	21	J. F. NICK & CO.
*CX PR	30	R. S. DODGE & CO., KERN SECURITIES CORP.
CYL	2	P. V. HALL & CO.

* Ten Share Unit Stocks

Symbol	Post	
CYM	17	COWEN & CO., F. H. SACKEN & CO.
CZ	7	E. H. STERN & CO.
CZ PR	7	E. H. STERN & CO.

—D—

Symbol	Post	
D	6	STOKES, HOYT & CO.
D PR	6	STOKES, HOYT & CO.
DAL	9	LENART, McHUGH & CO.
DAY	2	P. V. HALL & CO.
*DAY PR	30	R. S. DODGE & CO., KERN SECURITIES CORP.
DBD	10	BEAUCHAMP & CO.
DC	6	LIEF, FOSTER, WERLE & CO.
DCA	22	STERN BROS.
DCL	17	CAHILL, SMITH & GALLATIN
DCN	21	J. F. NICK & CO.
DCS	20	MURPHEY, MARSEILLES & SMITH
DD	1	MACKEY, SHEA & WINTER
DD PR A	1	MACKEY, SHEA & WINTER
DD PR B	1	MACKEY, SHEA & WINTER
DE	12	M. J. MEEHAN & CO.
DEL	5	WEIL & DUFFY
DEN	17	M. E. GOLDSTEIN & CO., INC., WISNER & DE CLAIRVILLE
DER PR A	4	EINHORN & CO.
DER PR B	4	EINHORN & CO.
DES	17	FREIDAY & CO.
DEW	22	ALBERT FRIED & CO.
DEX	22	STERN BROS.
DFC	1	SOMERS, SCHAFER & COLLINS
DG	10	CYRIL DE CORDOVA & BRO.
DGR	7	PICOLI & CO.
DHM	4	BLAIR S. WILLIAMS & CO.
DHM PR A	4	BLAIR S. WILLIAMS & CO.

* Ten Share Unit Stocks

Symbol	Post	
DHM PR B	4	BLAIR S. WILLIAMS & CO.
DI	4	GAINES, REIS & CO.
DI PR	4	GAINES, REIS & CO.
DI PR B	4	GAINES, REIS & CO.
DIA	10	BEAUCHAMP & CO.
DIA PR	10	BEAUCHAMP & CO.
DIA PR D	10	BEAUCHAMP & CO.
DIG	3	ASIEL & CO., GENGLER BROS.
DIG PR	3	ASIEL & CO., GENGLER BROS.
DIS	14	FAGENSON & FRANKEL CO., INC., J. STREICHER & CO.
DLL	16	ADOLPH SCHENKER & CO., KAUFMANN & CO.
DM	15	JOHN E. BARRETT & CO., INC.
DMK	13	ADLER, COLEMAN & CO.
DML	12	ARDEN & GITTERMAN, F. L. SALOMON & CO.
DMO	17	FREIDAY & CO.
DN	17	FREIDAY & CO.
DNB	3	ASIEL & CO., GENGLER BROS.
DNY	7	PICOLI & CO.
DOC	20	MURPHEY, MARSEILLES & SMITH
DOR	17	COWEN & CO., F. H. SACKEN & CO.
DOV	8	SPEAR, LEEDS & KELLOGG
DOW	9	S. M. PECK & CO., CARL H. PFORZHEIMER & CO.
DPL	2	CUNNIFF, ROMAINE, LAMM & STOUTENBURGH
DPL PR A	30	R. S. DODGE & CO., KERN SECURITIES CORP.
*DPL PR B	30	R. S. DODGE & CO., KERN SECURITIES CORP.
*DPL PR C	30	R. S. DODGE & CO., KERN SECURITIES CORP.

* Ten Share Unit Stocks

Symbol	Post	
*DPL PR D	30	R. S. DODGE & CO., KERN SECURITIES CORP.
DQU	9	LENART, McHUGH & CO.
*DQU PR A	30	R. S. DODGE & CO., KERN SECURITIES CORP.
*DQU PR B	30	R. S. DODGE & CO., KERN SECURITIES CORP.
*DQU PR C	30	R. S. DODGE & CO., KERN SECURITIES CORP.
*DQU PR D	30	R. S. DODGE & CO., KERN SECURITIES CORP.
*DQU PR E	30	R. S. DODGE & CO., KERN SECURITIES CORP.
*DQU PR G	30	R. S. DODGE & CO., KERN SECURITIES CORP.
DR	6	LIEF, FOSTER, WERLE & CO.
*DR PR A	30	R. S. DODGE & CO., KERN SECURITIES CORP.
DR PR B	6	LIEF, FOSTER, WERLE & CO.
DRV	10	CYRIL DE CORDOVA & BRO.
DRY	2	J. J. CONKLIN & CO.
DSN	19	WILCOX & CO.
DSN PR	19	WILCOX & CO.
DSO	5	JOHN K. CLOUD, THOMAS F. McKENNA
DSP	15	JOHN E. BARRETT & CO., INC., JOHN MUIR & CO.
DTE	4	EINHORN & CO.
DTE PR	4	EINHORN & CO.
DTL	21	FOWLER & ROSENAU
DUK	21	J. F. NICK & CO.
DUP	17	WILLIAMS, EISELE & CO.
DXC	17	M. E. GOLDSTEIN & CO., INC., WISNER & DE CLAIRVILLE

* Ten Share Unit Stocks

Symbol	Post	
	—E—	
EA	17	FREIDAY & CO.
EAF	3	SHAW & ADRIAN
EAL	13	ROBB, PECK, McCOOEY & CO.
EBF	15	JOHN E. BARRETT & CO., INC.
EBS	16	PHELAN & CO.
ECH	22	ALBERT FRIED & CO.
ECK	4	BLAIR S. WILLIAMS & CO.
ED	5	CHAUNCEY & CO.
ED PR A	5	CHAUNCEY & CO.
ED PR B	5	CHAUNCEY & CO.
*ED PR C	30	R. S. DODGE & CO., KERN SECURITIES CORP.
EDE	1	COROON & CO., SIMON B. BLUMENTHAL, SHASKAN & CO., INC.
EFD	17	COWEN & CO., F. H. SACKEN & CO.
EFU	13	ROBB, PECK, McCOOEY & CO.
EGG	19	BENTON & CO.
EJN	22	SILVER, BARRY & VAN RAALTE
*EJN PR	30	R. S. DODGE & CO., KERN SECURITIES CORP.
EK	13	ROBB, PECK, McCOOEY & CO.
ELG	2	J. J. CONKLIN & CO.
EMH	7	E. H. STERN & CO.
EMI	13	ADLER, COLEMAN & CO.
EMM	7	MALTZ, GREENWALD & CO.
EMM PR	7	MALTZ, GREENWALD & CO.
EMP	8	C. V. GIANNI & CO., GILLEN & CO.
EMR	11	MARCUS & CO., TRAVERS & HUME, JEWETT, NEWMAN & CO.

* Ten Share Unit Stocks

Symbol	Post	
EMR PR B	11	MARCUS & CO., TRAVERS & HUME, JEWETT, NEWMAN & CO.
ENG	14	FAGENSON & FRANKEL CO., INC., J. STREICHER & CO.
ENG PR	14	FAGENSON & FRANKEL CO., INC., J. STREICHER & CO.
ENW	5	WEIL & DUFFY
ENX	8	SPEAR, LEEDS & KELLOGG
ENX PR	8	SPEAR, LEEDS & KELLOGG
EOS	8	SPEAR, LEEDS & KELLOGG
EPI	9	LENART, McHUGH & CO.
EQT	9	LENART, McHUGH & CO.
ES	15	JOHN E. BARRETT & CO., JOHN MUIR & CO.
ESB	15	JOHN E. BARRETT & CO.
ESQ	8	SPEAR, LEEDS & KELLOGG
ET	3	H. L. GOLDBERG & CO.
*ET PR	30	R. S. DODGE & CO., KERN SECURITIES CORP.
EUA	19	FARRELL & CO., ALBERT ROTHENBERG, ROTHSCHILD & CO.
EVR	17	E. N. POTTER & CO.
EVY	5	JOHN K. CLOUD, THOMAS F. McKENNA
EXC	14	SESKIS & WOHLSTETTER
EXC PR	14	SESKIS & WOHLSTETTER
EY	12	M. J. MEEHAN & CO.
EY PR	12	M. J. MEEHAN & CO.

—F—

Symbol	Post	
F	12	M. J. MEEHAN & CO.
FAC	15	BENTON, CORCORAN, LEIB & CO.
FAL	14	STERN & KENNEDY

* Ten Share Unit Stocks

Symbol	Post	
FAM	5	WEIL & DUFFY
FAS	5	JOHNSTON & LUNGER
FBD	1	BENJAMIN JACOBSON & SONS
FBG WI	22	SILVER, BARRY & VAN RAALTE
FBO	16	PHELAN & CO.
*FBO PR	30	R. S. DODGE & CO., KERN SECURITIES CORP.
FCB	8	SPEAR, LEEDS & KELLOGG
FCF	15	BENTON, CORCORAN, LEIB & CO.
FCI	12	M. J. MEEHAN & CO.
FD	16	WAGNER, STOTT & CO.
FDM	2	J. J. CONKLIN & CO.
FDP	13	ADLER, COLEMAN & CO.
FDS	2	ZUCKERMAN, SMITH & CO.
FEN	12	ARDEN & GITTERMAN, F. L. SALOMON & CO.
FFI	10	CYRIL DE CORDOVA & BRO.
FFS	2	ZUCKERMAN, SMITH & CO.
FIR	10	HAUPT, MEFFERT, ANDREWS & HUG
FIS	5	WEIL & DUFFY
FJQ	17	DANIEL REEVES & CO.
FLA	8	C. V. GIANNI & CO., GILLEN & CO.
FLD	12	DURAND & CULLEN
FLG	12	ARDEN & GITTERMAN, F. L. SALOMON & CO.
FLM	8	COHEN, SIMONSON & REA, INC., ANDREWS, POSNER & ROTHSCHILD
FLR	22	SILVER, BARRY & VAN RAALTE
FLR PR B	22	SILVER, BARRY & VAN RAALTE
FLS	7	MALTZ, GREENWALD & CO.
FLT	20	BREGMAN & CO.
FLY	6	STOKES, HOYT & CO.
FMC	16	WAGNER, STOTT & CO.

* Ten Share Unit Stocks

Symbol	Post	
FMC PR	16	WAGNER, STOTT & CO.
FMF	17	M. E. GOLDSTEIN & CO., INC., WISNER & DE CLAIRVILLE
FMF PR	17	M. E. GOLDSTEIN & CO., INC., WISNER & DE CLAIRVILLE
FMO	4	THOMAS F. FAGAN & CO.
FN	8	SPEAR, LEEDS & KELLOGG
FNC	12	M. J. MEEHAN & CO.
FNL	3	H. L. GOLDBERG & CO.
FO	11	MARCUS & CO.
*FO PR	30	R. S. DODGE & CO., KERN SECURITIES CORP.
*FO PR A	11	MARCUS & CO.
*FO PR B	11	MARCUS & CO.
FOE	16	PHELAN & CO.
FOR	17	FREIDAY & CO.
FOR PR	17	FREIDAY & CO.
FOX	5	WEIL & DUFFY
FPC	7	MALTZ, GREENWALD & CO.
FPC PR	7	MALTZ, GREENWALD & CO.
FPL	3	SCHOLL & LEVIN
FQA	19	BENTON & CO.
FRA	15	JOHN E. BARRETT & CO., INC., JOHN MUIR & CO.
FS	7	MALTZ, GREENWALD & CO.
FSC	5	WEIL & DUFFY
FSS	8	COHEN, SIMONSON & REA, INC., ANDREWS, POSNER, & ROTHSCHILD
FST	18	J. W. TOOMEY & CO., VAUGHAN & CO., WRAGE & CO.
FT	7	PICOLI & CO.
FTE	11	MARCUS & CO.
FTE PR	11	MARCUS & CO.
FTR	21	J. F. NICK & CO.
FWC	4	THOMAS F. FAGAN & CO.

* Ten Share Unit Stocks

Symbol	Post	
FWC PR	4	THOMAS F. FAGAN & CO.
FWF	11	MARCUS & CO., TRAVERS & HUME

—G—

Symbol	Post	
G	8	SPEAR, LEEDS & KELLOGG
G PR B	8	SPEAR, LEEDS & KELLOGG
GA	12	M. J. MEEHAN & CO.
GA PR A	12	M. J. MEEHAN & CO.
GA PR B	12	M. J. MEEHAN & CO.
GA PR N	12	M. J. MEEHAN & CO.
GAC	4	GAINES, REIS & CO.
GAC PR	4	GAINES, REIS & CO.
GAF	6	STOKES, HOYT & CO.
GAF PR	6	STOKES, HOYT & CO.
GAK	21	J. F. NICK & CO.
GAM	21	SPRAGUE & NAMMACK
GAO	15	BENTON, CORCORAN, LEIB & CO.
GAP	21	SPRAGUE & NAMMACK
GAS	4	EINHORN & CO.
GAT	9	LENHART, McHUGH & CO.
GB	1	COROON & CO., SIMON B. BLUMENTHAL, SHASKAN & CO., INC.
GBS	17	FAGENSON & FRANKEL CO., INC., J. STREICHER & CO.
GCI	17	COWEN & CO., F. H. SACKEN & CO.
GCO	4	THOMAS F. FAGAN & CO.
GCO PR	4	THOMAS F. FAGAN & CO.
GCR	20	HIRSHON, ROTH & CO.
GD	10	BEAUCHAMP & CO.
GDC	11	MARCUS & CO., TRAVERS & HUME
GDV	3	SHAW & ADRIAN

Symbol	Post	
GE	6	STOKES, HOYT & CO.
GEB	3	H. L. GOLDBERG & CO.
GEM	9	S. M. PECK & CO., CARL H. PFORZHEIMER & CO.
GEM PR	9	S. M. PECK & CO., CARL H. PFORZHEIMER & CO.
GEN	8	COHEN, SIMONSON & REA, INC., ANDREWS, POSNER & ROTHSCHILD
GEN PR	8	COHEN, SIMONSON & REA, INC., ANDREWS, POSNER & ROTHSCHILD
GET	1	BENJAMIN JACOBSON & SONS
GET PR	1	BENJAMIN JACOBSON & SONS
GF	17	WILLIAMS, EISELE & CO.
GFC	19	BENTON & CO.
GFO	5	JEFFERSON H. MARCUS & CO., INC., IRWIN SCHLOSS & CO., INC.
GFO PR	5	JEFFERSON H. MARCUS & CO., INC., IRWIN SCHLOSS & CO., INC.
GG	17	JOHN P. DUFFY
GH	17	HENDERSON BROTHERS, INC.
GI	6	LIEF, FOSTER, WERLE & CO.
GID	12	DURAND & CULLEN
GIS	11	LAURO & CO.
GIS PR	11	LAURO & CO.
GK	19	WILCOX & CO.
GLB	13	ROBB, PECK, McCOOEY & CO.
*GLF PR A	30	R. S. DODGE & CO., KERN SECURITIES CORP.
*GLF PR B	30	R. S. DODGE & CO., KERN SECURITIES CORP.
GLI	20	HIRSHON, ROTH & CO.
GLM	20	MURPHEY, MARSEILLES & SMITH

* Ten Share Unit Stocks

Symbol	Post	
GLP	10	HAUPT, MEFFERT, ANDREWS & HUG
GLR	22	SILVER, BARRY & VAN RAALTE
GLW	16	WAGNER, STOTT & CO.
GM	4	BLAIR S. WILLIAMS & CO.
GM PR A	4	BLAIR S. WILLIAMS & CO.
GM PR B	4	BLAIR S. WILLIAMS & CO.
GMT	7	E. H. STERN & CO.
GMT PR	7	E. H. STERN & CO.
GN	5	CHAUNCEY & CO.
GNB	4	BLAIR S. WILLIAMS & CO.
GNI	18	J. W. TOOMEY & CO., VAUGHAN & CO., WRAGE & CO.
GO	16	WAGNER, STOTT & CO.
GOR	6	LIEF, FOSTER, WERLE & CO.
GP	12	M. J. MEEHAN & CO.
GP PR A	12	M. J. MEEHAN & CO.
GP PR B	12	M. J. MEEHAN & CO.
GPC	1	COROON & CO., SHASKAN & CO., SIMON B. BLUMENTHAL
GPO	10	CYRIL DE CORDOVA & BRO.
GPP	4	BLAIR S. WILLIAMS & CO.
GPP PR	4	BLAIR S. WILLIAMS & CO.
GPT	8	SPEAR, LEEDS & KELLOGG
GPU	13	ADLER, COLEMAN & CO.
GQ	10	BEAUCHAMP & CO.
GR	18	MURRAY & CO.
GRA	13	ADLER, COLEMAN & CO.
GRC	16	ADOLPH SCHENKER & CO., KAUFMANN & CO.
GRE	10	LAURO & CO., C. B. RICHARD, ELLIS & CO.
GRE PR A	10	LAURO & CO., C. B. RICHARD, ELLIS & CO.

Symbol	Post	
GRE PR B	10	LAURO & CO., C. B. RICHARD, ELLIS & CO.
GRL	2	P. V. HALL & CO.
GRL PR	2	P. V. HALL & CO.
GRW	3	ASIEL & CO., GENGLER BROS.
GRX	9	LENART, McHUGH & CO.
GRY	8	COHEN, SIMONSON & REA, INC., ANDREWS, POSNER & ROTHSCHILD
GS	10	HAUPT, MEFFERT, ANDREWS & HUG
GSI	18	MURRAY & CO.
GSK	14	SESKIS & WOHLSTETTER
GSK PR A	14	SESKIS & WOHLSTETTER
GSK PR B	14	SESKIS & WOHLSTETTER
GSR	17	M. E. GOLDSTEIN & CO., INC., WISNER & DE CLAIRVILLE
GSX	18	MURRAY & CO.
GSX PR	18	MURRAY & CO.
GT	13	ROBB, PECK, McCOOEY & CO.
GTU	17	M. E. GOLDSTEIN & CO., INC., WISNER & DE CLAIRVILLE
*GTU PR A	30	R. S. DODGE & CO., KERN SECURITIES CORP.
*GTU PR B	30	R. S. DODGE & CO., KERN SECURITIES CORP.
*GTU PR C	30	R. S. DODGE & CO., KERN SECURITIES CORP.
*GTU PR D	30	R. S. DODGE & CO., KERN SECURITIES CORP.
*GTU PR E	30	R. S. DODGE & CO., KERN SECURITIES CORP.
*GTU PR G	30	R. S. DODGE & CO., KERN SECURITIES CORP.
GTY	21	FOWLER & ROSENAU
*GTY PR	30	R. S. DODGE & CO., KERN SECURITIES CORP.

* Ten Share Unit Stocks

Symbol	Post	
GUL	12	DURAND & CULLEN
GUX	3	H. L. GOLDBERG & CO.
GVL	1	SOMERS, SCHAFER & COLLINS
GW	3	SCHOLL & LEVIN
GW PR A	3	SCHOLL & LEVIN
GW PR B	3	SCHOLL & LEVIN
GW PR C	3	SCHOLL & LEVIN
GW PR S	3	SCHOLL & LEVIN
GWD	6	H. L. KIMBALL & CO.
GWD PR	6	H. L. KIMBALL & CO.
GWF	1	MURPHY & CO.
GWU	6	LIEF, FOSTER, WERLE & CO.
GWU PR	6	LIEF, FOSTER, WERLE & CO.
GY	8	SPEAR, LEEDS & KELLOGG
*GY PR	30	R. S. DODGE & CO., KERN SECURITIES CORP.

—H—

HAL	3	ASIEL & CO., GENGLER BROS.
HAR	7	E. H. STERN & CO.
HAT	17	COWEN & CO., F. H. SACKEN & CO.
HAY	6	H. L. KIMBALL & CO.
HBB	17	FREIDAY & CO.
HBL	20	MURPHEY, MARSEILLES & SMITH
HBW	2	J. J. CONKLIN & CO.
HC	9	ERNST & CO., WARE & KEELIPS, HOMANS & CO.
HCA	7	E. H. STERN & CO.
HCA PR	7	E. H. STERN & CO.
HD	16	WAGNER, STOTT & CO.
HDL	5	JOHN K. CLOUD, THOMAS F. McKENNA
HE	9	LENART, McHUGH & CO.
HEC	16	PHELAN & CO.

* Ten Share Unit Stocks

Symbol	Post	
HEM	22	KINGSLEY, BOYE & SOUTHWOOD
HEM PR	22	KINGSLEY, BOYE & SOUTHWOOD
HES	14	STERN & KENNEDY
HFC	19	FARRELL & CO., ALBERT ROTHENBERG, ROTHSCHILD & CO.
HFC PR	19	FARRELL & CO., ALBERT ROTHENBERG, ROTHSCHILD & CO.
HFC PR B	19	FARRELL & CO., ALBERT ROTHENBERG, ROTHSCHILD & CO.
HGH	5	WEIL & DUFFY
HH	5	JOHN K. CLOUD, THOMAS F. McKENNA
HH PR	5	JOHN K. CLOUD, THOMAS F. McKENNA
HH PR A CV	5	JOHN K. CLOUD, THOMAS F. McKENNA
HI	6	LIEF, FOSTER, WERLE & CO.
HIA	17	CAHILL, SMITH & GALLATIN
HIA A	17	CAHILL, SMITH & GALLATIN
HII	2	P. V. HALL & CO.
HIR	21	WRESZIN, PROSSER, ROMANO & GAVIN
HIS	22	ALBERT FRIED & CO.
HIT	14	SESKIS & WOHLSTETTER
HIT PR	14	SESKIS & WOHLSTETTER
HJ	19	BENTON & CO.
HL	3	H. L. GOLDBERG & CO.
HLI	6	LIEF, FOSTER, WERLE & CO.
HLR	21	J. F. NICK & CO.
HLR PR	21	J. F. NICK & CO.
HLT	5	WEIL & DUFFY
HLY	17	FREIDAY & CO.

Symbol	Post	
HM	20	MURPHEY, MARSEILLES & SMITH
HMD	1	BENJAMIN JACOBSON & SONS
HML	14	FAGENSON & FRANKEL CO., INC., J. STREICHER & CO.
HMW	4	GAINES, REIS & CO.
HNG	1	SOMERS, SCHAFER & COLLINS
HNG PR A	1	SOMERS, SCHAFER & COLLINS
HNH	22	STERN BROS.
HNM	1	MACKEY, SHEA & WINTER
HNS	8	C. V. GIANNI & CO., GILLEN & CO.
HNZ	15	JOHN E. BARRETT & CO., INC.
HOB	7	E. H. STERN & CO.
HON	18	HENDERSON BROTHERS, INC.
HOU	4	BLAIR S. WILLIAMS & CO.
HP	5	WEIL & DUFFY
HPC	8	SPEAR, LEEDS & KELLOGG
HPC A	8	SPEAR, LEEDS & KELLOGG
HPG	16	WAGNER, STOTT & CO.
HPI	15	BENTON, CORCORAN, LEIB & CO.
HR	22	SILVER, BARRY & VAN RAALTE
HSC	1	MACKEY, SHEA & WINTER
HSM	3	H. L. GOLDBERG & CO.
HSY	6	LIEF, FOSTER, WERLE & CO.
HTN	10	CYRIL DE CORDOVA & BRO.
HVE	10	BEAUCHAMP & CO.
HW	14	SESKIS & WOHLSTETTER
HWA	8	SPEAR, LEEDS & KELLOGG
HWC	22	ALBERT FRIED & CO.
HWP	11	MARCUS & CO.
HZ	14	STERN & KENNEDY

Symbol	Post	
—I—		
IAD	9	S. M. PECK & CO., CARL H. PFORZHEIMER & CO.
IBC	18	J. W. TOOMEY & CO., VAUGHAN & CO., WRAGE & CO.
IBM	10	CYRIL DE CORDOVA & BRO.
IBP	14	STERN & KENNEDY
IC	15	LA BRANCHE & CO.
ICA	4	THOMAS F. FAGAN & CO.
ICS	14	CREEM & CREEM
ICS PR	14	CREEM & CREEM
IDA	17	M. E. GOLDSTEIN & CO., INC., WISNER & DE CLAIRVILLE
IDL	12	M. J. MEEHAN & CO.
IDL PR	12	M. J. MEEHAN & CO.
IEL	16	WAGNER, STOTT & CO.
IEX	14	STERN & KENNEDY
IFF	2	J. J. CONKLIN & CO.
IGL	13	ADLER, COLEMAN & CO.
IGL PR	13	ADLER, COLEMAN & CO.
IH	12	ARDEN & GITTERMAN, F. L. SALOMON & CO.
IHD	17	FREIDAY & CO.
IHD PR	17	FREIDAY & CO.
IHS	20	BREGMAN & CO.
IK	13	ADLER, COLEMAN & CO.
IKN	20	HIRSHON, ROTH & CO.
*IKN PR	30	R. S. DODGE & CO., KERN SECURITIES CORP.
IL	21	SPRAGUE & NAMMACK
IL PR	21	SPRAGUE & NAMMACK
ILS	22	SILVER, BARRY & VAN RAALTE
IM	6	STOKES, HOYT & CO.
INA	11	MARCUS & CO.
INB	17	CAHILL, SMITH & GALLATIN

* Ten Share Unit Stocks

Symbol	Post	
INP	21	WRESZIN, PROSSER, ROMANO, & GAVIN
INP PR	21	WRESZIN, PROSSER, ROMANO, & GAVIN
INR	18	MURRAY & CO.
INR PR A	18	MURRAY & CO.
INT	20	HIRSHON, ROTH & CO.
INT PR A	20	HIRSHON, ROTH & CO.
IOP	17	JOHN P. DUFFY
IP	5	WEIL & DUFFY
*IP PR	30	R. S. DODGE & CO., KERN SECURITIES CORP.
IPC	2	P. V. HALL & CO.
*IPC PR A	30	R. S. DODGE & CO., KERN SECURITIES CORP.
*IPC PR B	30	R. S. DODGE & CO., KERN SECURITIES CORP.
*IPC PR C	30	R. S. DODGE & CO., KERN SECURITIES CORP.
*IPC PR D	30	R. S. DODGE & CO., KERN SECURITIES CORP.
*IPC PR E	30	R. S. DODGE & CO., KERN SECURITIES CORP.
IPR	4	THOMAS F. FAGAN & CO.
IPR PR A	4	THOMAS F. FAGAN & CO.
IPS	15	JOHN E. BARRETT & CO., INC.
IPW	21	WRESZIN, PROSSER, ROMANO & GAVIN
IQ	11	MARCUS & CO., TRAVERS & HUME, JEWETT, NEWMAN & CO.
IQ PR A WI	11	MARCUS & CO., TRAVERS & HUME, JEWETT, NEWMAN & CO.
IR	6	H. L. KIMBALL & CO.
IR PR B	6	H. L. KIMBALL & CO.
IRF	14	STERN & KENNEDY

* Ten Share Unit Stocks

Symbol	Post	
ISD	9	ERNST & CO., WARE & KEELIPS, HOMANS & CO.
ISS	6	LIEF, FOSTER, WERLE & CO.
ISS PR	6	LIEF, FOSTER, WERLE & CO.
ITE	14	FAGENSON & FRANKEL CO., INC., J. STREICHER & CO.
ITK	9	LENART, McHUGH & CO.
ITS PR	16	WAGNER, STOTT & CO.
ITT	16	WAGNER, STOTT & CO.
*ITT PR C	16	WAGNER, STOTT & CO.
*ITT PR D	16	WAGNER, STOTT & CO.
*ITT PR E	16	WAGNER, STOTT & CO.
ITT PR F	16	WAGNER, STOTT & CO.
ITT PR H	16	WAGNER, STOTT & CO.
ITT PR I	16	WAGNER, STOTT & CO.
ITT PR J	16	WAGNER, STOTT & CO.
ITT PR K	16	WAGNER, STOTT & CO.
*ITT PR L	30	R. S. DODGE & CO., KERN SECURITIES CORP.
IU	8	SPEAR, LEEDS & KELLOGG
IU A	8	SPEAR, LEEDS & KELLOGG
IU PR	8	SPEAR, LEEDS & KELLOGG
IWG	6	STOKES, HOYT & CO.

—J—

J	9	ERNST & CO., WARE & KEELIPS, HOMANS & CO.
JAC	13	ROBB, PECK, McCOOEY & CO.
JAC PR	13	ROBB, PECK, McCOOEY & CO.
JAE	15	LA BRANCHE & CO.
JCP	13	ADLER, COLEMAN & CO.
JI	10	HAUPT, MEFFERT, ANDREWS & HUG
JI PR	10	HAUPT, MEFFERT, ANDREWS & HUG
JJN	20	BREGMAN & CO.

* Ten Share Unit Stocks

Symbol	Post	
*JJN PR	30	R. S. DODGE & CO., KERN SECURITIES CORP.
JL	17	FREIDAY & CO.
*JL PR	30	R. S. DODGE & CO., KERN SECURITIES CORP.
JM	11	MARCUS & CO., TRAVERS & HUME, JEWETT, NEWMAN & CO.
JNJ	7	E. H. STERN & CO.
JOL	20	MURPHEY, MARSEILLES & SMITH
JOR	21	FOWLER & ROSENAU
JOS	13	ROBB, PECK, McCOOEY & CO.
JOY	19	BENTON & CO.
JP	19	WILCOX & CO.
JPM	8	SPEAR, LEEDS & KELLOGG
JPN	21	FOWLER & ROSENAU
JSC	22	STERN BROS.
JSC PR A	22	STERN BROS.
JWC	12	M. J. MEEHAN & CO.
*JWC PR	30	R. S. DODGE & CO., KERN SECURITIES CORP.
JWC PR B	12	M. J. MEEHAN & CO.
JWC PR C	12	M. J. MEEHAN & CO.
JWC PR D	12	M. J. MEEHAN & CO.
JWL	5	WEIL & DUFFY
*JYP PR	30	R. S. DODGE & CO., KERN SECURITIES CORP.

—K—

K	1	BENJAMIN JACOBSON & SONS
KAN	19	FARRELL & CO., ALBERT ROTHENBERG, ROTHSCHILD & CO.
KB	7	PICOLI & CO.
KBI	20	BREGMAN & CO.

* Ten Share Unit Stocks

Symbol	Post	
KBR	1	SOMERS, SCHAFER & COLLINS
KCG	22	STERN BROS.
KCG PR	22	STERN BROS.
KCG PR B	22	STERN BROS.
KDE	17	CAHILL, SMITH & GALLATIN
KDE PR A	17	CAHILL, SMITH & GALLATIN
KDE PR B	17	CAHILL, SMITH & GALLATIN
KDT	19	FARRELL & CO., ALBERT ROTHENBERG, ROTHSCHILD & CO.
KEL	17	E. N. POTTER & CO.
KEN	18	HENDERSON BROTHERS, INC.
KES	17	FREIDAY & CO.
KFM	1	SOMERS, SCHAFER & COLLINS
KG	3	SHAW & ADRIAN
KGE	5	WEIL & DUFFY
KIR	9	S. M. PECK & CO., CARL H. PFORZHEIMER & CO.
KLM	14	FAGENSON & FRANKEL CO., INC., J. STREICHER & CO.
KLT	15	JOHN E. BARRETT & CO., INC.
*KLT PR A	30	R. S. DODGE & CO., KERN SECURITIES CORP.
*KLT PR B	30	R. S. DODGE & CO., KERN SECURITIES CORP.
*KLT PR C	30	R. S. DODGE & CO., KERN SECURITIES CORP.
*KLT PR D	30	R. S. DODGE & CO., KERN SECURITIES CORP.
*KLT PR E	30	R. S. DODGE & CO., KERN SECURITIES CORP.
KLU	16	PHELAN & CO.
KLU PR A CV	16	PHELAN & CO.
KLU PR B CV	16	PHELAN & CO.
KLU PR C CV	16	PHELAN & CO.
*KLU PR D CV	30	R. S. DODGE & CO., KERN SECURITIES CORP.

* Ten Share Unit Stocks

Symbol	Post	
KLU PR E CV	16	PHELAN & CO.
KMB	21	WRESZIN, PROSSER, ROMANO & GAVIN
KMG	11	MARCUS & CO.
KMG PR A	11	MARCUS & CO.
KMT	7	MALTZ, GREENWALD & CO.
KN	1	COROON & CO., SHASKAN & CO., INC., SIMON B. BLUMENTHAL
KNI	20	MURPHEY, MARSEILLES & SMITH
KNS	19	FARRELL & CO., ALBERT ROTHENBERG, ROTHSCHILD & CO.
KNS PR	19	FARRELL & CO., ALBERT ROTHENBERG, ROTHSCHILD & CO.
KNS PR B	19	FARRELL & CO., ALBERT ROTHENBERG, ROTHSCHILD & CO.
KNS PR D	19	FARRELL & CO., ALBERT ROTHENBERG, ROTHSCHILD & CO.
KNY	13	ADLER, COLEMAN & CO.
KO	7	E. H. STERN & CO.
KOE	14	STERN & KENNEDY
KOE PR H	14	STERN & KENNEDY
KOP	19	FARRELL & CO., ALBERT ROTHENBERG, ROTHSCHILD & CO.
*KOP PR	30	R. S. DODGE & CO., KERN SECURITIES CORP.
KR	5	JOHN K. CLOUD, THOMAS F. McKENNA, JOHNSTON & LUNGER
KRA	8	SPEAR, LEEDS & KELLOGG

* Ten Share Unit Stocks

Symbol	Post	
KSF	2	CUNNIFF, ROMAINE, LAMM & STOUTENBURGH
KSU	6	LIEF, FOSTER, WERLE & CO.
*KSU PR	30	R. S. DODGE & CO., KERN SECURITIES CORP.
KT	15	BENTON, CORCORAN, LEIB & CO.
KTY	12	ARDEN & GITTERMAN, F. L. SALOMON & CO.
KU	9	S. M. PECK & CO., CARL H. PFORZHEIMER & CO.
KW	13	ADLER, COLEMAN & CO.
KYR	2	ZUCKERMAN, SMITH & CO.

—L—

Symbol	Post	
LC	8	C. V. GIANNI & CO., GILLEN & CO.
LCE	13	ADLER, COLEMAN & CO.
LCE PR	13	ADLER, COLEMAN & CO.
LCR	8	C. V. GIANNI & CO., GILLEN & CO.
LCR PR	8	C. V. GIANNI & CO., GILLEN & CO.
LDN	17	E. N. POTTER & CO.
LDP	9	S. M. PECK & CO., CARL H. PFORZHEIMER & CO.
LDP PR	9	S. M. PECK & CO., CARL H. PFORZHEIMER & CO.
LEH	10	CYRIL DE CORDOVA & BRO.
LEH PR	10	CYRIL DE CORDOVA & BRO.
LEM	17	WILLIAMS, EISELE & CO.
LFB	22	STERN BROS.
LFB PR	22	STERN BROS.
LFC	16	PHELAN & CO.

* Ten Share Unit Stocks

Symbol	Post	
LFE	14	FAGENSON & FRANKEL CO., INC., J. STREICHER & CO.
LG	5	WEIL & DUFFY
LIL	4	BLAIR S. WILLIAMS & CO.
LIL PR B	30	R. S. DODGE & CO., KERN SECURITIES CORP.
LIL PR D	30	R. S. DODGE & CO., KERN SECURITIES CORP.
LIL PR E	30	R. S. DODGE & CO., KERN SECURITIES CORP.
LIL PR I	4	BLAIR S. WILLIAMS & CO.
LIO	9	ERNST & CO., WARE & KEELIPS, HOMANS & CO.
LIT	11	MARCUS & CO.
LIT PR A	11	MARCUS & CO.
LIT PR B	11	MARCUS & CO.
LIT PR CV	11	MARCUS & CO.
LJ	16	WAGNER, STOTT & CO.
LK	10	HAUPT, MEFFERT, ANDREWS & HUG
LKS	20	MURPHEY, MARSEILLES & SMITH
LLC	14	FAGENSON & FRANKEL CO., INC., J. STREICHER & CO.
LLC PR	14	FAGENSON & FRANKEL CO., INC., J. STREICHER & CO.
LLX	17	FREIDAY & CO.
LM	13	ADLER, COLEMAN & CO.
*LM PR	30	R. S. DODGE & CO., KERN SECURITIES CORP.
LM PR A	13	ADLER, COLEMAN & CO.
LMS	14	CREEM & CREEM
LN	9	S. M. PECK & CO., CARL H. PFORZHEIMER & CO.
LNR	17	M. E. GOLDSTEIN & CO., INC., WISNER & DE CLAIRVILLE
LNY	7	E. H. STERN & CO.

* Ten Share Unit Stocks

Symbol	Post	
LOF	4	EINHORN & CO.
LOF PR A	4	EINHORN & CO.
LON	15	JOHN E. BARRETT & CO., INC., JOHN MUIR & CO.
LOR	18	J. W. TOOMEY & CO., VAUGHAN & CO., WRAGE & CO.
LOU	15	LA BRANCHE & CO.
LPT	3	ASIEL & CO., GENGLER BROS.
LSC	14	STERN & KENNEDY
LSG	8	SPEAR, LEEDS & KELLOGG
LSI	11	LAURO & CO.
LSI PR	11	LAURO & CO.
LSO	2	CUNNIFF, ROMAINE, LAMM & STOUTENBURGH
LST	20	BREGMAN & CO.
LT	19	WILCOX & CO.
LTC	2	P. V. HALL & CO.
LTR	7	E. H. STERN & CO.
LTV	5	WEIL & DUFFY
LTV A	5	WEIL & DUFFY
LTV PR	5	WEIL & DUFFY
LUC	13	ROBB, PECK, McCOOEY & CO.
LUD	10	CYRIL DE CORDOVA & BRO.
LVO	2	P. V. HALL & CO.
LY	13	ROBB, PECK, McCOOEY & CO.
LY PR	13	ROBB, PECK, McCOOEY & CO.
LZ	17	M. E. GOLDSTEIN & CO., INC., WISNER & DE CLAIRVILLE

—M—

M	14	FAGENSON & FRANKEL CO., INC., J. STREICHER & CO.
M PR A	14	FAGENSON & FRANKEL CO., INC., J. STREICHER & CO.
MA	9	ERNST & CO., WARE & KEELIPS, HOMANS & CO.

Symbol	Post	
MA PR E	9	ERNST & CO., WARE & KEELIPS, HOMANS & CO.
MAC	21	FOWLER & ROSENAU
MAD	6	STOKES, HOYT & CO.
MAE	4	GAINES, REIS & CO.
MAF	12	ARDEN & GITTERMAN, F. L. SALOMON & CO.
MAG	16	WAGNER, STOTT & CO.
MAK	20	MURPHEY, MARSEILLES & SMITH
MAN	21	FOWLER & ROSENAU
MAR	7	E. H. STERN & CO.
MAS	5	WEIL & DUFFY
MAT	15	JOHN E. BARRETT & CO., INC., JOHN MUIR & CO.
MB	8	COHEN, SIMONSON & REA, INC., ANDREWS, POSNER & ROTHSCHILD
MC	17	COWEN & CO., F. H. SACKEN & CO.
MCA	2	P. V. HALL & CO.
MCC	22	STERN BROS.
MCD	22	STERN BROS.
MCG	19	FARRELL & CO., ALBERT ROTHENBERG, ROTHSCHILD & CO.
MCL	9	LENART, McHUGH & CO.
MCR	22	KINGSLEY, BOYE & SOUTHWOOD
MD	15	LA BRANCHE & CO.
MDA	3	SCHOLL & LEVIN
MDA PR	3	SCHOLL & LEVIN
MDC	3	SCHOLL & LEVIN
MDE	20	HIRSHON, ROTH & CO.
MDK	4	GAINES, REIS & CO.
MDP	18	HENDERSON BROTHERS, INC.
MEA	5	JOHNSTON & LUNGER

Symbol	Post	
MEA PR A	5	JOHNSTON & LUNGER
MEA PR B	5	JOHNSTON & LUNGER
MEI	10	CYRIL DE CORDOVA & BRO.
MES	12	ARDEN & GITTERMAN,
		F. L. SALOMON & CO.
*MES PR	30	R. S. DODGE & CO.,
		KERN SECURITIES CORP.
MET	11	LAURO & CO.
MF	9	S. M. PECK & CO.,
		CARL H. PFORZHEIMER & CO.
MFG	8	SPEAR, LEEDS & KELLOGG
MFS	22	KINGSLEY,
		BOYE & SOUTHWOOD
MG	1	BENJAMIN JACOBSON & SONS
MGD	1	BENJAMIN JACOBSON & SONS
MGI	22	STERN BROS.
MGM	7	E. H. STERN & CO.
MGR	21	FOWLER & ROSENAU
MGW	11	MARCUS & CO., TRAVERS &
		HUME, JEWETT, NEWMAN & CO.
MHC	10	BEAUCHAMP & CO.
MHG	17	CAHILL, SMITH & GALLATIN
MHP	17	COWEN & CO.,
		F. H. SACKEN & CO.
MHP PR	17	COWEN & CO.,
		F. H. SACKEN & CO.
MHS	13	ADLER, COLEMAN & CO.
MHT	13	ADLER, COLEMAN & CO.
MIC	19	FARRELL & CO.,
		ALBERT ROTHENBERG,
		ROTHSCHILD & CO.
MID	18	MURRAY & CO.
MIL	10	SESKIS & WOHLSTETTER
MIS	8	SPEAR, LEEDS & KELLOGG
MJW	17	JOHN P. DUFFY
MKC	22	SILVER, BARRY & VAN RAALTE
MKE	11	LAURO & CO.

* Ten Share Unit Stocks

Symbol	Post	
ML	16	WAGNER, STOTT & CO.
MLN	6	LIEF, FOSTER, WERLE & CO.
MLR	4	GAINES, REIS & CO.
MLR PR	4	GAINES, REIS & CO.
MLX	14	SESKIS & WOHLSTETTER
MM	2	CUNNIFF, ROMAINE, LAMM & STOUTENBURGH
MMC	2	ZUCKERMAN, SMITH & CO.
MME	13	ADLER, COLEMAN & CO.
MMM	21	FOWLER & ROSENAU
MMO	7	E. H. STERN & CO.
MNC	16	WAGNER, STOTT & CO.
MNP	5	WEIL & DUFFY
MO	13	ROBB, PECK, McCOOEY & CO.
MO PR A	30	R. S. DODGE & CO., KERN SECURITIES CORP.
*MO PR B	30	R. S. DODGE & CO., KERN SECURITIES CORP.
MOB	10	HAUPT, MEFFERT, ANDREWS & HUG
MOH	11	MARCUS & CO., TRAVERS & HUME
MON B	5	WEIL & DUFFY
MOP	15	LA BRANCHE & CO.
MOT	13	ADLER, COLEMAN & CO.
MOU	5	CHAUNCEY & CO.
MP	19	BENTON & CO.
MPD	2	CUNNIFF, ROMAINE, LAMM & STOUTENBURGH
MPH	8	SPEAR, LEEDS & KELLOGG
MPL	11	MARCUS & CO., TRAVERS & HUME, JEWETT, NEWMAN & CO.
MPV	8	C. V. GIANNI & CO., GILLEN & CO.
MQC	20	HIRSHON, ROTH & CO.
MRK	19	WILCOX & CO.

* Ten Share Unit Stocks

Symbol	Post	
*MRK PR	30	R. S. DODGE & CO., KERN SECURITIES CORP.
MRO	11	LAURO & CO.
MRP	20	MURPHEY, MARSEILLES & SMITH
MRS	14	CREEM & CREEM
MRX	19	WILCOX & CO.
MRY	7	E. H. STERN & CO.
MS	11	MARCUS & CO., TRAVERS & HUME, JEWETT, NEWMAN & CO.
*MS PR B	11	MARCUS & CO., TRAVERS & HUME, JEWETT, NEWMAN & CO.
*MS PR D	30	R. S. DODGE & CO., KERN SECURITIES CORP.
MSB	13	ROBB, PECK, McCOOEY & CO.
MSE	16	WAGNER, STOTT & CO.
MSG	6	LIEF, FOSTER, WERLE & CO.
MSL	22	STERN BROS.
*MSS	19	WILCOX & CO.
MST	19	BENTON & CO.
MSU	9	ERNST & CO., WARE & KEELIPS, HOMANS & CO.
MTB	6	STOKES, HOYT & CO.
MTC	14	STERN & KENNEDY
MTC PR WI	14	STERN & KENNEDY
MTP	21	WRESZIN, PROSSER, ROMANO & GAVIN
*MTT PR C	30	R. S. DODGE & CO., KERN SECURITIES CORP.
MUN	4	GAINES, REIS & CO.
MUR	19	FARRELL & CO., ALBERT ROTHENBERG, ROTHSCHILD & CO.

* Ten Share Unit Stocks

Symbol	Post	
MUR PR B	19	FARRELL & CO., ALBERT ROTHENBERG, ROTHSCHILD & CO.
MWO	19	BENTON & CO.
MYG	1	SOMERS, SCHAFER & COLLINS
MZ	1	SOMERS, SCHAFER & COLLINS
*MZ PR	30	R. S. DODGE & CO., KERN SECURITIES CORP.

—N—

N	5	WEIL & DUFFY
NAC	10	HAUPT, MEFFERT, ANDREWS & HUG
NAC PR	10	HAUPT, MEFFERT, ANDREWS & HUG
NAL	7	E. H. STERN & CO.
NAO	21	J. F. NICK & CO.
NAS	16	WAGNER, STOTT & CO.
NC	16	PHELAN & CO.
NCH	15	JOHN E. BARRETT & CO., INC.
NCR	12	M. J. MEEHAN & CO.
NEM	10	HAUPT, MEFFERT, ANDREWS & HUG
NEM PR A	10	HAUPT, MEFFERT, ANDREWS & HUG
NES	6	H. L. KIMBALL & CO.
NFG	7	MALTZ, GREENWALD & CO.
NFK	4	EINHORN & CO.
NG	15	LA BRANCHE & CO.
NG PR	30	R. S. DODGE & CO., KERN SECURITIES CORP.
NGC	13	ROBB, PECK, McCOOEY & CO.
NGE	13	ADLER, COLEMAN & CO.
NGE PR	30	R. S. DODGE & CO., KERN SECURITIES CORP.
NGS	1	BENJAMIN JACOBSON & SONS

Ten Share Unit Stocks

Symbol	Post	
NI	9	ERNST & CO., WARE & KEELIPS, HOMANS & CO.
NII	15	LA BRANCHE & CO.
NII PR A	15	LA BRANCHE & CO.
NII PR B	15	LA BRANCHE & CO.
NLC	17	FREIDAY & CO.
NMK	13	ADLER, COLEMAN & CO.
*NMK PR A	30	R. S. DODGE & CO., KERN SECURITIES CORP.
*NMK PR B	30	R. S. DODGE & CO., KERN SECURITIES CORP.
*NMK PR C	30	R. S. DODGE & CO., KERN SECURITIES CORP.
*NMK PR D	30	R. S. DODGE & CO., KERN SECURITIES CORP.
*NMK PR E	30	R. S. DODGE & CO., KERN SECURITIES CORP.
*NMK PR G	30	R. S. DODGE & CO., KERN SECURITIES CORP.
*NMK PR H	30	R. S. DODGE & CO., KERN SECURITIES CORP.
NNG	19	BENTON & CO.
*NNG PR A	30	R. S. DODGE & CO., KERN SECURITIES CORP.
*NNG PR B	30	R. S. DODGE & CO., KERN SECURITIES CORP.
*NNG PR C	30	R. S. DODGE & CO., KERN SECURITIES CORP.
*NNG PR D	30	R. S. DODGE & CO., KERN SECURITIES CORP.
*NNG PR E	30	R. S. DODGE & CO., KERN SECURITIES CORP.
*NNX	30	R. S. DODGE & CO., KERN SECURITIES CORP.
NOA	17	FREIDAY & CO.
NOB	15	JOHN E. BARRETT & CO., INC.
NOC	2	P. V. HALL & CO.

* Ten Share Unit Stocks

Symbol	Post	
NOC PR	2	P. V. HALL & CO.
NOM	5	JEFFERSON H. MARCUS & CO., INC., IRWIN SCHLOSS & CO., INC.
NP	8	ANDREWS, POSNER, & ROTHSCHILD, COHEN, SIMONSON & REA, INC.
NPH	4	EINHORN & CO.
NPK	17	WILLIAMS, EISELE & CO.
NPM	22	SILVER, BARRY & VAN RAALTE
NR	5	WEIL & DUFFY
NR PR	5	WEIL & DUFFY
NR PR B	5	WEIL & DUFFY
NRI	4	THOMAS F. FAGAN & CO.
NRT	1	MACKEY, SHEA & WINTER
NS	16	WAGNER, STOTT & CO.
NSC	20	BREGMAN & CO.
NSD	22	STERN BROS.
NSH	1	SOMERS, SCHAFER & COLLINS
NSI	22	ALBERT FRIED & CO.
NSI PR A	22	ALBERT FRIED & CO.
NSP	3	ASIEL & CO., GENGLER BROS.
*NSP PR A	30	R. S. DODGE & CO., KERN SECURITIES CORP.
*NSP PR B	30	R. S. DODGE & CO., KERN SECURITIES CORP.
*NSP PR C	30	R. S. DODGE & CO., KERN SECURITIES CORP.
*NSP PR D	30	R. S. DODGE & CO., KERN SECURITIES CORP.
*NSP PR E	30	R. S. DODGE & CO., KERN SECURITIES CORP.
*NSP PR G	30	R. S. DODGE & CO., KERN SECURITIES CORP.
*NSP PR H	30	R. S. DODGE & CO., KERN SECURITIES CORP.
*NSP PR I	30	R. S. DODGE & CO., KERN SECURITIES CORP.

* Ten Share Unit Stocks

Symbol	Post	
NSW	20	MURPHEY, MARSEILLES & SMITH
NTA	11	MARCUS & CO., TRAVERS & HUME
NTL	6	H. L. KIMBALL & CO.
NTS	1	COROON & CO., SHASKAN & CO., INC., SIMON B. BLUMENTHAL
NTT	18	HENDERSON BROTHERS, INC.
NTY	6	LIEF, FOSTER, WERLE & CO.
NU	17	JOHN P. DUFFY
NUM	11	MARCUS & CO., TRAVERS & HUME
NVF	17	E. N. POTTER & CO.
NVP	22	ALBERT FRIED & CO.
NWA	17	CAHILL, SMITH & GALLATIN
NWT	18	HENDERSON BROTHERS, INC.
NWT PR A	18	HENDERSON BROTHERS, INC.
NWT PR B	18	HENDERSON BROTHERS, INC.
NWT PR C	18	HENDERSON BROTHERS, INC.
NYH	1	MURPHY & CO.

—O—

Symbol	Post	
OAT	7	PICOLI & CO.
OAT PR	7	PICOLI & CO.
OCF	16	WAGNER, STOTT & CO.
OCQ	21	WRESZIN, PROSSER, ROMANO & GAVIN
OEC	16	PHELAN & CO.
*OEC PR A	30	R. S. DODGE & CO., KERN SECURITIES CORP.
*OEC PR B	30	R. S. DODGE & CO., KERN SECURITIES CORP.
*OEC PR C	30	R. S. DODGE & CO., KERN SECURITIES CORP.
*OEC PR D	30	R. S. DODGE & CO., KERN SECURITIES CORP.

* Ten Share Unit Stocks

Symbol	Post	
OEN	10	HAUPT, MEFFERT, ANDREWS & HUG
OG	19	BENTON & CO.
OG PR	19	BENTON & CO.
OGE	12	M. J. MEEHAN & CO.
*OGE PR A	30	R. S. DODGE & CO., KERN SECURITIES CORP.
*OGE PR B	30	R. S. DODGE & CO., KERN SECURITIES CORP.
OI	13	ADLER, COLEMAN & CO.
OI PR	13	ADLER, COLEMAN & CO.
OI PR A	13	ADLER, COLEMAN & CO.
OKT	17	WILLIAMS, EISELE & CO.
OLM	20	MURPHEY, MARSEILLES & SMITH
OM	5	JEFFERSON H. MARCUS & CO., INC., IRWIN SCHLOSS & CO., INC.
OMK	15	JOHN E. BARRETT & CO., INC., JOHN MUIR & CO.
ONG	12	M. J. MEEHAN & CO.
OPK	6	LIEF, FOSTER, WERLE & CO.
ORU	5	JOHNSTON & LUNGER
OT	1	SOMERS, SCHAFER & COLLINS
OTU	30	R. S. DODGE & CO., KERN SECURITIES CORP.
OVT	18	HENDERSON BROTHERS, INC.
OXM	17	DANIEL REEVES & CO.
OXY	21	WRESZIN, PROSSER, ROMANO & GAVIN
OXY PR A	21	WRESZIN, PROSSER, ROMANO & GAVIN
OXY PR B	21	WRESZIN, PROSSER, ROMANO & GAVIN
OXY PR C	21	WRESZIN, PROSSER, ROMANO & GAVIN

---

* Ten Share Unit Stocks

Symbol	Post	
—P—		
P	17	WILLIAMS, EISELE & CO.
PAC	21	SPRAGUE & NAMMACK
*PAC PR	21	SPRAGUE & NAMMACK
PAG	22	ALBERT FRIED & CO.
PAG PR	22	ALBERT FRIED & CO.
PAS	20	HIRSHON, ROTH & CO.
PBI	20	MURPHEY, MARSEILLES & SMITH
PC	18	J. W. TOOMEY & CO., VAUGHAN & CO., WRAGE & CO.
PCG	20	MURPHEY, MARSEILLES & SMITH
PCO	6	LIEF, FOSTER, WERLE & CO.
PCT	21	WRESZIN, PROSSER, ROMANO & GAVIN
PD	8	SPEAR, LEEDS & KELLOGG
PDC	18	HENDERSON BROTHERS, INC.
PDG	17	E. N. POTTER & CO.
PE	3	SHAW & ADRIAN
*PE PR A	30	R. S. DODGE & CO., KERN SECURITIES CORP.
*PE PR B	30	R. S. DODGE & CO., KERN SECURITIES CORP.
*PE PR C	30	R. S. DODGE & CO., KERN SECURITIES CORP.
*PE PR D	30	R. S. DODGE & CO., KERN SECURITIES CORP.
*PE PR E	30	R. S. DODGE & CO., KERN SECURITIES CORP.
PEG	7	PICOLI & CO.
PEG PR	30	R. S. DODGE & CO., KERN SECURITIES CORP.
*PEG PR A	30	R. S. DODGE & CO., KERN SECURITIES CORP.

* Ten Share Unit Stocks

Symbol	Post	
*PEG PR B	30	R. S. DODGE & CO., KERN SECURITIES CORP.
*PEG PR C	30	R. S. DODGE & CO., KERN SECURITIES CORP.
*PEG PR D	30	R. S. DODGE & CO., KERN SECURITIES CORP.
*PEG PR E	30	R. S. DODGE & CO., KERN SECURITIES CORP.
*PEG PR G	30	R. S. DODGE & CO., KERN SECURITIES CORP.
PEL	8	SPEAR, LEEDS & KELLOGG
PEO	22	KINGSLEY, BOYE & SOUTHWOOD
PEP	7	PICOLI & CO.
PET	21	SPRAGUE & NAMMACK
PET PR	21	SPRAGUE & NAMMACK
PET PR A	21	SPRAGUE & NAMMACK
PFE	20	BREGMAN & CO.
PFG	9	CARL H. PFORZHEIMER & CO., S. M. PECK & CO.
PFO	15	LA BRANCHE & CO.
PFR	18	HENDERSON BROTHERS, INC.
*PFT PR	30	R. S. DODGE & CO., KERN SECURITIES CORP.
PG	2	ZUCKERMAN, SMITH & CO.
PGB	21	J. F. NICK & CO.
PGL	16	ADOLPH SCHENKER & CO., KAUFMANN & CO.
PGN	3	ASIEL & CO., GENGLER BROS.
PH	8	COHEN, SIMONSON & REA, INC., ANDREWS, POSNER & ROTHSCHILD
*PHK PR	17	WILLIAMS, EISELE & CO.
PHL	20	BREGMAN & CO.
PIE	16	PHELAN & CO.
PIN	8	SPEAR, LEEDS & KELLOGG

* Ten Share Unit Stocks

Symbol	Post	
*PIN PR A	30	R. S. DODGE & CO., KERN SECURITIES CORP.
*PIN PR B	30	R. S. DODGE & CO., KERN SECURITIES CORP.
*PIN PR C	30	R. S. DODGE & CO., KERN SECURITIES CORP.
PKN	20	MURPHEY, MARSEILLES & SMITH
PKR	18	HENDERSON BROTHERS, INC.
PLO	18	MURRAY & CO.
PLT	5	JEFFERSON H. MARCUS & CO., INC., IRWIN SCHLOSS & CO., INC.
PMB	3	SHAW & ADRIAN
PN	16	WAGNER, STOTT & CO.
PNA	21	FOWLER & ROSENAU
PNV PR	18	J. W. TOOMEY & CO., VAUGHAN & CO., WRAGE & CO.
POM	5	WEIL & DUFFY
POM PR	5	WEIL & DUFFY
POR	22	ALBERT FRIED & CO.
PP	5	JEFFERSON H. MARCUS & CO., INC., IRWIN SCHLOSS & CO., INC.
PPD	2	J. J. CONKLIN & CO.
PPG	7	PICOLI & CO.
PPI	18	HENDERSON BROTHERS, INC.
PPL	8	SPEAR, LEEDS & KELLOGG
*PPL PR A	30	R. S. DODGE & CO., KERN SECURITIES CORP.
*PPL PR B	30	R. S. DODGE & CO., KERN SECURITIES CORP.
PPW	22	KINGSLEY, BOYE & SOUTHWOOD
PRC	21	WRESZIN, PROSSER, ROMANO & GAVIN
PRD	3	H. L. GOLDBERG & CO.
PRE	3	ASIEL & CO., GENGLER BROS.

* Ten Share Unit Stocks

Symbol	Post	
PRE PR A	3	ASIEL & CO., GENGLER BROS.
PRN	8	SPEAR, LEEDS & KELLOGG
PRX	19	WILCOX & CO.
PRX PR	19	WILCOX & CO.
PSA	12	ARDEN & GITTERMAN, F. SALOMON & CO.
PSD	21	SPRAGUE & NAMMACK
PSI	14	FAGENSON & FRANKEL CO., INC., J. STREICHER & CO.
PSM	1	MACKEY, SHEA & WINTER
PSM PR	1	MACKEY, SHEA & WINTER
PSM PR B	1	MACKEY, SHEA & WINTER
PSR	4	THOMAS F. FAGAN & CO.
PSY	20	HIRSHON, ROTH & CO.
PTC	17	COWEN & CO., F. H. SACKEN & CO.
PTO	4	THOMAS F. FAGAN & CO.
PTO PR A	4	THOMAS F. FAGAN & CO.
*PTT A	30	R. S. DODGE & CO., KERN SECURITIES CORP.
*PTT B	30	R. S. DODGE & CO., KERN SECURITIES CORP.
PU	9	ERNST & CO., WARE & KEELIPS, HOMANS & CO.
PUL	4	THOMAS F. FAGAN & CO.
PVH	12	ARDEN & GITTERMAN, F. L. SALOMON & CO.
*PYA PR	30	R. S. DODGE & CO., KERN SECURITIES CORP.
PZL	20	BREGMAN & CO.
PZL PR	20	BREGMAN & CO.

—R—

R	10	BEAUCHAMP & CO.
*R PR	30	R. S. DODGE & CO., KERN SECURITIES CORP.

* Ten Share Unit Stocks

Symbol	Post	
RAH	8	C. V. GIANNI & CO., GILLEN & CO.
RAL	3	H. L. GOLDBERG & CO.
RAL PR	3	H. L. GOLDBERG & CO.
RAY	1	COROON & CO., SHASKAN & CO., INC., SIMON B. BLUMENTHAL
RB	8	SPEAR, LEEDS & KELLOGG
RB PR	8	SPEAR, LEEDS & KELLOGG
RBD	12	DURAND & CULLEN
RCA	12	M. J. MEEHAN & CO.
*RCA PR	30	R. S. DODGE & CO., KERN SECURITIES CORP.
RCA PR B	12	M. J. MEEHAN & CO.
RCB	16	PHELAN & CO.
RCB PR	16	PHELAN & CO.
RCC	14	FAGENSON & FRANKEL CO., INC., J. STREICHER & CO.
RCI	14	FAGENSON & FRANKEL CO., INC., J. STREICHER & CO.
RCS	18	HENDERSON BROTHERS, INC.
RD	19	BENTON & CO.
RDG	18	HENDERSON BROTHERS, INC.
RDG PR A	18	HENDERSON BROTHERS, INC.
RDG PR B	18	HENDERSON BROTHERS, INC.
RDR	8	SPEAR, LEEDS & KELLOGG
RDS	21	WRESZIN, PROSSER, ROMANO & GAVIN
REE	1	SOMERS, SCHAFER & COLLINS
REE PR	1	SOMERS, SCHAFER & COLLINS
REE PR B	1	SOMERS, SCHAFER & COLLINS
REP	17	M. E. GOLDSTEIN & CO., INC., WISNER & DE CLAIRVILLE
RES	2	ZUCKERMAN, SMITH & CO.
REV	3	ASIEL & CO., GENGLER BROS.
REV PR	3	ASIEL & CO., GENGLER BROS.
RG	21	SPRAGUE & NAMMACK
RGI	7	PICOLI & CO.

* Ten Share Unit Stocks

Symbol	Post	
RGI PR	7	PICOLI & CO.
RGP	9	ERNST & CO., WARE & KEELIPS, HOMANS & CO.
RGS	20	MURPHEY, MARSEILLES & SMITH
RHH	18	HENDERSON BROTHERS, INC.
RHR	12	ARDEN & GITTERMAN, F. L. SALOMON & CO.
RI	10	HAUPT, MEFFERT, ANDREWS & HUG
RI CT UP	10	HAUPT, MEFFERT, ANDREWS & HUG
RI CT NW	10	HAUPT, MEFFERT, ANDREWS & HUG
RII	6	LIEF, FOSTER, WERLE & CO.
RJR	7	E. H. STERN & CO.
RJR PR B WI	7	E. H. STERN & CO.
RK	19	BENTON & CO.
RLM	5	JOHN K. CLOUD, THOMAS F. McKENNA
RLM PR A	5	JOHN K. CLOUD, THOMAS F. McKENNA
RLM PR B CV	5	JOHN K. CLOUD, THOMAS F. McKENNA
RNI	15	LA BRANCHE & CO.
ROF	5	JOHN K. CLOUD, THOMAS F. McKENNA
ROH	6	LIEF, FOSTER, WERLE & CO.
ROI	11	LAURO & CO.
ROK	15	BENTON, CORCORAN, LEIB & CO.
ROL	8	C. V. GIANNI & CO., GILLEN & CO.
RON	2	ZUCKERMAN, SMITH & CO.
ROP	21	SPRAGUE & NAMMACK
ROR	13	ADLER, COLEMAN & CO.
RPD	3	H. L. GOLDBERG & CO.

Symbol	Post	
RPD PR	3	H. L. GOLDBERG & CO.
RS	6	LIEF, FOSTER, WERLE & CO.
RST	17	WILLIAMS, EISELE & CO.
RTC	18	J. W. TOOMEY & CO., VAUGHAN & CO., WRAGE & CO.
RTN	19	BENTON & CO.
RTN PR	19	BENTON & CO.
RTS	22	KINGSLEY, BOYE & SOUTHWOOD
RTX	5	CHAUNCEY & CO.
RVB	1	SOMERS, SCHAFER & COLLINS
RVR	14	FAGENSON & FRANKEL CO., INC., J. STREICHER & CO.
RVS	2	P. V. HALL & CO.
RXM	14	STERN & KENNEDY
RYT	22	SILVER, BARRY & VAN RAALTE

—S—

S	21	SPRAGUE & NAMMACK
SA	8	SPEAR, LEEDS & KELLOGG
SAA	20	MURPHEY, MARSEILLES & SMITH
SAF	1	MACKEY, SHEA & WINTER
SAJ	19	WILCOX & CO.
SAV	2	J. J. CONKLIN & CO.
SAX	8	COHEN, SIMONSON & REA, INC., ANDREWS, POSNER & ROTHSCHILD
SB	5	JEFFERSON H. MARCUS & CO., INC., IRWIN SCHLOSS & CO., INC.
*SB PR	5	JEFFERSON H. MARCUS & CO., INC., IRWIN SCHLOSS & CO., INC.
SBC	16	PHELAN & CO.
*SBC PR	30	R. S. DODGE & CO., KERN SECURITIES CORP.
SBD	1	MACKEY, SHEA & WINTER

* Ten Share Unit Stocks

Symbol	Post	
SBI	15	LA BRANCHE & CO.
SBK	13	ADLER, COLEMAN & CO.
SBP	21	J. F. NICK & CO.
SC	13	ADLER, COLEMAN & CO.
SCE	9	S. M. PECK & CO., CARL H. PFORZHEIMER & CO.
SCG	13	ADLER, COLEMAN & CO.
SCG PR	13	ADLER, COLEMAN & CO.
SCI	1	MACKEY, SHEA & WINTER
SCM	9	S. M. PECK & CO., CARL H. PFORZHEIMER & CO.
SCO	4	GAINES, REIS & CO.
SCO PR B	4	GAINES, REIS & CO.
SCW	11	LAURO & CO.
SCX	13	ADLER, COLEMAN & CO.
SD	19	WILCOX & CO.
SDO	5	WEIL & DUFFY
SDF	1	MACKEY, SHEA & WINTER
SDV	7	E. H. STERN & CO.
SDV PR	7	E. H. STERN & CO.
SEA	13	ADLER, COLEMAN & CO.
SED	4	BLAIR S. WILLIAMS & CO.
SFF	1	MURPHY & CO.
SFF PR	1	MURPHY & CO.
SFI	4	GAINES, REIS & CO.
SFN	16	PHELAN & CO.
SFR	2	J. J. CONKLIN & CO.
SFZ	19	BENTON & CO.
SGA	20	HIRSHON, ROTH & CO.
SGL	4	THOMAS F. FAGAN & CO.
SGL PR	4	THOMAS F. FAGAN & CO.
SGM	18	J. W. TOOMEY & CO., VAUGHAN & CO., WRAGE & CO.
SGN	4	EINHORN & CO.
SGN PR A	4	EINHORN & CO.
SGN PR B	4	EINHORN & CO.
SGS	3	SHAW & ADRIAN

Symbol	Post	
SH	16	WAGNER, STOTT & CO.
SH PR	16	WAGNER, STOTT & CO.
SHG	15	LA BRANCHE & CO.
SHG PR	15	LA BRANCHE & CO.
SHG PR B	15	LA BRANCHE & CO.
SHK	1	SOMERS, SCHAFER & COLLINS
SHU	4	GAINES, REIS & CO.
SHW	22	KINGSLEY, BOYE & SOUTHWOOD
SHW PR B	22	KINGSLEY, BOYE & SOUTHWOOD
SIG	14	SESKIS & WOHLSTETTER
SII	5	CHAUNCEY & CO.
SIM	20	HIRSHON, ROTH & CO.
SJG	22	KINGSLEY, BOYE & SOUTHWOOD
SJM	19	FARRELL & CO., ALBERT ROTHENBERG, ROTHSCHILD & CO.
SJO	4	BLAIR S. WILLIAMS & CO.
SKC	8	C. V. GIANNI & CO., GILLEN & CO.
SKL	3	H. L. GOLDBERG & CO.
SKO	14	STERN & KENNEDY
SKW	7	PICOLI & CO.
SKW PR A	7	PICOLI & CO.
SKW PR B	7	PICOLI & CO.
SKY	22	ALBERT FRIED & CO.
SLB	7	PICOLI & CO.
SLF	1	SOMERS, SCHAFER & COLLINS
SLZ	20	BREGMAN & CO.
SMB	21	WRESZIN, PROSSER, ROMANO & GAVIN
SMC	21	SPRAGUE & NAMMACK
SMF	4	THOMAS F. FAGAN & CO.
SMF PR	4	THOMAS F. FAGAN & CO.
SMI	19	WILCOX & CO.

Symbol	Post	
SN	6	H. L. KIMBALL & CO.
SNH	13	ADLER, COLEMAN & CO.
SNH PR	13	ADLER, COLEMAN & CO.
SNK	5	JOHN K. CLOUD, THOMAS F. McKENNA
SNL	17	COWEN & CO., F. H. SACKEN & CO.
SNS	1	MACKEY, SHEA & WINTER
SNS PR	1	MACKEY, SHEA & WINTER
SO	16	PHELAN & CO.
SOA	17	COWEN & CO., F. H. SACKEN & CO.
SOC	8	SPEAR, LEEDS & KELLOGG
SOH	13	ROBB, PECK, McCOOEY & CO.
*SOH PR A	30	R. S. DODGE & CO., KERN-SECURITIES CORP.
SOH PR B	13	ROBB, PECK, McCOOEY & CO.
SOL	7	E. H. STERN & CO.
SOO	8	SPEAR, LEEDS & KELLOGG
SOS	3	SHAW & ADRIAN
SP	9	LENART, McHUGH & CO.
SPA	17	COWEN & CO., F. H. SACKEN & CO.
SPE	15	LA BRANCHE & CO.
SPG	16	PHELAN & CO.
SPK	7	E. H. STERN & CO.
SPK PR C	7	E. H. STERN & CO.
SPP	10	HAUPT, MEFFERT, ANDREWS & HUG
SPR A CV	18	HENDERSON BROTHERS, INC.
SPS	12	M. J. MEEHAN & CO.
SPT	18	HENDERSON BROTHERS, INC.
SPV	5	CHAUNCEY & CO.
SQB	13	ADLER, COLEMAN & CO.
SQB PR	13	ADLER, COLEMAN & CO.
SQD	11	MARCUS & CO.

* Ten Share Unit Stocks

Symbol	Post	
SR	2	CUNNIFF, ROMAINE, LAMM & STOUTENBURGH
SR PR	2	CUNNIFF, ROMAINE, LAMM & STOUTENBURGH
SRE	10	BEAUCHAMP & CO.
SRE PR	10	BEAUCHAMP & CO.
SRG	4	THOMAS F. FAGAN & CO.
SRL	12	ARDEN & GITTERMAN, F. L. SALOMON & CO.
SRP	9	ERNST & CO., WARE & KEELIPS, HOMANS & CO.
SRT	7	E. H. STERN & CO.
SRU	3	SHAW & ADRIAN
SRY	4	GAINES, REIS & CO.
SSC	4	GAINES, REIS & CO.
ST	4	GAINES, REIS & CO.
ST CT	4	GAINES, REIS & CO.
ST PR	4	GAINES, REIS & CO.
ST PR CT	4	GAINES, REIS & CO.
STA	13	ROBB, PECK, McCOOEY & CO.
STF	10	CYRIL DE CORDOVA & BRO.
STF PR A	10	CYRIL DE CORDOVA & BRO.
STN	16	WAGNER, STOTT & CO.
STO	16	PHELAN & CO.
STU	2	CUNNIFF, ROMAINE, LAMM & STOUTENBURGH
STU PR	2	CUNNIFF, ROMAINE, LAMM & STOUTENBURGH
STX	4	GAINES, REIS & CO.
STY	19	BENTON & CO.
STY PR	19	BENTON & CO.
SUB	19	BENTON & CO.
SUC	16	ADOLPH SCHENKER & CO., KAUFMANN & CO.
SUN	17	M. E. GOLDSTEIN & CO., WISNER & DE CLAIRVILLE

Symbol	Post	
SUN PR	17	M. E. GOLDSTEIN & CO., WISNER & DE CLAIRVILLE
SUO	17	CAHILL, SMITH & GALLATIN
SVE	8	SPEAR, LEEDS & KELLOGG
SVM	4	THOMAS F. FAGAN & CO.
SVU	17	COWEN & CO., F. H. SACKEN & CO.
SW	3	SCHOLL & LEVIN
SWA	11	MARCUS & CO.
SWK	17	DANIEL REEVES & CO.
SWL	19	BENTON & CO.
SWS	6	LIEF, FOSTER, WERLE & CO.
SWX	16	PHELAN & CO.
SX	21	J. F. NICK & CO.
SY	4	EINHORN & CO.
SYB	21	WRESZIN, PROSSER, ROMANO & GAVIN
SYB PR	21	WRESZIN, PROSSER, ROMANO & GAVIN
SYE	4	THOMAS F. FAGAN & CO.
SYP	20	BREGMAN & CO.

—T—

T	15	LA BRANCHE & CO.
TA	2	J. J. CONKLIN & CO.
TA PR	2	J. J. CONKLIN & CO.
*TA PR B	2	J. J. CONKLIN & CO.
TAL	20	HIRSHON, ROTH & CO.
TAN	10	CYRIL DE CORDOVA & BRO.
TBN	21	SPRAGUE & NAMMACK
TCL	14	FAGENSON & FRANKEL CO., INC., J. STREICHER & CO.
TDY	20	HIRSHON, ROTH & CO.
TDY PR	20	HIRSHON, ROTH & CO.
TDY PR B	20	HIRSHON, ROTH & CO.

* Ten Share Unit Stocks

Symbol	Post	
TE	22	KINGSLEY, BOYE & SOUTHWOOD
TED	15	BENTON, CORCORAN, LEIB & CO.
TEK	18	MURRAY & CO.
TET	12	M. J. MEEHAN & CO.
TF	13	ROBB, PECK, McCOOEY & CO.
TFB	21	WRESZIN, PROSSER, ROMANO & GAVIN
TFD	6	LIEF, FOSTER, WERLE & CO.
TG	12	DURAND & CULLEN
TGE	19	BENTON & CO.
TGT	16	WAGNER, STOTT & CO.
TGT PR	16	WAGNER, STOTT & CO.
THI	9	LENART, McHUGH & CO.
TIC	7	E. H. STERN & CO.
TIC PR	7	E. H. STERN & CO.
TII	6	H. L. KIMBALL & CO.
TIS	18	HENDERSON BROTHERS, INC.
TKR	8	SPEAR, LEEDS & KELLOGG
TL	4	EINHORN & CO.
TLC	6	STOKES, HOYT & CO.
TM	20	MURPHEY, MARSEILLES & SMITH
TMC	2	P. V. HALL & CO.
TNB	9	LENART, McHUGH & CO.
TOD	16	ADOLPH SCHENKER & CO., KAUFMANN & CO.
TPL	15	JOHN E. BARRETT & CO., INC.
TR	22	SILVER, BARRY & VAN RAALTE
TRA	3	H. L. GOLDBERG & CO.
TRI	15	JOHN E. BARRETT & CO., INC.
TRN	11	MARCUS & CO.
TRW	15	JOHN E. BARRETT & CO., INC., JOHN MUIR & CO.
TRW PR A	15	JOHN E. BARRETT & CO., INC., JOHN MUIR & CO.

Symbol	Post	
TRW PR B	15	JOHN E. BARRETT & CO., INC., JOHN MUIR & CO.
TRW PR D	15	JOHN E. BARRETT & CO., INC., JOHN MUIR & CO.
TSC	22	STERN BROS.
TSC PR	22	STERN BROS.
TU	15	LA BRANCHE & CO.
TWA	5	WEIL & DUFFY
TWA PR	5	WEIL & DUFFY
TWF	12	ARDEN & GITTERMAN, F. L. SALOMON & CO.
TX	3	ASIEL & CO., GENGLER BROS.
TXG	16	PHELAN & CO.
TXG PR	16	PHELAN & CO.
TXI	4	THOMAS F. FAGAN & CO.
TXN	5	JEFFERSON H. MARCUS & CO., INC., IRWIN SCHLOSS & CO., INC.
TXO	3	SHAW & ADRIAN
TXT	17	M. E. GOLDSTEIN & CO., INC., WISNER & DE CLAIRVILLE
TXT PR A	17	M. E. GOLDSTEIN & CO., INC., WISNER & DE CLAIRVILLE
TXT PR B	17	M. E. GOLDSTEIN & CO., INC., WISNER & DE CLAIRVILLE
TXU	3	SCHOLL & LEVIN
TY	9	ERNST & CO., WARE & KEELIPS, HOMANS & CO.
TY PR	9	ERNST & CO., WARE & KEELIPS, HOMANS & CO.

—U—

U	19	BENTON & CO.
UA	1	BENJAMIN JACOBSON & SONS
UAL	1	BENJAMIN JACOBSON & SONS
UBO	15	BENTON, CORCORAN, LEIB & CO.

Symbol	Post	
UC	14	SESKIS & WOHLSTETTER
UCC	4	BLAIR S. WILLIAMS & CO.
UCL	8	SPEAR, LEEDS & KELLOGG
UCL PR	8	SPEAR, LEEDS & KELLOGG
UCO	16	PHELAN & CO.
UEP	8	SPEAR, LEEDS & KELLOGG
*UEP PR A	30	R. S. DODGE & CO., KERN SECURITIES CORP.
*UEP PR C	30	R. S. DODGE & CO., KERN SECURITIES CORP.
*UEP PR D	30	R. S. DODGE & CO., KERN SECURITIES CORP.
*UEP PR E	30	R. S. DODGE & CO., KERN SECURITIES CORP.
*UEP PR G	30	R. S. DODGE & CO., KERN SECURITIES CORP.
UF	6	STOKES, HOYT & CO.
UFG	14	CREEM & CREEM
UFL	3	ASIEL & CO., GENGLER BROS.
UFO	21	FOWLER & ROSENAU
UGI	14	FAGENSON & FRANKEL CO., INC., J. STREICHER & CO.
UIC	8	SPEAR, LEEDS & KELLOGG
UIC PR	8	SPEAR, LEEDS & KELLOGG
UK	16	WAGNER, STOTT & CO.
UL	8	SPEAR, LEEDS & KELLOGG
UMM	7	E. H. STERN & CO.
UMT	7	E. H. STERN & CO.
UN	6	STOKES, HOYT & CO.
UNC	4	EINHORN & CO.
UNI	17	FREIDAY & CO.
UNP WI	20	HIRSHON, ROTH & CO.
UNR	8	COHEN, SIMONSON & REA, INC.. ANDREWS, POSNER & ROTHSCHILD
UNS	9	ERNST & CO., WARE & KEELIPS, HOMANS & CO.

* Ten Share Unit Stocks

Symbol	Post	
UOP	11	MARCUS & CO.
UP	20	HIRSHON, ROTH & CO.
UP PR	7	E. H. STERN & CO.
UPC	8	COHEN, SIMONSON & REA, INC., ANDREWS, POSNER & ROTHSCHILD
UPC PR B	8	COHEN, SIMONSON & REA, INC., ANDREWS, POSNER & ROTHSCHILD
*UPC PR C	30	R. S. DODGE & CO., KERN SECURITIES CORP.
UPJ	2	ZUCKERMAN, SMITH & CO.
UPK	14	STERN & KENNEDY
URB	3	ASIEL & CO., GENGLER BROS.
URC	6	LIEF, FOSTER, WERLE & CO.
USG	1	BENJAMIN JACOBSON & SONS
USG PR	1	BENJAMIN JACOBSON & SONS
USH	22	KINGSLEY, BOYE & SOUTHWOOD
USI	22	SILVER, BARRY & VAN RAALTE
USM	20	MURPHEY, MARSEILLES & SMITH
*USM PR	30	R. S. DODGE & CO., KERN SECURITIES CORP.
USM PR B	20	MURPHEY, MARSEILLES & SMITH
USR	9	S. M. PECK & CO., CARL H. PFORZHEIMER & CO.
UT	6	LIEF, FOSTER, WERLE & CO.
UT PR	6	LIEF, FOSTER, WERLE & CO.
UT PR A	6	LIEF, FOSTER, WERLE & CO.
UTP	8	C. V. GIANNI & CO., GILLEN & CO.
UV	11	MARCUS & CO., TRAVERS & HUME, JEWETT, NEWMAN & CO.

* Ten Share Unit Stocks

Symbol	Post	
UV PR	11	MARCUS & CO., TRAVERS & HUME, JEWETT, NEWMAN & CO.
UVV	3	H. L. GOLDBERG & CO.

—V—

VAR	13	ROBB, PECK, McCOOEY & CO.
VCR	20	BREGMAN & CO.
VEL	5	JEFFERSON H. MARCUS & CO., INC., IRWIN SCHLOSS & CO., INC.
*VEL PR A	30	R. S. DODGE & CO., KERN SECURITIES CORP.
*VEL PR B	30	R. S. DODGE & CO., KERN SECURITIES CORP.
*VEL PR C	30	R. S. DODGE & CO., KERN SECURITIES CORP.
*VEL PR D	30	R. S. DODGE & CO., KERN SECURITIES CORP.
*VEL PR E	30	R. S. DODGE & CO., KERN SECURITIES CORP.
VEN	22	KINGSLEY, BOYE & SOUTHWOOD
VFC	19	WILCOX & CO.
VIL	19	FARRELL & CO., ALBERT ROTHENBERG, ROTHSCHILD & CO.
VLV	17	COWEN & CO., F. H. SACKEN & CO.
VMC	2	P. V. HALL & CO.
VNO	2	J. J. CONKLIN & CO.
VON	2	P. V. HALL & CO.
VR	8	C. V. GIANNI & CO., GILLEN & CO.
VSI	8	COHEN, SIMONSON & REA, INC., ANDREWS, POSNER & ROTHSCHILD
VWR	15	JOHN E. BARRETT & CO., INC.

* Ten Share Unit Stocks

Symbol	Post	
—W—		
W	7	PICOLI & CO.
W PR	30	R. S. DODGE & CO., KERN SECURITIES CORP.
*WA PR	30	R. S. DODGE & CO., KERN SECURITIES CORP.
WAG	10	CYRIL DE CORDOVA & BRO.
WAL	19	MURRAY & CO.
WAR	15	JOHN E. BARRETT & CO., INC.
WBB	11	MARCUS & CO.
WBC	2	J. J. CONKLIN & CO.
WBL	4	THOMAS F. FAGAN & CO.
WCS	22	ALBERT FRIED & CO.
WD	16	PHELAN & CO.
WDS	14	FAGENSON & FRANKEL CO., INC., J. STREICHER & CO.
WEY	9	ERNST & CO., WARE & KEELIPS, HOMANS & CO.
WGL	17	FREIDAY & CO.
WH	17	JOHN P. DUFFY
WHD	17	CAHILL, SMITH & GALLATIN
WHR	13	ROBB, PECK, McCOOEY & CO.
WHX	3	H. L. GOLDBERG & CO.
*WHX PR	30	R. S. DODGE & CO., KERN SECURITIES CORP.
*WHX PR B	30	R. S. DODGE & CO., KERN SECURITIES CORP.
WID	22	KINGSLEY, BOYE & SOUTHWOOD
WID PR A	22	KINGSLEY, BOYE & SOUTHWOOD
WIE	17	M. E. GOLDSTEIN & CO., WISNER & DE CLAIRVILLE
WIN	6	LIEF, FOSTER, WERLE & CO.
WIN B	6	LIEF, FOSTER, WERLE & CO.
WIT	19	BENTON & CO.
WIT PR	19	BENTON & CO.

* Ten Share Unit Stocks

Symbol	Post	
WIX	16	ADOLPH SCHENKER & CO., KAUFMANN & CO.
WJ	11	MARCUS & CO.
WKR	20	BREGMAN & CO.
WKT	5	JEFFERSON H. MARCUS CO., INC., IRWIN SCHLOSS & CO., INC.
WKT PR	5	JEFFERSON H. MARCUS CO., INC., IRWIN SCHLOSS & CO., INC.
WLA	22	KINGSLEY, BOYE & SOUTHWOOD
*WLE	30	R. S. DODGE & CO., KERN SECURITIES CORP.
WM	6	LIEF, FOSTER, WERLE & CO.
WMB	19	BENTON & CO.
WMC	19	WILCOX & CO.
WMC PR	19	WILCOX & CO.
WMK	17	DANIEL REEVES & CO.
WOA	17	SESKIS & WOHLSTETTER
WOM	18	HENDERSON BROTHERS, INC.
WPC	6	LIEF, FOSTER, WERLE & CO.
WPM	7	E. H. STERN & CO.
WPS	9	LENART, McHUGH & CO.
WRC	8	COHEN, SIMONSON & REA, INC., ANDREWS, POSNER & ROTHSCHILD
WRC PR B	8	COHEN, SIMONSON & REA, INC., ANDREWS, POSNER & ROTHSCHILD
WRS	1	MURPHY & CO.
WS	16	WAGNER, STOTT & CO.
WSC	6	LIEF, FOSTER, WERLE & CO.
*WSP PR	30	R. S. DODGE & CO., KERN SECURITIES CORP.
*WSP PR B	30	R. S. DODGE & CO., KERN SECURITIES CORP.
*WSP PR C	30	R. S. DODGE & CO., KERN SECURITIES CORP.

* Ten Share Unit Stocks

Symbol	Post	
WSS	10	HAUPT, MEFFERT, ANDREWS & HUG
WSW	16	WAGNER, STOTT & CO.
WSW PR A	16	WAGNER, STOTT & CO.
WSW PR B	16	WAGNER, STOTT & CO.
WSW PR C	16	WAGNER, STOTT & CO.
WTC	9	LENART, McHUGH & CO.
WU	19	FARRELL & CO., ALBERT ROTHENBERG, ROTHSCHILD & CO.
WU PR A	19	FARRELL & CO., ALBERT ROTHENBERG, ROTHSCHILD & CO.
WU PR B	19	FARRELL & CO., ALBERT ROTHENBERG, ROTHSCHILD & CO.
WU PR C	19	FARRELL & CO., ALBERT ROTHENBERG, ROTHSCHILD & CO.
WUR	8	COHEN, SIMONSON & REA, INC., ANDREWS, POSNER & ROTHSCHILD
WW	15	JOHN E. BARRETT & CO., INC.
WWP	3	SCHOLL & LEVIN
WWW	1	MURPHY & CO.
WWY	18	MURRAY & CO.
WX	15	BENTON, CORCORAN, LEIB & CO.
*WX PR B	30	R. S. DODGE & CO., KERN SECURITIES CORP.
WY	21	SPRAGUE & NAMMACK

---

* Ten Share Unit Stocks

Symbol	Post
—X—	
X	19 BENTON & CO.
XLO	8 SPEAR, LEEDS & KELLOGG
XRX	16 WAGNER, STOTT & CO.
XTR	22 ALBERT FRIED & CO.
—Y—	
Y	1 SOMERS, SCHAFER & COLLINS
Y PR	1 SOMERS, SCHAFER & COLLINS
YSD	13 ADLER, COLEMAN & CO.
—Z—	
Z	10 CYRIL DE CORDOVA & BRO.
Z PR A	10 CYRIL DE CORDOVA & BRO.
ZA	22 ALBERT FRIED & CO.
ZAL	2 CUNNIFF, ROMAINE, LAMM & STOUTENBURGH
ZAL PR	2 CUNNIFF, ROMAINE, LAMM & STOUTENBURGH
ZB	15 JOHN E. BARRETT & CO., INC., JOHN MUIR & CO.
*ZB PR	30 R. S. DODGE & CO., KERN SECURITIES CORP.
ZE	4 GAINES, REIS & CO.
ZOS	17 CAHILL, SMITH & GALLATIN
ZOS PR	17 CAHILL, SMITH & GALLATIN
ZRN	13 ROBB, PECK, McCOOEY & CO.
ZY	4 THOMAS F. FAGAN & CO.

* Ten Share Unit Stocks

Index

Index